SPECIAL ABBREVIATIONS USED IN THIS BOOK

BC	Between columns (see Lesson 14)	SM	Side margin
CH	Column heading	SP	Supplementary practice
Col.	Column	SS	Single space (spaces, spaced, spacing)
CW	Cumulative words (see Lesson 10)	St	Stroke intensity (see Lesson 15)
DS	Double space (spaces, spaced, spacing)	Sy	Syllabic intensity (see Lesson 15)
LM	Left margin	TR	Timing Record (for straight copy timings), see p. 7.
MR	Margin release (key)	TR–NS	Timing Record (for number and symbol timings). See p. 32.
NS	Number and symbol (copy containing many numbers and symbols)	TS	Triple space (spaces, spaced, spacing) or Tab stop
PF	Practice Form (see p. 115)	WL	Writing line (see p. 6)
RM	Right margin		
S	Space, spaces, spaced, spacing		

TWO-LETTER STATE ABBREVIATIONS

Alabama	AL	Indiana	IN	Nebraska	NE	South Carolina	SC
Alaska	AK	Iowa	IA	Nevada	NV	South Dakota	SD
Arizona	AZ	Kansas	KS	New Hampshire	NH	Tennessee	TN
Arkansas	AR	Kentucky	KY	New Jersey	NJ	Texas	TX
California	CA	Louisiana	LA	New Mexico	NM	Utah	UT
Colorado	CO	Maine	ME	New York	NY	Vermont	VT
Connecticut	CT	Maryland	MD	North Carolina	NC	Virginia	VA
Delaware	DE	Massachusetts	MA	North Dakota	ND	Washington	WA
Florida	FL	Michigan	MI	Ohio	OH	West Virginia	WV
Georgia	GA	Minnesota	MN	Oklahoma	OK	Wisconsin	WI
Hawaii	HI	Mississippi	MS	Oregon	OR	Wyoming	WY
Idaho	ID	Missouri	MO	Pennsylvania	PA		
Illinois	IL	Montana	MT	Rhode Island	RI		

MARKING AND COUNTING STROKING ERRORS

Circle your errors as shown below.

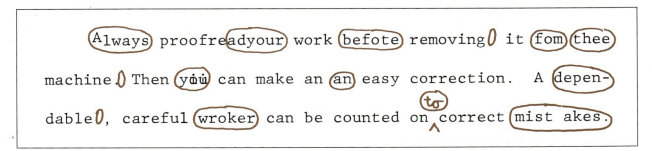

Line 1: High capital, omitted space, misstroke, extra space, omitted letter, extra letter
Line 2: Wrong spacing, strikeovers (1 error per word), repeated word, wrong word division
Line 3: Wrong spacing, transposition (1 error per word), omitted word, extra space

1 Spacing errors are separate from word errors.

2 Any capital not even with the line of writing is an error.

3 Count as 1 error the omission of several words or lines *in succession.* If omissions are separated, count each omission as a separate error.

4 In computing speed, subtract omitted words from (and add repeated or inserted words to) total words typed before dividing by time in minutes.

5 For copy typed from a wrong hand position (*we tgubj tgat*) for (*we think that*), count each five consecutive words as 1 error.

MODERN COLLEGE TYPEWRITING

A BASIC COURSE

LEONARD J. WEST
PROFESSOR OF EDUCATION
BARUCH COLLEGE OF THE CITY UNIVERSITY OF NEW YORK

 HARCOURT BRACE JOVANOVICH, INC.   NEW YORK   CHICAGO   SAN FRANCISCO   ATLANTA

ISBN: 0-15-560550-X

Library of Congress Catalog Card Number: 76-58775

Printed in the United States of America

PREFACE

MODERN COLLEGE TYPEWRITING: A BASIC COURSE serves a dual purpose. First, it provides realistic personal and vocational skills for students who will take only this introductory course. At the same time, as a precursor to the 225-lesson Complete Course, it lays a solid foundation for the development of higher-level skills in later, advanced courses.

The materials and procedures used in MODERN COLLEGE TYPEWRITING are firmly grounded on reputable, up-to-date evidence about what typists do and how typing is best learned. The book preserves those practices from the past that are supported by experience and research; but where traditional practices have proved to be unsound or ineffective, I have replaced them with materials and procedures that are in the closest possible accord with current knowledge. The new methods derive from two sources: general research in the psychology of skill learning (conducted by psychologists) and research particular to typewriting (conducted largely by business educators).

The feature of MODERN COLLEGE TYPEWRITING that most distinguishes it from other typewriting textbooks is its implementation of the findings of research conducted since the late 1960s on production typing—findings that are not yet widely known. That research has uniformly shown that early attention to production skills—as compared to traditional practices—results in vastly superior production skills at no cost whatever to stroking skills.

MODERN COLLEGE TYPEWRITING therefore introduces production typing early and teaches the student to perform realistic typing tasks under realistic conditions. To that end, the keyboard and skill-building materials and procedures are specifically designed to develop sufficient stroking skill to support such early attention to production typing.

Two other dominating features of the book are its adaptability to variations in course length and objectives and its thorough accounting for individual differences in students' aptitudes, skill levels, and needs—particularly during keyboard learning and in the program for building stroking speed and accuracy.

A number of other characteristics distinguish MODERN COLLEGE TYPEWRITING:

1. In addition to its 75 numbered lessons, the book includes large collections of separate, self-contained materials. One is *Supplementary Practice* for each keyboard lesson, as well as for selected later lessons, that serve three purposes: keeping the faster typists profitably occupied, permitting more attention to particular instructional topics, and providing vital practice on the planning features of production tasks. A second is *Optional Practice* of four kinds—targeted at improving selected aspects of stroking skills and intended for general or remedial stroking skills practice or for keeping the faster typists usefully busy.

2. Also in a self-contained section of the book are two types of material used in a structured program for building stroking speed and accuracy, *Progressive Practice* and *Paced Practice*. The materials cover the entire range of skills found among postsecondary students throughout the introductory course, and the applicable procedures totally individualize skill-building practice. At no cost to ease of classroom management, all students at all times practice for speed or for accuracy according to individual needs, present skill level, and goals. A simple record form maintained by the student provides instant knowledge of his or her present status and immediate goals. (Other simple, student-maintained forms apply (a.) to scores on periodic 5-minute test timings and (b.) to progress with Optional Practice materials.)

3. Whether taken alone or with *Supplementary Practice,* the materials for keyboard learning greatly exceed those in other beginning books, providing in each new lesson far more occurrences of each new key and vastly more cumulative review of all earlier-taught letters. Dictionary words, phrases, and sentences—not nonsense sequences or drills—are used, and they deliberately provide practice at the variety of "reaches" to each new key.

4. Physiological research has shown that in learning *any* motor skill, including typing, a beginner cannot rely on muscular sensations at the start. The early lessons in this book therefore foster an easy, gradual transition to touch operation. Also, early stroking errors are treated according to an established tactic for all of human learning. Accuracy development in the structured skill-building program corrects the erroneous notion that accuracy depends on the internal characteristics of the practice materials, on concoctions of "drill" materials; it is based instead on the central

generalization about accuracy in all motor skills: Accuracy depends on the right speed.

5. Production typing takes the student step by step from fully guided work, through partially assisted work, to wholly unarranged materials. To that end, the student is taught early and explicitly how to make the pertinent decisions on margins, tab stops, and the like, and is given practice in making those decisions on tasks stripped down to essentials. Then, tasks of varied lengths and features are typed—without advance placement information from the textbook. As one of many examples, business letters are not accompanied by a word count; instead, the student is first taught *how* to estimate letter length. (Can you imagine any employer asking an employee to "type this 137-word letter"?) Throughout, the focus is on realistic tasks carried out under realistic conditions. Another aspect of realism is the inclusion of the leading stylistic variations (for correspondence and reports); the instructor can choose from among them or teach all the variations, as may be desired. Contributing to the flexible use of the book for different course objectives is a *Cross-Classified Production Task Inventory* that enables the instructor to identify instantly the page numbers for work of any given kind.

6. Cumulative tests (or reviews) appear at intervals in the lessons; procedures for scoring and grading timings and production typing for both speed and accuracy are supplied. Completion-time is used as the basis for speed scoring in production typing, and its procedures are described in detail in the Instructor's Manual.

7. Significant portions of the materials to be typed (especially in the timing and reports) provide up-to-date information on how typing is best learned and on the real-world activities of personal and vocational typists. The

thesis is that students learn best when they know how to go about learning.

8. This book gives more attention to manuscript or report typing (in much of Lessons 59-70) than any other introductory typing text for postsecondary students. That strategy permits all students to type term papers for other courses as early as possible and is especially beneficial for those who take only one course of typing instruction. Those who have less interest in report typing can use, instead, the substantial collection of *Supplementary and Optional Practice* materials. In all other respects, the kinds of typing skills covered serve equally the vocational and personal typist at no cost to the longer-range objectives of either—because a common body of skills applies to the early (first-course) instruction of all typists.

Space does not permit my listing the names of all the people who have helped me as I was preparing MODERN COLLEGE TYPEWRITING. I am grateful to my colleagues over the years for their encouragement and to the many academics who reviewed the manuscript—particularly Professors Rosemarie McCauley of Montclair State College and Patricia A. Parzych of Hostos Community College of the City University of New York. I am especially grateful to my students who have used significant portions of the materials on a trial basis in my classes. I also wish to thank Mrs. Gertrude S. Altholz, now retired, formerly Chairperson of the Secretarial Science Department at Midwood High School in New York City, where I did my first high-school teaching. In accord with the rationale of this book, Mrs. Altholz prepared portions of the materials and edited an early draft of the manuscript.

LEONARD J. WEST

CONTENTS

Contents

This inventory lists the lesson (and Supplementary Practice) sections and their page numbers on which various kinds of production typing tasks appear. By referring to this inventory, the instructor who may wish from time to time to devote lessons or parts of them to certain kinds of work other than those contained in particular lessons can immediately locate the desired materials.

For inventory purposes, the number of tasks of each kind is shown (a) in brackets after each kind of task and (b) when there is more than one item of its kind in a given lesson section, in parentheses after the page number. For example, TABLES [51] means that there are 51 instances of table typing or planning in the book; 50B/68(2) in the listing for standard business letters means that in Lesson 50B on page 68, there are two such letters. Tasks with several features are shown for each such feature. For example, a table with a minor heading and a footnote is shown with each of those subcategories; but the total for each major category counts each task once, whatever its features.

Details on the three major types of tasks are given first, in the order in which they first appear in the book (tables, correspondence, manuscripts or reports). Miscellaneous other kinds of tasks follow. Next, tasks whose contents provide information needed by typists are listed. Finally, as an addition to this inventory of production typing tasks, Comparison Practice and straight copy test timings are tallied.

TABLES [51]

Note. "Guided" refers to placement instructions. Fully guided tables are accompanied by complete placement instructions; unguided tables are free of advance information on margins, tab stops, between-column space, and the like. Even if no more than between-column space is specified in advance, the table is classified as partially guided. All the tables "With additional or special features" are partially guided.

Simple (no column headings) [37]

Fully guided [4]   13C/24, 27B/42, 38D/54, 39C/55

Partially guided [17]   13C-E/24(3), 14A/24(2), 14C/25(2), 15A/25, 16A/28, 22D/36, 27B/42, 28E/43, 29-30H/45, 31D/46, 32C/47, 33C/48(2)

Planned but not typed [16]   32C/47(4), 33D/48(3), SP 32/111(9)

Standard (with column headings but without special features) [6]

Fully guided [1]   34C/49

Partially guided [4]   35B/50(2), 41A/57, 48-49D/66
Unguided [1]   73-75I/97

With additional or special features [8]

Blocked [3]   21D/35, 28E/43, 69C/90

Footnote(s) [3]   65B/84(2), 69C/90

Minor heading(s) [6]   39C/55, 55C/74(2), 57-58D/77, 65B/84, 69C/90

Two-line column headings [3]   65B/84(2), 69C/90

Unequal between-column space [3]   38B/53, 39C/55, 65B/84

CORRESPONDENCE [87, excluding envelopes]

Note. Starred items include enclosures in at least one of the letters in the lesson section. The types of correspondence are listed in the order in which they first appear in the book. Beginning in Lesson 52, all the correspondence is unguided.

Envelopes [46]   25B/40(8), 28B/43(2), 29-30C/45, 43B/60, 44C/61, 45B/61(2) 47C/65, 48-49F/66(2), 50C/68(2), 55B/73(6), 57C/77(2), 62C/81, 69B/90, 73-75D/97(2), SP 25/109(20)

Postal cards [12]   26B/41(7), 28C/43, 29-30G/45, 73-75H/97, SP 26/110(8)

Personal notes or letters [16]   42B/58-59(4), 48-49K/61, 51D/69*, 62C/81*, 69B/90*, 73-75E/97, SP 42/111(7)

Personal-business letters [19]   43B/59(3), 44C/61(2), 45B/61(2), 48-49E/66, 54C/73, 57-58C/77*, 73-75G/97, SP 44/112(8)

Business letters [37, excluding planned but not typed]

Short (fewer than 60 words) [10]   46B/63(4), 47C/64, 48-49C/66, 52B/70*, 54C/73*, 56C/75*, SP 52-56/114*

Standard [27]   47B/63, 50B/68(2), 51C/69(2), 52B/70, 53D/72, 54C/73*, 56C/75*, 57-58C/77(2), 73-75C/96(2)*, SP 47/113(8), SP 52-56/114(6)*

Planned but not typed [6]   52B/70(6)

Memos [3]

Half-sheet [2]   p. 99
Full sheet [1]   p. 99

MANUSCRIPTS AND MANUSCRIPT PARTS [27]

Note. All the manuscripts after Lessons 59-60 are unguided.

In outline form [5] 36C/51, 41B/57, 64C/83, 67B/88, 71-72B/92-94

Simple (without footnotes) [6]

    Unbound (SM-1") [2] 59-60B/78-79, 61B/80
    Unbound (WL-6") [2] 59-60D/79, 68A/88
    Sidebound [2] 59-60C/79, 62B/81

With footnotes [5] 64C/83, 67B/88, 68B/89, 70B/91, 73-75J/98

With long quotations [1] 70B/91

In journal style [2] 67A/87, 68A/88

Manuscript parts [14]

    Footnotes [9]
        Planned but not typed [4] 64D/83
        Typed [5] 63B/82(3), 64D/83, 69A/89
    References page [4] 66B/85-86(2), 68B/89, 73-75K/98
    Title page [1] 62D/81

MISCELLANEOUS OTHER TASKS [33]

Note. Bracketed frequencies for major categories are task counts, not number of items within tasks. Example: The 36 words for word division practice count as 4 tasks because they are distributed among 4 tables.

Centering (excluding table and manuscript headings or titles) [18]

    Horizontal only [3: 18 lines] 15C/26(11), 15E/26(3), 17D/30(4)

    Vertical (groups of lines or paragraphs) [12] 18D/31(2) 18E/31, 24C/38, 28D/43, 29-30D/45, 73-75F/97, SP 18/107(5)

        Planned but not typed [3] 24C/38

Error correction [3: 16 corrections] 45C/62(9), 56B/75(4), 61B/80(3)

Outlines [3] 35C/50(2), 48-49J/67

Rough draft (sentences and paragraphs) [5]

    Sentences [7] 37B/52(4), 40C/56(3)
    Paragraphs [3] 37B/53, 40C/56, 48-49I/67

Word division (in table form) [4:36 words] 14C/25, 15A/25, 16A/28, 28E/43

TASKS CONTAINING INFORMATION NEEDED BY TYPISTS

Carbon copies

    Assembling a carbon pack 62B/81
    Correcting errors on carbons 62B/81

Correspondence procedures

    Addressing envelopes 25C/40
    Estimating letter length 54B/72

Kinds of work typists do

    Frequency of manuscript or report typing 57-58B/76
    Frequency of rough draft typing 38C/54
    Frequency of table typing 34B/49
    Infrequency of straight copy typing p. 144/36 wpm.

Manuscript or report procedures

    Basic features 59-60B/78-79

Citation of sources 57B/76, 67A/87, 70B/91
Estimating footnote space 64B/83
Highpoints 61B/80, 62C/81
Reference listings 67B/88

Production typing procedures review 71-72B/92-94

Stroking skills

    Chaining of motions 44B/60, p. 140/20 wpm.
    Development of speed and accuracy 29B/44, pp. 141-143, 155/24, 30, 34, 60 wpm.
    Kinesthesis 15B/27, p. 141/26 wpm.
    Nature and purpose of 5-minute timings 19B/32, 40D/56, 73-75A/95
    What accuracy depends on 29B/44, p. 142/28 wpm.

Table placement by spacing and counting 41B/57

STRAIGHT COPY COMPARISON AND TEST TIMINGS

Comparison practice timings (3 or 4 minutes) [4] 36B/51, 38C/54, 40D/56, 47B/64

Test timings [44] Note. Two timings in the same lesson are starred.

    Ordinary prose [31]
        1-minute [5] Lessons 1, 2, 3, 4*
        2-minute [5] Lessons 5, 6, 7, 8, 9

    3-minute [2] Lessons 10, 11
    4-minute [1] Lesson 12
    5-minute [18] Lessons 15*, 19, 25, 29-30*, 34, 39, 44*, 48-49*, 54, 57-58*, 64, 73-75*

Numbers and symbols [13]
    3-minute [4] Lessons 16, 17, 19, 20
    4-minute [4] Lessons 21, 22, 23, 24
    5-minute [5] Lessons 24, 29, 49, 48, 73-75

Preparing to type

A ARRANGE YOUR WORK AREA

1 Clear desk of everything you don't need.

2 If your typewriter is not already bolted down into position, move its front edge even with the edge of your desk or table.

3 Place this book to the right of your typewriter. Turn it towards you at a comfortable reading angle.

B SIT IN TYPING POSITION

1 Squarely in front of typewriter

2 Base of spine well back in chair

3 Leaning slightly forward from the hips

4 Feet flat on floor

5 Chair a proper distance from machine

Adjust chair distance so that, with curved fingers in place on second row of keys from the bottom (see Section H, p. 5), elbows are alongside your body. Avoid the most common posture fault—sitting too close to the typewriter, a position that causes muscle fatigue and errors.

Details:

Fingers curled—more tightly on a manual than on an electric typewriter.

Back of hands at same upward slant as slant of keyboard—that is, wrists low, but do **not** rest heel of hand on edge of typewriter or desk.

Upper arms hanging loosely, neither hugging nor flying away from body.

Too close

Too far

Table 2
Grades for Total Errors in One and in Two 5′ Timings for Each of Three Grading Systems
A (2 epm = 75), B (3 epm = 65), C (3 epm = 60)
(E = Number of errors)

In One 5-Minute Timing

E	A	B	C	E	A	B	C	E	A	B	C
1	98	98	97	16	60	63	57	31	22	28	17
2	95	95	95	17	58	60	55	32	20	25	15
3	92	93	92	18	55	58	52	33	18	23	12
4	90	91	89	19	52	56	49	34	15	21	9
5	88	89	87	20	50	53	47	35	12	18	7
6	85	86	84	21	48	51	44	36	10	16	4
7	82	84	81	22	45	49	41	37	8	14	1
8	80	81	79	23	42	46	39	38	5	11	0
9	78	79	76	24	40	44	36	39	2	9	
10	75	77	73	25	38	42	33	40	0	7	
11	72	74	71	26	35	39	31	41		4	
12	70	72	68	27	32	37	28	42		2	
13	68	70	65	28	30	35	25	43		0	
14	65	67	63	29	28	32	23				
15	62	65	60	30	25	30	20				

In the Sum of Two 5-Minute Timings

E	A	B	C	E	A	B	C	E	A	B	C	E	A	B	C
1	99	99	99	16	80	81	79	31	61	64	59	46	42	46	39
2	98	98	97	17	79	80	77	32	60	63	57	47	41	45	37
3	96	97	96	18	78	79	76	33	59	62	56	48	40	44	36
4	95	95	95	19	76	78	75	34	58	60	55	49	39	43	35
5	94	94	93	20	75	77	73	35	56	59	53	50	38	42	33
6	92	93	92	21	74	76	72	36	55	58	52	51	36	40	32
7	91	92	91	22	72	74	71	37	54	57	51	52	35	39	31
8	90	91	89	23	71	73	69	38	53	56	49	53	34	38	29
9	89	90	88	24	70	72	68	39	51	54	48	54	32	37	28
10	88	88	87	25	69	71	67	40	50	53	47	55	31	36	27
11	86	87	85	26	68	70	65	41	49	52	45	56	30	35	25
12	85	86	84	27	66	68	64	42	48	51	44	57	29	34	24
13	84	85	83	28	65	67	63	43	46	50	43	58	28	32	23
14	82	84	81	29	64	66	61	44	45	49	41	59	26	31	21
15	81	82	80	30	62	65	60	45	44	48	40	60	25	30	20

Overall Speed and Error Grade. Of the three methods below, use the one specified by your instructor.

SA Equal weight to speed and accuracy
2SA Twice as much weight to speed as to accuracy
S2A Twice as much weight to accuracy as to speed

Example. Assume, in Week 6, an average gross wpm in two 5′ timings of 29 (speed grade of 88) and a total of 8 + 13 = 21 errors (error grade of 72, assuming use of Standard C).

SA (88 + 72) ÷ 2 = 80
2SA (88 + 88 + 72) ÷ 3 = 82.7 = 83
S2A (88 + 72 + 72) ÷ 3 = 77.3 = 77

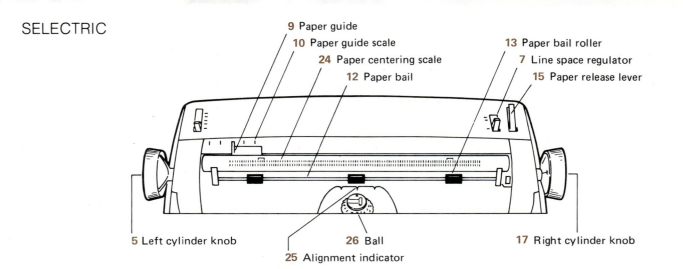

9 Paper guide
10 Paper guide scale
24 Paper centering scale
12 Paper bail
13 Paper bail roller
7 Line space regulator
15 Paper release lever

5 Left cylinder knob
26 Ball
17 Right cylinder knob
25 Alignment indicator

MANUAL

Typewriter Parts. Most typewriter parts are located in the same place and work in the same way on all machines. In a few instances, there are differences in the location and operation of machine parts. The parts you will use in the early lessons are described and illustrated here. Your instructor will help you learn to use them. Later you will learn to use other parts.

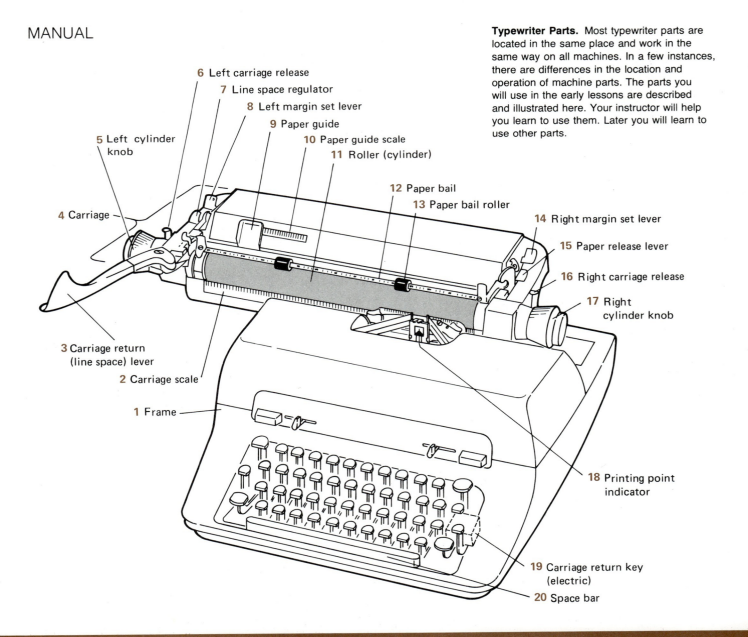

6 Left carriage release
7 Line space regulator
8 Left margin set lever
9 Paper guide
10 Paper guide scale
11 Roller (cylinder)
5 Left cylinder knob
4 Carriage
12 Paper bail
13 Paper bail roller
14 Right margin set lever
15 Paper release lever
16 Right carriage release
17 Right cylinder knob
3 Carriage return (line space) lever
2 Carriage scale
1 Frame
18 Printing point indicator
19 Carriage return key (electric)
20 Space bar

STRAIGHT COPY TIMINGS

Score for gross wpm and number of errors. When there are two 5' timings, average the speeds and sum the errors. Use the grading tables for speed (at the right) and for errors in 10 minutes (next page).

When there is only one 5' timing, use the 5' error grading table (next page).

NUMBER AND SYMBOL (NS) TIMING

First

If your NS GWPM is	Add to it
Below 10	3
10–14	5
15–19	7
20–24	9
25–29	11
30–39	13
40+	15

Then

Use the grading table at the right.

Examples

For NS speed of 13 wpm, add 5, making 18 wpm—for a grade in Week 6 of 70.

For NS speed of 23 wpm, add 9, making 32 wpm—for a grade in Week 10 of 88.

ERROR GRADING FOR 5' TIMINGS

Table 2 on the next page, for 1 and for 2 timings, provides for 3 grading standards:

A 2 epm (errors per minute) earn the average grade of 75.

B 3 epm earn a lowest passing grade of 65

C 3 epm earn a lowest passing grade of 60

For a standard of 1/75 (1 epm = average grade of 75), from 100 points for 0 errors, deduct 5 points per error in a 5' timing and 2½ points per error in the sum of two 5' timings.

Your instructor will tell you which standard to use, according to your stage of training.

Table 1
Grades for Straight Copy Speed in 5' Timings
(First Semester)

GWPM	Weeks of Training						
	6	8	10	12	14	16	18
6	50						
7	52	50					
8	53	52	49				
9	55	53	51	50	49		
10	57	55	53	52	51	49	
11	58	57	55	54	52	51	50
12	60	59	56	55	54	52	51
13	62	60	58	57	55	54	52
14	63	62	59	58	57	55	54
15	65	63	61	60	58	57	55
16	67	65	62	61	60	58	57
17	68	67	64	63	61	60	58
18	70	68	65	64	63	61	60
19	72	70	67	66	64	63	61
20	73	72	69	68	66	64	63
21	75	74	70	69	67	66	64
22	77	75	72	71	69	67	66
23	78	77	73	72	70	69	67
24	80	78	75	74	72	70	69
25	82	80	77	75	74	72	70
26	83	81	78	77	75	74	72
27	85	83	80	79	77	75	73
28	87	85	81	80	78	77	75
29	88	86	83	82	80	78	76
30	90	88	85	83	81	80	78
31	92	90	86	85	83	81	79
32	93	91	88	86	84	83	81
33	95	93	89	88	86	84	82
34	97	94	91	90	87	86	84
35	98	96	93	91	89	87	85
36	100	98	94	93	91	89	87
37		99	96	94	92	90	88
38		100	97	96	94	92	90
39			99	97	95	93	91
40			100	99	97	95	93
41				100	98	96	94
42					99	98	96
43					100	99	97
44						100	99
45							100

C INSERT AND STRAIGHTEN PAPER

1 On all machines *except* those of the "ball" type, such as the Selectric (preceding page), center the **Carriage** [**4**]. Hold it firmly by one of the **Cylinder knobs** [**5, 17**]; depress or hold forward (with thumb) the **Carriage release** [**6, 16**] and move carriage [**4**] to approximate center of machine (aligned over the **Frame** [**1**]).

Note. Except on machines of the "ball" type, the carriage moves across the top of the frame as you type. On ball machines the carriage (called the "carrier" by the manufacturer) on which the **Ball** [**26**] is mounted moves across within the frame.

2 Set **Paper guide** [**9**] at zero (or equivalent mark) on **Paper guide scale** [**10**] or **Paper centering scale** (Selectric, preceding page) [**24**].

3 Pull the **Paper bail** [**12**] forward. If it does not move or stay forward, raise it.

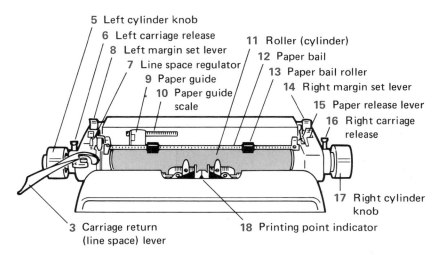

5 Left cylinder knob
6 Left carriage release
8 Left margin set lever
7 Line space regulator
9 Paper guide
10 Paper guide scale
11 Roller (cylinder)
12 Paper bail
13 Paper bail roller
14 Right margin set lever
15 Paper release lever
16 Right carriage release
17 Right cylinder knob
18 Printing point indicator
3 Carriage return (line space) lever

4 Hold paper near upper left corner. Let bottom edge rest lightly behind **Roller** [**11**] (also called **Cylinder** or **Platen**), with left edge of paper against raised edge of paper guide [**9**]. Strongly twirl or spin **Cylinder knob** [**5, 17**] away from you (thumb underneath, first two fingers on top) until at least one inch of paper shows in front of roller [**11**].

5 Pull PAPER RELEASE (lever) [**15**] forward and pull paper higher up in front of ROLLER [**11**]. Touch front against back part of paper and line up side edges exactly, keeping left edges against the paper guide [**9**]. Then push back **Paper release** [**15**].

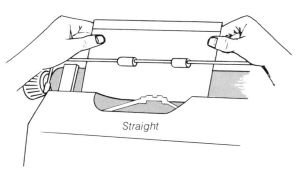

Straight

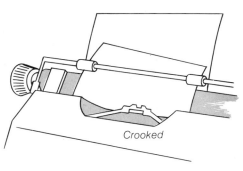

Crooked

6 Push back or bring down the paper bail [**12**] against the paper. Position the two (or three) small **Paper bail rollers** [**13**] to divide the paper into thirds (or quarters). Turn the roller [**11**] (by cylinder knob [**5, 17**]) until the little rollers are just on the top edge of the paper—*not* underneath.

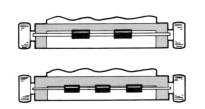

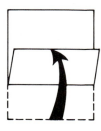 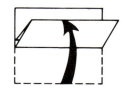 

A Folding full–sheet letter for insertion in large envelope.

B Folding of full–sheet letter for insertion in small envelope.

TYPES OF MAJOR AND MINOR ERRORS IN BUSINESS LETTERS

1 A "mailable" letter is one in which there are no errors of any kind that require retyping the entire letter—no "major" errors. "Minor" errors do **not** affect mailability, whether or not they have been corrected.

2 According to employers, as determined in a number of studies, the major and minor errors are those listed below.

3 Count each instance as a separate error (e.g., 3 high capitals are 3 minor errors; 2 incorrect word divisions are 2 major errors).

MAJOR ERRORS THAT MAKE A LETTER UNMAILABLE

1 Word errors (omitted, added, substituted, transposed, repeated) that affect meaning

2 Misspelled words (especially proper names)

3 Noticeably poor correction

4 Grossly poor placement: too high or low, too far to one side or the other

5 Incorrect word division

6 Violation of conventional format (e.g., wrong spacing between parts or parts out of order)

7 Irregular paragraph indention

8 Grossly irregular left or right margin

9 Frequent typographical errors (more than one per line or two of typing)—ones that are visible even though corrected

10 Grossly uneven touch (shading of strokes)

MINOR ERRORS THAT SHOULD DEFINITELY BE CORRECTED

a Notably misaligned capital letter or letter within a word

b Noticeable strikeover

c Failure to capitalize

d Omitted or nearly invisible letter

e Uncorrected typographical error (misstroke)

f Space within a word or no space between words

MINOR ERRORS THAT SHOULD PREFERABLY BE CORRECTED

g Two spaces between words

h Wrong spacing before or after punctuation mark

i Piling or spreading of letters within a word

j Nearly invisible strikeover

k Slightly high capital letter

l Small deviation from good placement or conventional format*

*Errors of this kind are usually not correctable.

D SET LINE SPACE REGULATOR [3] (for SS)

Some machines can be set at 1 or 2 or 3 for single, double, or triple spacing (SS, DS, TS). Other machines permit 1–1½–2 spacing (SS, 1½S, DS); still others allow 1–1½–2–2½–3 spacing.

```
        ┌ 1   These two lines are
        │ 2   SS (single spaced).      These two lines
one     │ 3
inch    │ 4   This is a DS below.      use 1½ spacing.
deep    │ 5
        │ 6
        └ 7   This is a TS below.      This is 2½S below.
```

Notice that in SS there are no blank lines between typed lines; in DS there is one blank line and in TS two blank lines between typed lines. Six SS lines equal 1 inch.

E SET THE RIBBON SELECTOR

The **Ribbon selector** is located in different places on different machines. Set it for typing on the *upper part* of your ribbon.

F IDENTIFY YOUR SIZE OF TYPE

On most machines the type size is either pica (10 spaces to the inch) or elite (12 spaces to the inch).

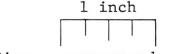

1 inch

```
Pica:   correspond   (10 spaces)
Elite:  corresponded  (12 spaces)

This is a sample of pica type.
This is a sample of elite type.
```

Standard size typing paper (8½ inches wide and 11 inches long) allows 8½ × 10 = 85 pica spaces or 8½ × 12 = 102 elite spaces across the page. *To determine your size of type,* hold left edge of paper at zero on the **Carriage scale** [2] or **Margin scale** [22]. If right edge is at 85, you have pica type; if at 102, you have elite type.

G SET SIDE MARGINS

1 Use the process (below and on the next page) that applies to your typewriter.

a Margin set levers [8, 14] at each end of carriage [4] (toward the rear): To set left margin, hold left lever forward *while* you move the carriage to desired point on carriage scale [2], as shown by **Printing point indicator** [18]; then release the lever. To set right margin, repeat the process, using the right lever.

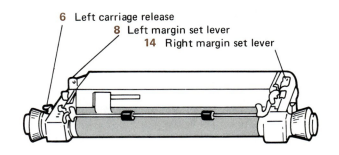

6 Left carriage release
8 Left margin set lever
14 Right margin set lever

Reference materials

EXACT LETTER PLACEMENT

1 On a full sheet, place a simple, 2-paragraph letter with a 3-line inside address as follows:

Dictionary words in body	Spaces in writing line Pica	Spaces in writing line Elite	Side margins[a] Pica	Side margins[a] Elite	Moving date line[b]	Date fixed on line 14[c]
Short Up to 100	45	45	20–65	30–75	On line 21 for a message of up to 60 words. Raise 1 line for each additional 20 words or fraction of 20 words. Lower 1 line for less than 50 words. In personal letters with no inside address, use line 23, not 21, as a base.	For up to 60-word message, 12 carriage returns between date (on line 14) and inside address. Use 1 return less for each additional 20 words or fraction of 20 words. Add 1 return for less than 50 words.
Medium 100–200 201–250	55 65	55 65	15–70 10–75	25–80 20–85		
Long Over 250[d]	65	78	10–75	12–90		

[a]To minimize use of the margin release key, set right margin 3 spaces farther to the right than is shown above. On Remington typewriters use the lower carriage scale.

[b]Space down 4 times (3 blank lines) between date and inside address and never type the date higher than line 12. To keep on 1 page what would otherwise require 2 pages, reduce the date-to-address distance by 1 or 2 lines.

[c]Never leave less than a double space between date and inside address.

[d]Applies to elite type. In pica type, a letter of more than 200 words is considered long.

2 BASIC LETTER has: 2 paragraphs, a 3-line inside address, no firm name, and nothing below the typed signature plus title of the dictator. If additional features are added:

For each TWO added lines **raise** the date higher on the page (or **reduce** the date-to-address distance) by ONE line.

Examples of two added lines:

A 4-paragraph letter
A 3-paragraph letter with a 4-line inside address
A firm name after the closing

An enclosure notation
A 5-line inside address
A typed return address in a personal or personal-business letter

3 Ordinarily, type the reference initials on the same line as the typed signature. Lower the initials a few (1–3) lines if the letter would otherwise be too high on the page. Always check the approximate equality of top and bottom margins **before** typing the initials. A letter that starts too high can be lowered by lowering the initials; a letter that starts too low cannot be remedied.

LETTER PLACEMENT BY EYE JUDGMENT

Letter length	Side margins	Moving date line (Distance from top of page)	Date fixed on line 14 (Distance from top of page to inside address)
Short	About 2 "	3–3½ inches	4–4½ inches
Medium	About 1½ "	2½–3 inches	3½–4 inches
Long	About 1 "	About 2 inches	About 3 inches

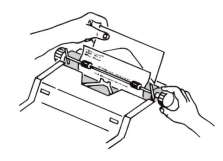

Envelope Spin-in/Spin-out

Upon completing the last address line, drop the next envelope behind the roller. Then, spin the completed envelope out and the new one in—with one strong flip of the cylinder knob.

b Margin stops [21, 23] on a margin scale [22] (just above the keyboard or behind the roller [11]): Depress or push in and slide the stops to the desired points on the MARGIN SCALE [22].

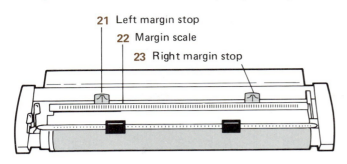

21 Left margin stop
22 Margin scale
23 Right margin stop

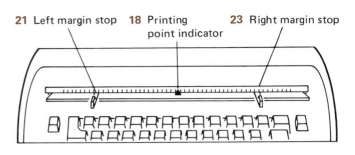

21 Left margin stop   18 Printing point indicator   23 Right margin stop

c Margin (set or reset) key [27] (on the keyboard or just above the keyboard):

(1) To set new left margin, first push or return carriage [4] to present left margin. Next, hold down **Margin key [27]** *while* moving carriage [4]—using other hand—to new left margin. Then release **margin key [27]**.

(2) To set new right margin, first move carriage [4] to present right margin. Next, hold down margin key [27] *while* moving carriage [4]—using other hand—to new right margin. Then release margin key [27].

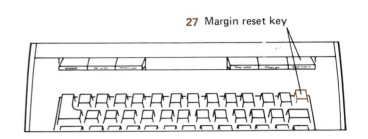

27 Margin reset key

2 *In the early lessons* you will use side margins of 1 inch (SM–1″). On pica machines set LM (left margin) at 10 and RM (right margin) at 75. On elite typewriters set LM at 12 and RM at 90.

3 *In later lessons* you will set SMs for a *centered* writing line (WL). The WL is the number of spaces between LM and RM—as in WL–50 (a writing line of 50 spaces), or WL–55, or WL–60, and so on.

As illustrated in the example for a 60-space WL at right, to find the left margin subtract half the WL spaces (½ of 60) from the center point; to find the right margin add half the WL spaces to the center point. The pica center is at ½ of 85= 42; the elite center is at ½ of 102= 51.

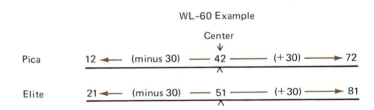

WL–60 Example

Center ↓

			Center		
Pica	12 ←	(minus 30) —	42	— (+30) →	72
Elite	21 ←	(minus 30) —	51	— (+30) →	81

H PLACE FINGERS ON GUIDE KEYS

The second row of keys from the bottom is the "home" row—the base from which all keys are struck. Place your fingers, well curled, on the eight "guide keys," with thumbs just over—but *not* touching—the **Space bar [20]**. With your fingers in this position, check distance of chair from machine; adjust chair if necessary.

Two principles are the basis for building typing speed and accuracy. First, speed gains require typing at a rate slightly faster than a comfortable one. Under that condition, many errors are natural; and since worrying about mistakes prevents faster stroking, speed practice is done without concern for errors. Second, accuracy depends on the right speed—— slightly below the high—error speeds of speed practice. An effective skill building program consists, then, of building more speed than you can control, then of dropping back to a rate you can control. Upon attaining good accuracy at your previous best rate, you return to speed practice.

Paced practice adds a special, additional feature: marking of the materials in quarter—minute intervals to guide your stroking rate. As each passing quarter minute is announced, you adjust your stroking rate, aiming to just reach each marked point as its time is announced. If you fall behind, purposely speed up; if you are ahead, deliberately slow down. The time announcements are designed to assist you to type at just the right rate. If you adjust your stroking rate accordingly, gains will result.

During speed practice, success requires finishing within five strokes on either side of the exact point when time is called——regard- less of errors. Success at accuracy practice requires, in addition, mak- ing no more than two errors per minute. If you succeed, you move ahead; otherwise you repeat the same copy towards the same goal.

I KEYSTROKING AND SPACING

Note. On an electric typewriter, turn the switch to ON position.

1 Tap electric keys; strike manual keys with more force. On all machines use a quick downward motion. Start the key down but do *not* follow it down. Bounce OFF instead.

2 To space (between words, for example), tap the space bar [20] quickly with side of right thumb. Bounce lightly OFF.

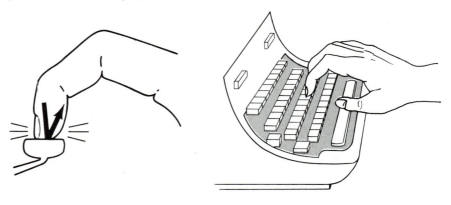

J RETURNING THE CARRIAGE [4]

Electric and Selectric. Lightly depress the **Return key** [19] with right little finger, keeping index finger on its guide key; then instantly return other fingers to guide keys.

Manual. Brace the fingers of your left hand. Take up the slack in the **Carriage return (or Line space) lever** [3] and send the carriage across with a flick of the wrist. Return hand to keyboard while carriage is moving across.

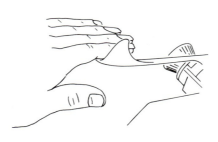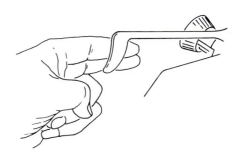

K REMOVING PAPER FROM MACHINE

1 Pull forward or raise paper bail [12].

2 Pull forward the paper release [15].

3 Pull paper from machine.

4 Push back paper release [15] and paper bail [12].

5 Center the carriage [4].

ARE YOU NOW READY TO TYPE?

1 Is your work area arranged?

2 Is your paper properly inserted?

3 Are you set for SS (single spacing)?

4 Do you know your size of type?

5 Are your side margins 1 inch (SM–1"): pica 10 and 75, elite 12 and 90?

6 Are you seated the right distance from the machine, with fingers well curled on the eight guide keys?

7 Is your carriage at the LM (left margin)?

If your answer is **Yes** to each of the seven questions above, you are ready for Lesson 1.

What would life be like with no electrical power? It is not necessary to leave this question to the imagination. Late in the afternoon
of November 9, 1965, radio and TV, mass transportation by subway, and
industries run by electricity all stopped. The greatest electric power
failure in history had taken place. A group of highly skilled techni-
cians searched for days before finding the source of a failure that
left most of the northeast and parts of Canada in the dark. One out of
every four people in this country was affected. The area hardest hit
was metropolitan New York. More than half a million people were trapped
in subways and elevators. Traffic, left without its controlling stoplights, crawled out of the city. Luckily, the moon was full; the sky
was clear; and the New Jersey cities across the Hudson River still had
their electrical power. Thus, planes that could not land safely at
darkened La Guardia and Kennedy Airports were able to land safely at
well-lit Newark Airport in New Jersey.

What could have been a tragedy was merely annoying. New Yorkers
responded to the occurrence with humor and good will instead of panic.
People looked after each other while waiting for the lights to come
back on. It is unsettling to suppose what might have happened if people had not kept calm. The blackout showed not only how cooperative
we can be in an emergency, but also how important electricity is to
our existence.

1 A □ S □ D □ F □ J □ K □ L □ ;

SPACE BAR

Machine settings: SM–1″ (side margins of 1 inch: pica 10–75, elite 12–90). Line space regulator set for SS (single spacing).

PROCEDURES AND ADVICE FOR ALL KEYBOARD LESSONS

1 Type each practice line **once,** omitting the line numbers.

2 To leave a blank line between typed lines, return the carriage twice.

3 Bounce OFF each key.

4 Use quick tap with side of your right thumb on the space bar.

Read the comments below when you reach the practice lines alongside them.

1 aa ss dd ff jj kk ll ;; asdfjkl; asdfjkl; asdfjkl;

2 aaa sss ddd fff jjj kkk lll ;;; as ad af aj ak all

3 a;a; slsl dkdk fjfj dkdk slsl a;a; slsl dkdk fjfjf

Space once after a semicolon (;).

4 a as ask asks; ad ads; add adds; al all; lass alas

5 sa sad salad salads; da dad dads; fa fad fads; lad

6 lads lass; all fall falls; ask flask flasks; salad

For lines 7–14, DS (double space) after each pair of SS (single spaced) typed lines.

7 ask all; all fads; sad lad; as a salad; all flasks

8 dad adds; sad lass; fall ads; lads ask; add flasks

   <u>Manual</u>: Click the carriage return lever (line spacer) once; then give it a full throw.

9 ask a lad; add a salad; a flask falls; alas a lass

10 a sad lad; a lass asks; all fall fads; a lad falls

   <u>Electric</u>: Depress the return key twice.

11 add all flasks; sad ads alas; as a fad; ask a lass

12 as all dads ask; a lad asks a lass; as flasks fall

If you finish early, repeat lines 7–14 as many times as you can.

13 all sad lads ask dad; dad falls as lads ask a lass

14 add all salads; all flasks fall; a lass asks a lad

. . . . 1 . . . . 2 . . . . 3 . . . . 4 . . . . 5 . . . . 6 . . . 7 . . . . 8 . . . . 9 10

RECORDING YOUR PERFORMANCE

At the end of this lesson, you will take a 1-minute timing on lines 13–14. Use the word-counting scale just below line 14 to find your speed in wpm (words per minute). Notice that every 5 typewriter strokes—including spaces—count as 1 word.

Most of the early lessons end with a brief timing to measure your skill. You will find in your kit of supplies (or your instructor will give you) a Timing Record (TR) form like the one at the right to enable you to keep a record of your progress from now on.

TIMING RECORD—STRAIGHT COPY

Date	Lesson	Minutes	WPM	No. of Errors*	Grade*
9/6	1	1	8		
9/7	2	1	9		
9/8	3	1	11		

*Your instructor may prefer that recording errors and assigning a grade be postponed until later. (For marking errors, see inside the front cover.)

Although he died early in the fourth decade of this century and did most of his chief work more than sixty years ago, even now the world's best known inventor is no doubt Thomas Alva Edison. To him we owe the microphone, the phonograph, the electric light and lighting systems, the motion picture camera, and many other devices of great benefit to mankind that we take for granted today. Edison had very little formal education, but he early in life showed a genius for tinkering and a passion for experiment. He had, as well, great patience, the drive to work for hours on end without sleep until a problem was solved, a rare talent for leading and inspiring other men, a great concern with practical benefits for mankind, and the good sense to hire trained scientists as helpers. Without their trained knowledge many of his inventions would never have seen the light of day.

As a chief figure in the whole history of science and invention up to now, Edison stands halfway between the craftsman of the early nineteenth century and the theoretical scientist of our time. Our scientific knowledge has increased so greatly in recent years that no one without special training could expect to make major contributions of the sort Edison could make in his time. It was, you might know, Edison who coined the remark: "Genius is one percent inspiration and ninety-nine percent perspiration."

HOW TO MAKE LEARNING TO TYPE
QUICK AND EASY

The two things to learn at the start are where the keys are and how to strike them. To do so:

1 <u>Use the correct finger on each key.</u> Using the wrong fingers on keys reduces speed and causes errors. Be sure you know which finger to use **before** you strike a key. That may take some time at first, but will quite soon become automatic. Be patient at the start; it will pay off in your use of the typewriter throughout your life.

2 <u>Strike keys; don't press them.</u> Bounce OFF each key! On an electric typewriter, tap quickly and bounce OFF. On a manual, strike with more force and bounce OFF. If you strike manual keys properly, all the letters will be equally dark. If your typescript (the typing on your paper) shows some light and some dark letters, fuzzy letters, or skipped spaces, then you are pressing keys instead of striking them. A good way to insure sharp, bouncy stroking is to say each letter to yourself in a sharp whisper as you strike its key. Sharp whispering produces bouncy keystroking.

During your earliest practice you will probably watch your fingers as you type. That will enable you to locate the right key quickly and to strike it sharply. BUT you must stop watching your fingers as soon as possible. Test yourself. Try to type without looking. If you do not know the location of a key, glance down quickly and find it. Then look away before you strike it. In that way, minute by minute you will be typing less and less by sight and more and more by touch. (Whispering each letter sharply to yourself as you strike its key will not only aid your stroking technique; it will also help you to learn where the keys are.)

Don't worry about errors at the start. Most of your early work should be typed at a speed just a bit faster than is comfortable. There are three reasons why it is important to type with as little delay as possible between strokes:

a To develop good stroking technique

b To learn the keyboard more quickly

c To touch type sooner—without looking at the keyboard

SUMMARY OF WHAT TO DO

1 Look at the keyboard only if you are unsure of a key location. Then look away and strike the key without looking.

2 Be certain to use the correct finger on each key.

3 Whisper each letter sharply to yourself as you strike its key.

4 Tap electric keys, strike manual keys. Bounce OFF—do not press—the keys.

5 Practice at a rate a bit faster than a comfortable one.

6 If you use a manual typewriter, examine your work occasionally to see if all letters are equally dark and clear, without skipped spaces.

Man has wondered for centuries whether our Earth is the only heavenly body on which life exists. We have long known that our own solar system is just one among the billions upon billions in the Milky Way. And the Milky Way is just one of the many galaxies in the universe. In fact, the number of planets in the universe has been estimated to be 10 to the 17th power--100 quadrillion. The laws of probability in connection with what we already know about the universe suggest that there must certainly be many other heavenly bodies on which life exists, perhaps in a more advanced form than on Earth.

Our new radio telescopes are the first devices powerful enough to send signals (and to receive them from) far enough into space. But what sort of signals? In what "language" could communication take place among heavenly bodies? The answer is: in the completely abstract language of numbers, of counting. A series of "beeps" could be transmitted and listened for, such as a one-two-three series or a series of squares (1 beep, 4 beeps, 9 beeps, and so on) or a series of prime numbers (ones not divisible by a whole number without remainder except by 1 and by themselves, such as 3, 5, 7, 11, etc.). The receipt of such signals from outer space would be a clear indication that intelligent forms of life exist elsewhere in the universe.

1 Study the directions and illustrations for striking each new key. "Anchor" the little finger on its guide key and raise other fingers slightly. (**Anchor** means "touch lightly.")

2 Each lesson ends with a 1-minute or a 2-minute test timing. Each line in that timing contains all keys taught. Do not type the timing lines until your instructor tells you to do so.

3 If you finish the practice lines early, continue with the Supplementary Practice (SP) materials for your lesson until your class is ready for the end-of-lesson test timing.

2 E □ T □ N

Machine settings: 1. SM–1″ (side margins of 1 inch: pica 10–75, elite 12–90).
2. SS (line space regulator set for single spacing).

REVIEW

1 aaa sss ddd fff jjj kkk lll ;;; as ad af aj ak all
2 lads ask a lass as dad falls; add flasks; sad fads

Are you spelling in a sharp whisper as you type?

Line 1 contains all keys taught: line 2, all except *j*.

e (lines 3–4)
*Left middle finger (**d** finger) up and a little to the left for e. Anchor **a** and lift other fingers slightly.*

t (lines 5–6)
*Left forefinger (**f** finger) up and to the right for t. Anchor **a** and lift other fingers slightly.*

n (lines 7–8)
*Right forefinger (**j** finger) down to the left for n. Anchor **;** and lift other fingers slightly.*

NEW KEYS

e
3 ded ded deed deeded see seed seeded fed feed jells
4 led less eked keeled added leased sealed desk deaf

t
5 ftf ftf aft set jets lest late stall dealt settled
6 deft lets felt kettle fasted stated jested deleted

n
7 jnj jnj snake tank tend knee lent dense fanned ant
8 sadness jeans fanjet deafness fatness tallness net

PRACTICE

Each word in lines 9–10 contains all three new keys.

9 nest nets neat netted teens tens tent taken fatten
10 sent tenant tense nested attends fastens flattened

Are you bouncing off each key? Is your typescript equally dark and clear?

11 add salt; feel a need; a tea kettle; attend a sale
12 all tasks; ten ladles; tanned knees; faded flannel

13 faded fast; talk sense; leased land; ate at a desk
14 flat feet; all lanes; left at last; eat at a feast

Type quickly! Don't drag out strokes or delay between them.

15 a sad end; take a jet; less talent; send ten tanks
16 as stated; sleet fell; needs a seat; stand at ease

17 a late date; a neat feat; faded jeans; sent a sled
18 felt tense; jade flasks; lean steaks; tasted stale

. . . . 1 . . . . 2 . . . 3 . . . . 4 . . . . 5 . . . . 6 . . . . 7 . . . . 8 . . . . 9 10

If there is any radio program that will go down in history it is probably the Mercury Theater broadcast on Halloween night in 1938. On that night a play was presented called "The Men from Mars," adapted from H. G. Wells' famous story, "The War of the Worlds." It all began innocently enough. In fact, there was considerable feeling in advance that the whole thing was pretty silly. After all, who in this day and age would be entertained by a lot of nonsense about Martians visiting this planet and laying waste to a good part of New Jersey? The answer is: millions of people. And entertainment is not the right word; for the program was done so realistically--in the form of "news" announcements to the effect that men from Mars with leathery tentacles and pale-eyed faces were wading the Hudson River and using poison gas to kill the populace--that millions who tuned in late accepted this fiction as fact. Utter panic followed. In many cities and towns mobs milled about the streets; the police were deluged with inquiries and pleas for protection. There were even some casualties, mostly not serious. All this from a radio presentation completely fictional. There was no intent to hoax the public, but it turned out to be the most effective bit of deception ever perpetrated.

| 19 | lease and lend; tell a tall tale; sent a teak desk |
| 20 | a steel needle; a saddened lass; tested a deaf lad |

Continue with SP (supplementary practice) for Lesson 2 (p. 101)
until your class is ready for the final timing. *Remember:* Do not
type the timing lines below until your instructor tells you to do so.

TIMING

1' (1-minute) timing on lines 21–22. Each phrase includes all keys taught. Type at a comfortable rate. Enter your score on your TR (Timing Record).

| 21 | faded jeans and anklets; leaked and jelled as fast |
| 22 | fallen jets and tanks; a sad jest and a false talk |

. . . . 1 . . . . 2 . . . . 3 . . . . 4 . . . . 5 . . . . 6 . . . . 7 . . . . 8 . . . . 9 10

IMMEDIATE ERROR CORRECTION

If, during practice, you notice right away that you have struck the wrong key, immediately strike the correct key right after it, or space once and retype the word, like this:

tjhe   *or*   tj the

Error correction helps only if it is immediate, so ignore errors you do not notice right away. Do **not,** however, watch your paper to catch errors; keep your eyes on your copy as much as possible. Retype only if you instantly sense or notice that you have made an error.

Use immediate error correction only during untimed practice, never during tests or any other timed practice.

---

3 R □ I □ H

Machine settings: 1. SM–1″ (side margins of 1 inch: pica 10–75, elite 12–90).
2. SS (line space regulator set for single spacing).

Think before you type. Use the correct finger on each key.

REVIEW

Each of lines 1–2 contains all keys taught.

| 1 | sent a jade flask; left a neat desk; faded anklets |
| 2 | and jell as fast; add a flank steak; defense talks |

NEW KEYS

r | 3 | frf frf free red reed deer leer far fare dare serf
  | 4 | jerk starts lard earn trade draft arrears fearless

i | 5 | kik kik kid kin kind kill kilt fist sit sift liked
  | 6 | dike jiff dial lair diet rein ride side tire sniff

h | 7 | jhj jhj hike hill her heard think rehire deathless
  | 8 | rajahs khan inhales freshness fishtail halfhearted

. . . . 1 . . . . 2 . . . . 3 . . . . 4 . . . . 5 . . . . 6 . . . . 7 . . . . 8 . . . . 9 10

r (lines 3–4)
Left forefinger (**f** *finger) up and a little to the left for* r. *Anchor* **a** *and lift other fingers slightly.*

i (lines 5–6)
Right middle finger (**k** *finger) up and a little to the left for* i. *Raise* **j** *finger slightly.*

h (lines 7–8)
Right forefinger (**j** *finger) to the left on home row for* h. *Anchor* **;** *finger and slide other fingers to the left.*

50 wpm (Sy 1.50)

The work that Binet and his associate, Simon, carried out with French boys and girls at the turn of the century was the forerunner of our modern intelligence tests. The culture of France, however, differs in some ways from the culture of our own country. Therefore, it was necessary to adapt the test for use with American children. That fine work was done in 1916 by the American psychologist, Lewis M. Terman, of Stanford University. The most recent revision of what we now call the Stanford-Binet was in 1972, and it is one of the most highly regarded measures of academic aptitude in wide use in this country today.

Many school children these days have taken an intelligence test at one time or another, but probably not the Stanford-Binet——because that test requires an examiner with special training and must be given to one person at a time rather than to groups. Such tests are quite expensive and tend to be used in special cases; for example, to identify the very bright or the very dull child or for a person whose poor schoolwork is thought to stem from emotional sources. It is interesting to note, by the way, that the best single measure of your intelligence is the size of your vocabulary. Those who read widely score high.

PRACTICE

Each word in lines 9–10 and each phrase in lines 11–22 contains
all three new keys.

9   hire thirst thrill thrift shirt shirk either third
10 inherited sharkskin their shinier sheriff shiftier

Remember: Type the word again if you notice right away that you
have struck the wrong key.

11 fresh air; drink this; held a trial; either street
12 a kind father; finish the jar; inherit fine health

13 linen threads; thinner ankles; it rained in sheets
14 dried his hands; kindle the fire; he is his friend

15 raise a threat; three fair ideas; a harsh disaster
16 little hair; share the risks; a hardheaded thinker

17 tried hard; different hats; jeers at their trifles
18 sit there; the first draft; like her; rather tired

19 he jarred the line; fifth trial; his leather jeans
20 attend the affair; left this ajar; the third aisle

21 eat fresh fish; strain at the leash; she is afraid
22 a radish in the salad; terrified her; neither kind

. . . . 1 . . . . 2 . . . . 3 . . . . 4 . . . 5 . . . . 6 . . . . 7 . . . . 8 . . . . 9 10

Continue with SP-3 (supplementary practice for Lesson 3), p. 101.

Timing hint. To do your best work on test timings, type at a comfortable speed. Neither
rush for the sake of extra speed nor crawl in the hope of avoiding all errors. Let nothing
interrupt a continuous flow of strokes.

Instructions for all test timings. If you finish the test copy before time is up, type it again.

TIMING

1′ timing on lines 23–24. Each sentence
contains all keys taught. Enter score on your
TR (Timing Record).

23 she jerked at a fishline; the frank lad is in jail
24 he stated she has the jitters after darkness falls

. . . . 1 . . . . 2 . . . . 3 . . . . 4 . . . 5 . . . . 6 . . . . 7 . . . . 8 . . . . 9 10

4 Shift key □ Period

Machine settings: SM–1″/SS (side margins of 1 inch, single spacing).

REVIEW

Each of lines 1–2 contains all keys taught.

1   it jars her if friends take less than a fair share
2   she jerked at her dark hat and then left the train

. . . . 1 . . . . 2 . . . . 3 . . . . 4 . . . 5 . . . . 6 . . . . 7 . . . . 8 . . . . 9 10

Of the many things psychologists do, the measurement of intelligence is one of the most fascinating. Just before the turn of the century, the French government asked Alfred Binet to find a way to identify those children so retarded mentally that one could not expect them to profit from normal schooling. He shortly hit on the key concept that what the average person of a given age could do represented average intelligence for that age. In that way a five-year-old child who knew or could do the things typical of the average six-year-old was said to have a mental age of six years.

For more than half a century the intelligence quotient was expressed as the ratio of mental to chronological age (multiplied by 100 to get rid of decimals). In that way the child just described would have an IQ of 120; that is, 6/5 x 100. These days, intelligence is figured in a different way; but its levels are interpreted in the same way. An IQ of 100 is "average"; while one of 120 is called "superior"; one of 140, "gifted." Just about six persons in one thousand qualify as gifted.

IQ tests do not measure every kind of ability, but mostly academic intelligence--the ability to do well in school.

Shift key. Shift with the *opposite* hand: To capitalize a right-hand letter, depress left shift key; to capitalize a left-hand letter, depress right shift key. Depress shift key firmly with little finger; hold key down until letter key has been struck; then instantly return little finger to guide key.

Spacing. The general rule is: Space once between words and twice between sentences. When the period ends a sentence, space TWICE *after* it. Do *not* space before it.

Left shift (lines 3–4)
*Use **a** finger. Anchor **f** on guide key and stretch open other fingers.*

Period (lines 4–6)
*Right ring finger (**ell** finger) down and to the right. Anchor **;** and lift other fingers slightly.*

Right shift (lines 5–6)
*Use **;** finger. Anchor **j** on guide key and stretch open other fingers.*

NEW KEYS

Left shift and period

3   Ja Ka La Na Ia Ha Jan Hal Hall Ken Len Ian Nan Ned
4   Jan left. Les ran. Ned fled. I fell. He dared.

Right shift and period

5   Ella Slade Al Tiller Silas Dill Anne Finn Alf Rink
6   She fished. Ellen dressed. Ann jested. Aid Sid.

Both shifts and period

7   Jane Keller and Fred Sterne ate here. It is fine.
8   He raised alfalfa. Ella Kress did that. I tried.

PRACTICE   Each of lines 9–26 contains all keys taught.

As shown in lines 9–10, space once after a period following an initial in a name.

9   Dr. L. K. Janes treated three friends. Dan aided.
10   Fran H. and Kate J. Lad are sisters. I like Kate.

How are you doing about typing without looking? Are you getting better at it?

11   Jake left at nine. Al finished earlier than that.
12   Learn the details. Frank and Jane are interested.

13   Jake left Indiana. He and Alfred are in Arkansas.
14   Dr. Fenn dislikes rare steak. His taste is jaded.

15   Ken filled the jar. It is needed at their dinner.
16   Dr. Karl F. Linnert treated Jane. She had a rash.

Are you typing quickly—going from stroke to stroke without delay?

17   Take the faster jet. It lands in Dallas at three.
18   Helen Fish said it in jest. She has a kind heart.

19   Al has the jitters. He thinks he failed his test.
20   The jail is in darkness. The sad jailer has left.

21   Alf started it. He jerked and rattled the handle.
22   Jenkins listened. He heard Fred and Al tell lies.

Continue with SP–4, p. 102.

TIMING

1′ timing on lines 23–24; then a second 1′ timing on lines 25–26. Each line contains all keys taught. For your TR entry, average the two scores.

Example: For 10 and then 11 wpm, record 10½ or 10.5 wpm; for 2 and then 3 errors, record 2½ or 2.5 errors.

23   Jean feels ill. She ails. Dr. Krankheit is here.
24   Drs. J. Keller and T. I. Felter had three friends.

25   Jan and Frank left. Alan said he had thanked her.
26   Alfred jilted the kind lass and left her in tears.

. . . . 1 . . . . 2 . . . . 3 . . . . 4 . . . . 5 . . . . 6 . . . . 7 . . . . 8 . . . . 9 10

46 wpm (Sy 1.48)

One of the most interesting and exciting men who ever lived was Mithridates, King of Pontus. He lived during the first century before Christ,
when Julius Caesar was a young man and the Roman empire was approaching the
zenith of its power. Pontus is now part of Turkey, but in those days Asia
Minor consisted of a number of small kingdoms, most of which owed allegiance
and paid heavy taxes and tribute to Rome with its feared legions.

Mithridates was of Persian ancestry, and, as was the fashion among
oriental rulers in those days, murder was the usual way to secure and hold
a throne. Young Mithridates began by doing away with his mother and brother
and then, just to be on the safe side, married his sister. Each day of his
life he swallowed a small dose of poison, and then an antidote, thus building up complete and lifelong immunity. Through wise administration he secured the complete loyalty of his subjects and set about freeing the neigh-
boring kingdoms from the yoke of Rome and bringing them under his own aegis.
In his sixties he personally led his armies and was for decades a thorn in
the side of the mighty Roman empire.

5 O □ C □ , (Comma)

Machine settings: SM–1″/SS

Fingering. To permit easy stroking, anchor the little finger on its guide key and raise other fingers slightly.

Shifting. "Beheaded" capitals or an extra space after a capital will result if the shift key is not depressed all the way or is released too soon.

Spacing. Remember: TWICE between sentences.

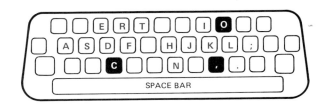

REVIEW

Each of lines 1–2 contains all keys taught.

1 Frank sent Jennie a letter. She read it and left.
2 Indeed he has different interests. He likes jade.

Are you retyping immediately when you know you've made an error?

NEW KEYS

o (lines 3–4)
*Right ring finger (**ell** finger) up to the left for o. Anchor ; and lift **j–k** fingers slightly.*

o
3 lol lol loan hole rook John nose Leon honor Trojan
4 food soft notion does toil Koran aorta jot odor of

c (lines 5–6)
*Left middle finger (**d** finger) down to the right for c. Anchor **a** and lift other fingers slightly.*

c
5 ded ded deck arc talc soccer acre Jack Scotch acne
6 tactics ashcan cancer cliff icicle offcast handcar

As shown in lines 7–8, space once after—not before—the comma.

, (lines 7–8)
*Right middle finger (**k** finger) down to the right for comma. Anchor ; and lift other fingers slightly.*

,
7 k,k k,k Joe Cooke, Richard Locke, and I left soon.
8 Al, Jeff, and I took the short road to the arcade.

PRACTICE

The abbreviation *etc.* (et cetera) on line 9 is Latin for *and so forth.*

9   Len, Joe, and Dick ate lots of ices, cookies, etc.
10 Jock Corder, his friend, located the second clock.

Are you glancing at the keyboard only when you have to?

11 Catch the old crook. Do so at once. John Alcott.
12 Jock attends the local technical school. So do I.

13 A cracked, old lock is enclosed. Cone checked it.
14 A short, cool rain fell. It cooled off Oscar Coe.

15 A doctor is needed. Call Dr. Condon to the scene.
16 Check the coil. If it has a red color, it is hot.

Are you getting clear typescript from bouncy strokes?

17 Load the cotton on the cart. Take it to C Street.
18 Cook, a critic, disliked the second act. So do I.

19 Harold called. He told Scott to cancel the check.
20 That is a fact, not fiction. Clare Locke said so.

21 Lock the door, Cora. Let no one enter the office.
22 Oakland, San Jose, and Stockton are in California.

. . . . 1 . . . . 2 . . . . 3 . . . . 4 . . . . 5 . . . . 6 . . . . 7 . . . . 8 . . . . 9 10

How did the universe begin and what is its future? Those questions
have been a puzzle to mankind from the first days to today. As of the mid—
1970's there were three theories. All three of them agree that it all be—
gan with a "big bang" millions of years ago and that it has been expanding
ever since. The theories differ, though, on the future of the universe.

One theory says that the universe will keep on expanding into the in—
finite future. A second says that expansion will be followed by contrac—
tion, bringing the universe to an end in the far distant future. The third
theory posits expanding, contracting, and exploding in an endless cycle.

Still earlier notions had to be cast aside as optical telescopes gave
way to the far more powerful radio telescopes that reach out billions of
light years to galaxies we do not yet know. Since light travels at 186,000
miles per second—about 16 billion miles per day—the vastness of just that
part of the universe within the reach of our instruments is most impressive.
In this boundless space, this vast cosmos, our Earth is but a speck.

Note commas in lines 23–26: between place names and enclosing the state—but *no* space before the comma.

23	Dr. Clarkson crossed the Atlantic to Nice, France.
24	Kodiak, Alaska, is a cold location. Ron is there.
25	I left Little Rock, Arkansas, for Cairo, Illinois.
26	Ed Johnson is in Laconia, N. H., north of Concord.

Continue with SP–5, p. 102.

2′ timing, lines 27–29. Repeat if you finish beforehand. Each line includes all keys taught. To get wpm, divide total words typed by 2. TR

(TR stands for Timing Record. It means: Enter your wpm and number of errors on that record.)

TIMING

27	Ask if Dick, Jane, or Lester can check. I cannot.
28	Dr. Jacks, his friend, left. He had another call.
29	Jeff likes rich, dark cookies. So do Stan and Ed.

....1....2....3....4....5....6....7....8....9....10.

6 P □ U □ M

Machine settings: SM–1″/SS

Posture reminders. Lean slightly forward from the hips; feet flat on floor; elbows hanging loosely at sides, just a little ahead of your body. Curve fingers over guide keys with wrists low—but keep heel of hand off your machine.

REVIEW

Each of lines 1–2 contains all keys taught.

| 1 | Janet ran a fish store in Akron, Ohio. It closed. |
| 2 | Take the first, second, or third jet. Land there. |

NEW KEYS

p
| 3 | ;p; ;p; pops napkin inkpot appear Alpine sharpness |
| 4 | split paprika septic flapjack ripcord ashpit photo |

u
| 5 | juj juj just dual fuel pull suit sunup pluck Rufus |
| 6 | uncut nature chauffeur huddle arduous pickup Dukes |

m
| 7 | jmj jmj jump mumps topmost calm Freshman farmhouse |
| 8 | jams commit unmake condemn aimless trackman smells |

PRACTICE

Each word in lines 9–10 contains all 3 new keys.

| 9 | dump rump pump hump umpire pumice uppermost markup |
| 10 | lump triumph supplement punishment ampule pulmotor |

p (lines 3–4)
Right little finger (; finger) up to the left for p. *Anchor* **j**. *Lift* **k–l** *fingers slightly.*

u (lines 5–6)
Right forefinger (**j** *finger) up and a little to the left for* u. *Anchor* **;** *and lift other fingers slightly.*

m (lines 7–8)
Right forefinger (**j** *finger) down to the right for* m. *Anchor* **;** *and lift other fingers slightly.*

42 wpm (Sy 1.46)

One of the most heroic exploits in the annals of man is Sir Ernest
Shackelton's expedition to the Antarctic in 1915. Gripped by the spirit
of adventure, Shackelton sailed from Buenos Aires with a crew of 27 men,
determined to cross the great land mass of the Antarctic continent on foot.
Hardly had they arrived when their boat was ground to pieces by the massive
ice floes, moaning and shrieking as they pressed relentlessly on the little
ship. For months afterward they shifted their supplies as the ice floes
cracked beneath them, waiting for a break in the weather to make a dash by
small boat to a whaling station on South Georgia Island, some eight hundred
miles off across the stormiest and most treacherous seas in the world. Finally, a small group started out, against immense odds, across the wintry
seas, promising to send back a rescue boat for those left behind. After
tremendous hardships, every member of the expedition reached safety––a
tribute to Sir Ernest's staunch leadership, and to the skill, daring, and
fortitude of man.

11 The account is due. Peter marked it paid in full.
12 Please that customer. He has a particular demand.

13 Patrick married Mildred. He met her at our house.
14 Maude mends clothes. That supplements her income.

Whisper each letter sharply as you strike its key.

15 James is a professional man. He studied medicine.
16 Jackson is in Mississippi, just east of Louisiana.

17 Paul and Pam Coe planned a trip to Miami, Florida.
18 Samuel met an important client in Tulsa, Oklahoma.

19 Pat attempts, as a rule, to prepare a full report.
20 Tom Maple opened a store four miles from his home.

Are you using the correct finger on each key?

21 Jim, of course, should help to complete the plans.
22 In our opinion, Pamela made a mistaken assumption.

23 Mr. Thompson found numerous opportunities to help.
24 Under the circumstances, it seems peculiar to him.

25 His machines are manufactured in Peoria, Illinois.
26 Mr. Tupman could include a sample of his products.

27 Unless people return on time, he must postpone it.
28 I think St. Paul, Minnesota, is the state capital.

Continue with SP–6, p. 103.

TIMING

2′ timing, lines 29–31. Each line contains all keys taught. Divide total words by 2 to get wpm. TR

29 In the near future, Jack plans a trip to Mud Lake.
30 Speak up; use a loud, clear sound for Jim to hear.
31 Jack tracked his first puma across the hot plains.

. . . . 1 . . . . 2 . . . . 3 . . . . 4 . . . . 5 . . . . 6 . . . . 7 . . . . 8 . . . . 9 10

7 W □ Y □ G

Machine settings: As usual (SM–1″/SS)

When returning the carriage try to strike the first key on the new line just as the carriage clicks to a stop.

Are you gaining skill almost every day: more practice lines each day and better end-of-lesson scores?

REVIEW

Each of lines 1–2 contains all keys taught.

1 A trickle of rain just seeped under the farm door.
2 An occupant of Apartment K has left his door ajar.

. . . . 1 . . . . 2 . . . . 3 . . . . 4 . . . . 5 . . . . 6 . . . . 7 . . . . 8 . . . . 9 10

In a delightful essay in "The World of Mathematics" Kasner and Newman tell about the coining, by Dr. Kasner's nine-year-old nephew, of a word to represent the biggest possible number a person could imagine; namely, googol. A googol is a 1 followed by a hundred zeros. The important thing to recognize is that the number is finite, not infinite. In fact, the authors poke fun at people who use the word infinite when they mean some big number like a billion billion, which would hardly dent a number as big as a googol. To give you an idea of how big a googol is, consider that the number of atoms in the average thimble is a good deal more than the number of grains of sand on a large beach. Nevertheless, it is still much less than a googol. Even with a particle as tiny as an electron, all the electrons in the entire universe do not exceed perhaps one followed by seventy-nine zeros. Still, if a googol is not enough for you, how about a googol-plex, which is ten to the googol power?

NEW KEYS

w (lines 3–4)
*Left ring finger (**s** finger) up to the left for w. Anchor **a** and lift other fingers slightly.*

y (lines 5–6)
*Right forefinger (**j** finger) up and <u>stretch</u> to the left for y. Anchor **;** and lift other fingers slightly.*

g (lines 7–8)
*Left forefinger (**f** finger) to the right on home row for g. Anchor **a**; slide other fingers slightly to the right.*

w
3 sws sws swum jewel twist lawful Newton awhile paws
4 writes lowdown halfwit woodwork showcases Sherwood

y
5 jyj jyj jury my you sky type occupy synonym mayhem
6 why key rye Friday coyly yawl windy showy identify

g
7 fgf fgf fig guy Gwen high ogre magic ridge kingdom
8 jug rangy forget pigtail goggles mortgage leggings

PRACTICE

Are you bouncing off each key and getting clear, equally dark
typescript?

9 Gwen was wrong.   The money was owed to Judge Page.
10 Do drag the yellow wagon away.   It wiggles wildly.

11 Gregory purchased a new typewriter last Wednesday.
12 Enjoy the warm spring weather after a long winter.

13 We stayed in Atlanta, the capital city of Georgia.
14 Twice a year his family goes on a trip to Wyoming.

Are you beginning to sense—without looking—when you have
made an error, and are you retyping when you know you've made
an error?

15 Wagner employs a new system of studying for tests.
16 Years ago, Jack Godfrey worked fifty hours a week.

17 I lay awake many a long night, tossing restlessly.
18 Roy will not pay for the goods.   They are damaged.

19 George is fully aware of the difficulty they face.
20 It was a gray day yesterday.   Tuesday was lighter.

How's your speed? Are you avoiding delays between strokes?
between words? between sentences? between practice lines?
when shifting for capitals?

21 Mr. Gwynn agreed to wait until Monday for payment.
22 Mr. Dewey was willing to go on Thursday or Friday.

23 Gladys went to her engagement early last Saturday.
24 We earn a good wage working for the power company.

25 They saw a ray of light shining in the dark night.
26 Sy may yet get away today or early Sunday morning.

. . . . 1 . . . . 2 . . . . 3 . . . . 4 . . . . 5 . . . . 6 . . . . 7 . . . . 8 . . . . 9 10

Most Civil Service tests for typists and many typing tests used in business consist of typing from nicely printed paragraphs like this one. On Civil Service tests the faster you type, the more errors you may make and still earn a passing score. Some business tests are scored in the same way; others allow no more than a certain number of mistakes, no matter what the speed.

Such tests are, of course, quite unlike real typing. No employed typist copies line by line from perfect print, without correcting errors. Real typing includes, instead, filling in forms, typing addresses on envelopes and file cards, preparing correspondence and reports, setting up information in table form. Much work is done from longhand, and mistakes must be corrected.

The chief reason for the kind of testing that is done is that it costs little to give and score such tests. Better testing costs too much.

Astronomy is no doubt the oldest science; for the motions of the sun and earth are an obvious part of man's surroundings. Since there were no telescopes in ancient times, and all relied on their own eyes, it is not hard to see why they thought that the sun revolved around the earth. This theory we owe to Ptolemy, who lived in Egypt in the second century. For fourteen hundred years this was the dominant concept. It was Copernicus, the Polish scholar, who first put forth the heliocentric or sun-in-the-center theory. He was soon followed by Kepler, a German, who worked out the laws that govern the motions of the planets and who laid the basis for the work of that great English genius, Sir Isaac Newton. The rapid growth of our knowledge about the heavens during the sixteenth and seventeenth centuries was due, in no small part, to the invention of the telescope by Galileo. Our opera glasses are of the same form as the early telescope.

27 Greg suggested that it was necessary to reply now.
28 Yes, Mrs. Grew, we know what he was saying to you.

Continue with SP–7, p. 104.

TIMING

2′ timing, lines 29–31. Each line contains all keys taught. WPM = total words typed ÷ 2. TR.

29 Jackson, Hughes, and Weiss were formerly partners.
30 My judgment was for Mrs. Plank to take the chairs.
31 I know they just might fail to read the copy soon.

. . . . 1 . . . . 2 . . . . 3 . . . . 4 . . . . 5 . . . . 6 . . . . 7 . . . . 8 . . . . 9 10

8 X □ B □ Q

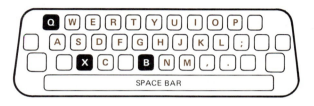

Machine settings: As usual

About fatigue. Long periods of typing won't tire you—unless your posture is poor or you are using more energy than is needed. To save energy: tap—don't press—the keys. If you get tired, exhale and relax completely for a moment.

x (lines 3–4)
Anchor **a**; *drop other fingers downward. Strike x with left ring finger (**s** finger) down to the right.*

b (lines 5–6)
*Left forefinger (**f** finger) down and* stretch *to the right for* b. *Anchor* **a** *and slide other fingers down to the right.*

q (lines 7–8)
*Left little finger (**a** finger) up to the left for* q. *Anchor* **f** *and raise other fingers slightly.*

REVIEW

Each of lines 1–2 contains all keys taught.

1 To make major gains, we changed our fiscal policy.
2 Frank Fulwell enjoys taking physics and chemistry.

NEW KEYS

x 3 sxs sxs six xray exact except Oxford flaxseed Marx
   4 jinxed mixture Maxwell exult exhale oxygen Kleenex

b 5 fbf fbf offbeat ragbag abrupt obstacle standby but
   6 job web oxblood backbone obtain chubby Macbeth orb

q 7 aqa aqa aqua quip jonquil frequented squaw bequest
   8 exquisite quickly squeamish grotesque acquire quit

PRACTICE

To avoid "flying" elbows when striking **x** or **q,** let arms hang loosely alongside your body.

9   A quarter of our budget, maybe more, is for taxes.
10 Bob explained our job. There were many questions.

11 B. J. Quimber acquired the annex on Baxter Street.
12 His explanations are quite unclear and disturbing.

By now, using the correct finger on each key should nearly always be automatic.

13 The liquid mixture will be put into quart bottles.
14 Mr. Bixby inquired about the bill. It was higher.

Are you spelling sharply as you type, bouncing off each key and getting clear, equally dark typescript?

. . . . 1 . . . . 2 . . . . 3 . . . . 4 . . . . 5 . . . . 6 . . . . 7 . . . . 8 . . . . 9 10

32 wpm (Sy 1.41)

Efficient typing depends on more than just skill in striking keys. Setting up a routine before you start to type is also required. If you adopt regular, orderly procedures, you can save some headaches after you start to type.

It goes without saying that the typewriter cover should be folded neatly and stored so that it will not be in your way. Laying out your supplies for easy access is a second point. Are they in easy reach, each thing always in the same place? There are three especially important steps to take even before you insert paper into the machine. First, set the paper guide exactly at zero. Next, set the line space regulator for the vertical spacing you want to use. Then set your margins. Unless you take those steps first, you may have to begin your work all over again.

34 wpm (Sy 1.42)

Several things characterize the development from beginner to skillful typist. One important change is the getting rid of excess motions--movements that hold back, rather than aid, your performance.

What are some of the unnecessary motions that might be delaying your progress? Perhaps you swivel your head to look back and forth between the copy and your machine. More confidence is all you need. Your fingers will move in the right direction without watching them. Do you look up at the end of each line before returning the carriage? Why? On a manual typewriter the line space lever is so big you simply cannot miss it. Too, perhaps you are pushing it across like a weakling. Instead, give it a good swift throw. Try to type the first stroke on the next line just as the carriage clicks across. In that way you save valuable seconds.

15 Extra big boxes will no doubt be required, I feel.
16 Express your opinion, but do not quarrel with Bob.

17 Robin fixed the broken table. It was quite a job.
18 Mabel bought an exquisite handbag, quite a luxury.

19 An extremely large quantity of rubbish was burned.
20 His next experiment will probably be done quickly.

By now, you should need to glance at the keyboard only very occasionally.

21 Bert expects frequent inquiries. He will be busy.
22 Robbins has quite a bit of experience as a broker.

23 Excuse my babbling. I am quite excited about him.
24 Upon request, Ben examined the beautiful jonquils.

25 Rebecca quit abruptly, after six weeks on the job.
26 Mr. Quentin relaxed on the bed. He was exhausted.

27 Barbara is responsible for equipment and fixtures.
28 Exchange the goods. They are not of best quality.

29 Robert will be able to acquit himself excellently.
30 We question the expense of his habits and hobbies.

Continue with SP–8, p. 104.

TIMING

2′ timing, lines 31–33. Each line contains all keys taught. TR

31 Jim acquired an exact copy of the work by Glasser.
32 Fields was kept quite busy exchanging major items.
33 Weem enjoys the exquisite display of big crockery.

. . . . 1 . . . . 2 . . . . 3 . . . . 4 . . . . 5 . . . . 6 . . . . 7 . . . . 8 . . . . 9 10

9

Machine settings: As usual

"Touch" typing means typing without looking at the keys. You can touch type when your finger muscles tell you—without your looking—whether you have struck the right key. To type more and more by touch:

1. Try for faster speeds.
2. Spell sharply as you type.
3. Look down at the keyboard only when you have to; otherwise, resist the temptation to do so.

REVIEW

Each of lines 1–2 contains all keys taught.

1 We just inquired about the package left by Maxine.
2 My phlox and jonquils were taken by Cliff Gibbons.

. . . . 1 . . . . 2 . . . . 3 . . . . 4 . . . . 5 . . . . 6 . . . . 7 . . . . 8 . . . . 9 10

28 wpm (Sy 1.39)

Some people think that the way to become an accurate typist is to practice at drills that contain certain letters or sequences of letters. They think that making few errors rests on the content of the practice lines. But nothing could be further from the truth. The plain fact is that the language of the drill copy has no effect on accurate stroking. Instead, striking the right key depends on nothing more than controlling the time between motions, on typing at the right speed.

The right speed is neither a fast speed nor a slow one, but one just below the speed at which you make too many errors. Any large difference from an easy, unrushed speed has harmful effects on stroking accuracy.

30 wpm (Sy 1.40)

Two things measure your skill at what is called straight copy typing: speed and errors. One thing that has been discovered about typing speed and errors is that they are unrelated. Typists at all levels of accuracy are found at all levels of speed. Some fast typists make many errors, some commit few. The same applies to slow typists.

What that means is that the causes of accuracy are different from the causes of speed. It is not possible to practice toward both goals at the same time. Practice for speed by intentionally rushing, without concern for errors. When you have gained about half-a-dozen words per minute in speed, you then slow down just a bit and most of the errors disappear. On exams, just stroke at a comfortable rate.

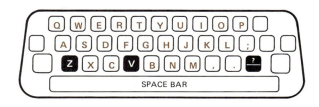

NEW KEYS

v (lines 3–4)
*Left forefinger (**f** finger) down to the right for v. Anchor **a**.*

v $\begin{bmatrix} 3 \\ 4 \end{bmatrix}$ fvf fvf favor vivid hive jovial vex evasive quiver
service envy Slovak vim pave gave vow travel above

z $\begin{bmatrix} 5 \\ 6 \end{bmatrix}$ aza aza jazzy Zulu Balzac waltz quizzical Ezra zip
lizards fuzes vizier Muzhik zigzag ozone maximized

Space twice after the question mark.

z (lines 5–6)
*Left little finger (**a** finger) down to the right for z. Anchor **f** (or **s**) if you can.*

? $\begin{bmatrix} 7 \\ 8 \end{bmatrix}$;?; ;?; Why not? Who came? Where is it? Did he?
Is there? Can they? Have we? Should I? Was it?

PRACTICE

Retype mistyped words—but only if you happen to notice or sense the error right away.

9 Will you do me a favor? Analyze the varied plans.
10 Their children visited the zoo. Were they amazed?

11 Are the prizes expensive? Hazel hopes to win one.
12 Eva froze. Was it very icy, near zero, in Quebec?

13 Were the avenues iced over? Was travel hazardous?
14 The citizens voted. They surely have civic pride.

Type fast—but not so fast that your muscles tense up.

15 Does the correct zip code appear on each envelope?
16 Was Liza given valuable advice? I recognize that.

? (lines 7–8)
*Left shift; right little finger down to the right for ?. Anchor **j**.*

17 David realizes that the magazine must be improved.
18 Have you ever visited Arizona in November? I did.

By now, you should hardly ever have to look at a key in advance.

19 Did Mr. Sanchez give Evelyn Levison a bronze vase?
20 Can Elizabeth solve the several marvelous puzzles?

21 Which improvement will be emphasized above others?
22 Mr. Diaz travels to Brazil on every vacation trip.

23 Why not take advantage of the freeze? Save money.
24 Was Mr. Van vexed to discover the sizable overage?

25 Have they been delivered? Revised? Alphabetized?
26 Have five companies invested heavily in Venezuela?

27 Why involve Victor? A dozen others are available.
28 Was a bazaar authorized? Was firm approval given?

29 I believe that various postal zones were involved.
30 Why did Vera criticize the service Lopez provided?

. . . . . 1 . . . . 2 . . . . 3 . . . . 4 . . . . 5 . . . . 6 . . . . 7 . . . . 8 . . . . 9 10

Continue with SP–9, p. 105.

Part of the idea behind these [1/4] practice materials is stated toward [1/2] the end of the second [3/4] paragraph of the section on the [1] next page marked for practice [1/4] at thirty words per minute. If an increase in speed is [1/2] your objective, you work toward a [2] substantial gain in speed, without [1/4] concern for errors. Then you [1/2] slow down a bit, resulting in a large [3/4] decrease in mistakes. [3]

In this practice, pacing by a time [1/4] signal every quarter [1/2] minute is meant to help you [3/4] adjust your stroking rate to [4] just the right speed for your purposes. [1/4] If you can stroke at [1/2] the desired speed, you may [3/4] expect gains from this practice. [5]

At the outset of learning to [1/4] type, it is necessary to see the [1/2] results of your stroking in order [3/4] to determine whether it is correct. [1] At the be- ginning, very likely [1/4] you looked at your fingers a lot [1/2] or at the keyboard or at the [3/4] paper in the typewriter to assist [2] or verify your stroking.

Quite [1/4] soon, however, a motion comes to [1/2] feel right or wrong, as the case may be. [3/4] The sensations in your [3] muscles tell you the distance and [1/4] direction of the movement you [1/2] have made. When that happens, [3/4] you need no longer see the results [4] of your work. The change--from [1/4] vision to your muscles as the [1/2] source of information about your work [3/4]--is, of course, a gradual one. [5]

2' timing, lines 31–33. Each line is alphabetic.
TR

31	Just why does Dave M. Franklin expect my big quiz?
32	A quick brown fox lazily jumps over the black dog.
33	Jeff Bover played quick, exciting music with zeal.

....1....2....3....4....5....6....7....8....9....10

10 Hyphen (word division) □ Dash □ Paragraph indention

Machine settings: As usual

The **hyphen key** is as important as any letter key. Employers often require complete retyping of a job containing a word-division error; so it is essential to master the bases for syllabication and the rules for dividing words at the typewriter. They begin here.

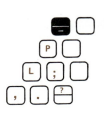

Hyphen (-)
Anchor **j**. *Stretch other fingers up to the right and strike hyphen with* **;** *finger.*

REVIEW

Each of lines 1–2 contains the entire alphabet.

1	Has Ward Z. Farberg excused my trivial jokes and quips?
2	Jim just quit and packed extra heavy bags for Liz Owen.

NEW KEY PRACTICE

USE THE HYPHEN

1 In compound words

3	;-; ;-; a self-made man, fifty-four days, one-half full
4	a trade-in allowance, a short time-out, a quick tune-up

2 In compound expressions

5	a second-class ticket, a seventh-grade class, a change-
6	of-address card, soft- and loud-voiced persons, up-and-
7	down motions, pre- and posttest scores, high-test fuels

3 To separate syllables

  a After word beginnings (prefixes)

8	in-sist, pre-fers, de-lay, ex-act, be-tween, con-spired
9	dis-place, per-mit, re-sume, en-joy, for-give, ad-justs

  b Before word endings (suffixes)

10	scorch-ing, state-ments, pay-able, good-ness, frac-tion
11	grate-ful, crea-tures, preach-ers, par-tial, blame-less

  c Between double letters (but see lines 16–17)

12	oc-cur-rence, dif-fer-ence, as-sure, man-ner, rac-coons
13	ac-com-mo-date, par-rots, ped-dler, rub-bish, ap-proves

14	If a final consonant is doubled before a suffix, divide
15	as in tar-ring, tip-ping, can-ning, rub-bing, nag-ging.

16	Divide after double letters when a syllable is added to
17	a word stem, as in pass-ing, stall-ing, spell-ers. But
18	double letters sometimes need to be divided to spell an
19	added suffix correctly, as in re-ces-sion, ac-ces-sion.

  d In general, where the voice pauses

20	im-por-tant, en-ve-lopes, dis-cus-sions, ac-quaint-ance
21	or-gan-i-za-tion, es-ti-mates, spe-cial-ist, fa-vor-ite

TWO hyphens—without spacing—make a dash (a mark of punctuation).

22	stay--do not go; strike three--out; our loss--your gain
23	Sound--not meaning--is a chief basis for word division.

....1....2....3....4....5....6....7....8....9....10....11

Before a little boy has learned to add, he cannot tell you the sum of eight plus three, for example. Afterwards, he can give you the correct sum. We see, therefore, that learning always involves a change in behavior. But not all changes are due to learning. Some, like blinking when a bright light shines in your eyes, are reflex actions. Still other changes are due to growth. Only some kinds of changes in your responses are due to learning.

In the beginning stages of learning to type, one thinks and types letter by letter. Indeed, sharply pronouncing each letter to yourself as you strike its key not only helps you to learn the keyboard, but also develops good stroking techniques.

Later on, you find you no longer have to name each letter as you type it. You come to be able to type short words and parts of longer words without having to think of each separate letter. When that happens, you are well on the road to genuine skill.

In earlier paragraphs it was pointed out that some behavior is due to learning, but that other kinds of behaviors are reflex actions or are the result of growth. For instance, the change in the voice of a teenage boy is due purely to growth. The thing that sets learning apart from other types of behavior is that it stems from practice. For a few things, one trial is enough. Most often, quite a few trials are needed before we can count on the right response being made nearly all the time. Only then may we say that learning has taken place.

Use the tab key to indent the first line of a paragraph (¶) 5 spaces. (Tabulating is explained more fully in ¶s 2–4 of 13C, p. 24.) In SS typing, always DS (double space) between ¶s by returning the carriage twice.

24	He did a tip-top job--in fact, the best Mrs. Axel-	10
	man ever saw. She needed a dozen good copies--quickly.	21
25	Word division--the correct use of a hyphen at syl-	32
	labic breaks--is needed for regular right-hand margins.	43

. . . . 1 . . . . 2 . . . . 3 . . . . 4 . . . . 5 . . . . 6 . . . . 7 . . . . 8 . . . . 9 . . . . 10 11

Begin again from line 3 of this lesson.

TIMING

Type ¶s 24–25 again, now as a 3′ timing. Indent for ¶s and remember to DS between them. As always, if you finish before time is up, start over.

¶24 is alphabetic.

Use the CW (cumulative words) column for lines you complete; use the dotted word-count line below ¶25 to add part of a line to your full-line total.

WPM = total words ÷ 3. TR

11 Setting side margins □ Margin release key □ Paragraph practice

SETTING MARGINS FOR AN EXACT WRITING LINE (WL)

To set side margins for any WL (as illustrated in G2, p. 5): Set LM at center point minus ½ the WL; set RM at center point plus ½ the WL. *Example for WL–55* (½ of 55 = 27 and 28): For pica type, set LM at 42 − 27 = 15, RM at 42 + 28 = 70; for elite type, set LM at 51 − 27 = 24, RM at 51 + 28 = 79 (or, in round numbers, set at 25 and 80). Typewriter bell rings 6–12 spaces before RM. Listen for the bell; type at least 4–10 more strokes; then return the carriage to LM.

REVIEW (Alphabetic)
Set SMs (side margins) for WL-55

| 1 | We shall make--with just a few exceptions--the ad- |
| | justments in zoning ordinances requested by the voters. |

MARGIN RELEASE (MR) KEY and PARAGRAPH PRACTICE

READ INSTRUCTIONS 1–6 BELOW BEFORE YOU CONTINUE TO TYPE.

Margin locks here.
Bell rings about here.

2	He gave us an up-to-the-minute account of the novel
	developments.
3	He told me--in confidence, you understand--of marked
	interest in my project.
4	Her son-in-law was appointed a vice-president of the
	local bank.
5	If you want a first-class job done, call on Ms. Clay
	to do the work.
6	Two- and three-letter words are easier to type than
	longer words--among experts. For beginners, it does not
	matter how long the words are.

1 The MR (margin release) key is on or just above the keyboard. Tapping it when you are at LM or RM **temporarily** unlocks or opens the margin stop, permitting you to type past it.

2 To complete (or divide) a word at the end of a line that otherwise would not fit within your RM, tap the MR key.

3 Use MR key in copying ¶s 2–13 exactly as shown. In this lesson **omit immediate error correction.**

. . . . 1 . . . . 2 . . . . 3 . . . . 4 . . . . 5 . . . . 6 . . . . 7 . . . . 8 . . . . 9 . . . . 10 11

10 wpm (Sy 1.30)

At the dawn of[¼] mankind's[½] life on earth,[¾] there was[1] no one to explain[¼] things.[½] Many a question[¾] had no[2] quick answer.[¼] Today, there[½] are answers[¾] to many things[3] that puzzle[¼] people,[½] young or old.[¾] We stand on[4] the shoulders[¼] of our ancestors[½] through[¾] the ages.[5]

12 wpm (Sy 1.31)

To have an open[¼] mind is to have[½] something of[¾] real worth as we[1] go through life.[¼] It means that[½] we are willing[¾] to modify our[2] opinions if[¼] there are good[½] reasons for changing[¾] them. It[3] means that we[¼] are willing to[½] consider new ideas,[¾] however strange[4] they may[¼] at first seem to[½] be. Life never[¾] stands still.[5]

14 wpm (Sy 1.32)

Nobody knows who first[¼] notched a reed,[½] drilled holes[¾] in it, and blew the[1] first notes on[¼] what we now call[½] a wind instrument.[¾] Nobody knows around[2] what campfire[¼] Man first began[½] to sing musical notes[¾] or to thump with[3] sticks on stretched[¼] skins, the[½] first type of drum.[¾] We know nothing[4] definite about the[¼] beginnings of[½] music long back in[¾] Man's history.[5]

16 wpm (Sy 1.33)

To say that a person[¼] has learned something[½] is to say that you[¾] can count on that[1] person nearly every[¼] time to make a certain[½] response on a specified[¾] occasion--as[2] a result of practice.[¼] The child who gives[½] thirteen as the[¾] sum of eight plus five[3] is said to have[¼] learned that sum. A[½] person who regularly[¾] names Madrid when[4] called to state the[¼] capital city of Spain[½] has learned the capital[¾] city of Spain.[5]

4 Paragraphs 7–13 contain important information. Read them **now**—before you type.

5 In a choice between falling short of or overrunning the RM (using the MR key), choose the one that will end the line closer to the exact margin. If short spaces equal runover spaces, run over (type past the margin).

6 Set a tab stop and use the tab key or bar to indent 5 spaces for each new ¶ (see 13C, p. 24). DS between ¶s: On a manual typewriter, click the return lever and then give the carriage a full throw; on an electric, depress the return key twice.

7   The bell does not signal a carriage throw; it means
you have a few more spaces to type on that line.

8   Skill at word division and the use of the hyphen key
is one of the features that distinguishes the fine typist from the second-rater.

9   Make a reasonably even right-hand margin one of your
primary objectives in typing.

10   Sometimes, both the margin release and a word division are required to preserve a good right-hand margin.

11   By careful word division and use of the margin release key, you make your typing attractive to the eye.

12   Scan down the right-hand margin of these paragraphs.
It would have been far less regular if the margin release
key had not been used or some words not divided.

13   Notice that none of the full lines on this page differs from any other full line by more than two strokes.

Repeat as much as you can of ¶s 2–13.

3′ timing on ¶s 14–15. Each is alphabetic. Follow the typing and scoring directions given at the end of Lesson 10.

WPM = total words ÷ 3. TR

		CW
14	Judge Way——our former mayor——ordered the fire haz-	10
	ards to be removed next Tuesday as quickly as possible.	21
15	Tuesday——tomorrow, that is——we shall have our jun-	32
	ior clerk type a list of expenses, including the charge	43
	for the prizes distributed at the banquet.	51

. . . . 1 . . . . 2 . . . . 3 . . . . 4 . . . . 5 . . . . 6 . . . . 7 . . . . 8 . . . . 9 . . . .10 11

12 Call-the-throw practice □ Setting the right margin stop □ Double-spaced paragraphs

12A REVIEW (Alphabetic)

WL–55, SS. Use MR key.
Space twice between ¶s.
Repeat if time permits.

1   Mr. Quizmay can join us to work out plans for bridg-
ing the vexing gaps.

2   Extra Roquefort cheese was served to many at the big
lunch for Mr. Jack Peizer.

12B CALL-THE-THROW PRACTICE   About 15–18 half-minute (½′) timings; SS, SM–1″

1 In preparation for practicing a speedier carriage return, take a 1′ timing on ¶s 14–15 of Lesson 11. Score for wpm.

2 Then select from Series A (pp. 127–130) the practice sentence which, when completed in ½ minute, is 1 wpm **more** than your 1′ timing speed.

3 "Throw" will be called every 30 seconds. When you hear the call—regardless of errors and whether or not you finished the sentence—return the carriage and continue to type without awaiting any other signal. If, when "Throw" is called, you finished the earlier sentence, continue with the next sentence. If you did not finish, repeat the earlier sentence. You move ahead when you finish; you repeat when you do not finish.

4 Use SS, without ¶ indention. Do **not** type the sentence numbers. After every fourth timing, at the signal "Double down," space down **twice** and rest before the next set of four timings. (You SS within a set of four timings and DS between one set and the next.) If you finish ahead of time, wait for the signal, "Throw." Make PF entry when finished (see p. 115).

1 As described in the 60-wpm materials (p. 155), paced practice is designed to guide you to type at just the right speed—during timings of 3–5+ minutes and in steps of 2 wpm at a time.

2 As illustrated in the sample schedules below, the rule during the first two cycles of practice is:

Up 6, down 2

Later it becomes:

Up 4, down 2

You work (2 wpm at a time) for a speed gain of 6 (later 4) wpm. Then you drop back 2 wpm for accuracy practice. When you can type with good accuracy at your previous best speed, you return to speed practice for another 6 (or 4) wpm gain.

Speed rule. Finish within 5 strokes on either side of the exact point in the copy (within a range of 11 strokes) when "stop" is called—*regardless of errors*.

Accuracy rule. Same as the speed rule, plus make no more than 2 epm (errors per minute).

3 *Accuracy Practice Error Maximums* (in parentheses) for the various timing durations are:

| 2¾', 3' | (6) | 3¾', 4' | (8) | 4¾', 5' | (10) |
| 3¼', 3½' | (7) | 4¼', 4½' | (9) | 5¼', 5½' | (11) |

4 After starting paced practice at the next even-numbered speed above your previous 5' timing speed, you thereafter practice entirely according to your paced practice performance, without further 5' timings.

5 When you finish your first paced practice session, enter *your* paced practice schedule on your Timed Practice Form (see the examples below). Then, line out the items at which you succeeded (see footnote **d**, p. 115). Thereafter, line out each entry as you succeed at it.

Nine Sample Practice Schedules
(S = Speed, A = Accuracy)

5' wpm = Start at	1–9 10		10–11 12		12–13 14		14–15 16		16–17 18		20–21 22		26–27 28		32–33 34		36–37 38	
	S	A	S	A	S	A	S	A	S	A	S	A	S	A	S	A	S	A
	10S		12S		14S		16S		18S		22S		28S		34S		38S	
	12S		14S		16S		18S		20S		24S		30S		36S		40S	
	14S		16S		18S		20S		22S		26S		32S		38S		42S	
		12A		14A		16A		18A		20A		24A		30A		36A		40A
		14A		16A		18A		20A		22A		26A		32A		38A		42A
	16S		18S		20S		22S		24S		28S		34S		40S		44S	
	18S		20S		22S		24S		26S		30S		36S		42S		46S	
	20S		22S		24S		26S		28S		32S		38S		44S		48S	
		18A		20A		22S		24A		26A		30A		36A		42A		46A
		20A		22A		24S		26A		28A		32A		38A		44A		48A
	22S		24S		26S		28S		30S		34S		40S		46S		50S	
	24S		26S		28S		30S		32S		36S		42S		48S		52S	
		22A		24A		26A		28A		30A		34A		40A		46A		50A
		24A		26A		28A		30A		32A		36A		42A		48A		52A
	26S		28S		30S		32S		34S		38S		44S		50S		54S	
	28S		30S		32S		34S		36S		40S		46S		52S		56S	
		26A		28A		30A		32A		34A		38A		44A		50A		54A
		28A		30A		32A		34A		36A		40A		46A		52A		56A
	30S		32S		34S		36S		38S		42S		48S		54S		58S	
	32S		34S		36S		38S		40S		44S		50S		56S		60S	
		30A		32A		34A		36A		38A		42A		48A		54A		58A
		32A		34A		36A		38A		40A		44A		50A		56A		60A
	Etc.		Etc.		Etc.		Etc.		Etc.		Etc.		Etc.		Etc.		

12C SETTING THE RIGHT MARGIN STOP

To make RM no wider than LM and to reduce use of MR key, set RM 3 spaces beyond where lines are to end (e.g., set at 68 if lines are to end at 65).

Since the bell rings 6–12 spaces before RM, be certain to type 5–10 more strokes before returning the carriage. If you return it too soon (when the bell rings), your RM will be much too wide.

12D DOUBLE-SPACED PARAGRAPHS

Set the line space regulator for DS. Use WL–55 and set the RM according to the instructions in 12C. Type the ¶s at the right, noticing where the bell rings. In DS typing, use only **one** return between paragraphs.

```
     Instruct the truck drivers to rotate the tires at

frequent, regular intervals.  Return three trip tickets.

     Theresa had terrible troubles; they were truly a

great trial to her.  She tried to be Spartan about them.
```

12E TIMING (4')

DS and set margins for WL–65, according to 12C. Use MR key if necessary. Divide total words by 4 to get WPM. Each ¶ is alphabetic. TR

	CW
As a consequence of the talk which exposed the fraud, a large	12
group of citizens demanded an investigation to establish responsi-	25
bility and bring the criminal to justice.	34
The ten members of the search party returned quite exhausted	46
but happy; for in the maze of trees and bushes in the dark jungle	59
they had found the child, weary but alive and well.	70

```
. . . . .1. . . . .2. . . . .3. . . . .4. . . . .5. . . . .6. . . . .7. . . . .8. . . . .9. . . .10. . . . .11. . . .12. . . .13
```

13 Tabulating for typing in columns □ Stroke refinement practice

13A REVIEW (Alphabetic)

DS, WL–60 (pica margins at 42 ± 30; elite at 51 ± 30)

Set tab stop (see 13C) for 5-space ¶ indention. Remember: in DS, **one** carriage return between ¶s. Repeat if time permits.

	CW
This device––a very delicate one, I might add––works	11
best if you equalize the pressure by adjusting the axis pin.	23
By systematizing these complex processes, we find we	34
avoid waste and attain our object quickly.	42

```
. . . .1. . . . .2. . . . .3. . . . .4. . . . .5. . . . .6. . . . .7. . . . .8. . . . .9. . . .10. . . . .11. . . .12
```

13B CALL-THE-THROW PRACTICE

Twelve ½-minute timings (p. 127). Reset margins for SM–1″, SS.

Consult your PF (Practice Form) for your proper starting sentence. Make a PF entry when you finish today's practice. Remember to throw only when you hear the call and to advance to the next sentence only if you complete the previous sentence within the time allowed.

	WPM in
	1' 2'

42 Our championship golf tournament, a $90,000 event (first prize $18,000, 20% of the total) will be held on May 5. TV/4 will cover the action *live* on the 14th–18th holes of the par-71, 7,360-yard course. 42 21

43 The envelopes most commonly used with business correspondence are the #6¾ (size 6½" by 3-⅝") and the #10 (size 9½" by 4-⅛"). The #6¾ envelopes are generally called BUSINESS envelopes; the #10, LEGAL envelopes. 44 22

44 To celebrate our twelfth anniversary, we're offering a 2-year subscription to our magazine, *Home Gardens,* at the SPECIAL RATE of $9.50 (about 36½¢ a copy). Take advantage of this once-in-a-lifetime offer! 46 23

45 Marx & Brayland publish the magazine *Today.* It costs 35¢ a copy on newsstands. Subscriptions for 6 bi-monthly issues a year cost $1.75. Subscribe now, and they'll include issues #1 and #2 free. Get 6 issues for the price of 5. 48 24

46 Up! up! up! Everything's gone up! Taxes are at least 25% higher. The price of food: Bread has jumped from 38¢ to 46¢; eggs from 74¢ to 87¢; fruit up 20%; meat sky high. Clothes —one could purchase a very good dress for $25; now it's at least $50. 50 25

47 Enjoy the delightful dessert, "Yum-Yum," at our expense. Pick up a box at your grocer's this very day—it costs only 25¢. Send the box top to us: Quilly & Company, Detroit, Michigan. We'll *immediately* refund the purchase price to you. 52 26

48 Our "Debs" angora sweaters are a real buy! Sizes 32–38 come in several colors (blue, green, brown). They were $34.95, but we have reduced them 15% to bring them to you @ $29.70. We are open from 9 to 5:30 p.m. weekdays and until 9 p.m. on *Saturdays.* 54 27

49 Parry's Lake Hotel is located in the Adirondacks, about 1400 feet above sea level. Average *maximum* summer temperature is just 78.3; the average *minimum* isn't quite 62. Large-size rooms (double occupancy), meals included, are only $160 to $245 weekly. 56 28

50 There's still time—though not much—to make your reservations for PRINCE LINE's 7-day "Cruise to Nowhere." Prices start at $498 (with a 10% reduction on winter cruises). Do send for our illustrated booklet #15 today. Address: Prince Line, 346 West 107 Street, New York, New York 10025. 58 29

51 Did you notice the advertisement in today's *Courier* of the CLOSING SALE at Kay & Dun's Linen Shop? They're offering bed sheets, size 66" x 104", @ $7.25, reduced from $8.40; also the 81" x 104" size, reduced from $9.60 to $8.30. I'm going tomorrow. I'd like to meet you at 9 or 9:30. 60 30

52 Here's an *excellent* chance to learn about today's changing market! Write to the main office of Boyd & Kahn, 285 East 37 Street, New York, N. Y. 10016, for a copy of Bulletin #49 entitled "Selected Securities." Among the securities listed, you'll find more than 50 selling below $10 a share. 62 31

53 Fly from O'Hare International Airport in Chicago to Kennedy International Airport in New York on one of our luxurious superjets *every* hour on the half-hour (or from New York to Chicago —every hour on the hour). For a second family member, you pay only ½ fare—50% off! Call us at 732-4319 for our folder #C4. 64 32

1 SET MARGINS at extreme left and right.

2 CLEAR TAB STOPS. Use Total Tab Clear key if your machine has one. If not, move carriage to right edge of paper and hold down tab clear key **while** returning the carriage.

3 SET EACH TAB STOP by moving carriage to desired position (on carriage scale) and depressing tab set key.

4 TO TABULATE on most manuals, hold down tab key or tab bar until carriage stops. On other manuals, depress and release tab key or tab bar. On an electric typewriter, tap tab key with little finger. Use forefinger (**f** or **j** finger) on tab bar; use little finger on tab key.

5 TO CLEAR A SINGLE TAB STOP, tabulate to desired point and depress tab clear key.

TASK 1 For the columns at the right:

a Pica: Set left margin at 21. Elite: Set left margin at 30. Remington: Use lower carriage scale.

b Set right margin at right edge of paper, clear tab stops, set for DS.

c At left margin, type *she*. Space 10 times, set tab stop, type *can*. Space 10 times, set tab stop, type *win*. Space 10 times, set tab stop, type *the*.

d Then return the carriage and type each remaining row, tabulating **across** from column to column.

she	can	win	the
old	pin	and	ask
for	the	new	one

TASK 2 Reset pica left margin at 18, elite left margin at 27. Clear all tab stops and retype the rows of Task 1, setting tab stops for 12 spaces between columns.

TASK 3 Try again with pica left margin at 24, elite left margin at 33. Clear all tab stops and set new ones for 8 spaces between columns.

13D STROKE REFINEMENT

Read the descriptive ¶s at the top of p. 122. Then type the practice lines on p. 121 until it is time for 13E. When you finish, make a PF entry according to the instructions on p. 115.

13E SKILL EVALUATION (Tabulating)

Clear tab stops and set margins to extreme left and right. Retype the table of 13C; use 6 spaces between columns and set pica left margin at 27, elite left margin at 36. The table contains the equivalent of 9–10 words. Can you complete it—including all machine settings —in 1½ minutes? 1¼ minutes? 1 minute? 45 seconds?

14 Word division rules □ Table (word division)

14A REVIEW (Alphabetic)

LM: pica 22/elite 31; BC–7. Use DS and the procedures of Lesson 13C. If you finish early, repeat the table, moving LM 3 spaces to the left; BC–9.

Note. LM = left margin, BC = between columns (BC–7 means "Leave 7 spaces between columns").

quick	vital	waxes	funny
zebra	drape	laugh	major

		WPM in
		1'	2'

25 May & Sons have reduced their *entire* stock 20%. Lee's coat (formerly $100) now costs only 4/5 as much—$80.   24 12

26 Bank interest at 5% (compounded daily) amounts to 5.68% in 5 years. The interest on a 4¾% bond for $500 is $23.75 a year.   25 12½

27 Have they joined our *Bond-a-Month* plan? Freedom Shares earn 6.74% in just 4½ years (if held to maturity).   26 13

28 According to today's *Courant,* 8 trains were late because of the tie-up (some as much as 45 minutes late). Were you late?   27 13½

29 Flynn & Clark make a huge machine (Heavy Duty Model #84), containing over 1¼ tons of steel. It works with the *utmost* precision.   28 14

30 The steamer *Americana* (leaving Pier #64 at 9:30) sails up the Hudson daily. Round trip fares: $7½; children under 12, ½ fare.   29 14½

31 The 90-minute film, "A Day with the Packers," (in color) will be shown on February 2 from 8:45 to 10:15 p.m. TUNE US IN for 1½ interest-filled hours.   30 15

32 Tom's clock radio (called the "Timer") uses only *one* 9-volt battery. It's easily portable, weighing only 7¼ lbs. Suggested dealer's price: $29.75   31 15½

33 I enclose my check for $18.80 in payment for my season reserved seats #L–105 and #L–106 for the June 23 matinee performance of "Who's Afraid of Virginia Woolf?"   32 16

34 My teacher, Mr. Crane, told us, "Remember the following kinds of fractions: proper fractions, like 4/7; improper fractions, like 8/3; and mixed numbers, like 2-5/6.   33 16½

35 He then gave us these easy examples, with their answers: 1. Change 10-2/5 to an improper fraction. (Answer: 52/5.) 2. Change 7/4 to a mixed number. (Answer: 1¾.)   34 17

36 Our FM/AM radio (Model A136L) works on 5 flashlight batteries. It weighs only 10½ pounds and sells at $42.98. See it today! You'll *want* it! and you'll *buy* it!   35 17½

37 For the week of June 24 through 30, save 9¢ on each 16-ounce container of Jay's cottage cheese, selling @ 79¢. You'll be *amazed* at such fine quality at so low a price!   36 18

38 I made an appointment to meet Mary at Kane's Tuesday at 9:45. But alas! on the way, I fell and saw stars (***)! I was still seeing stars when I met her. I got there ¼ or ½ hour late.   37 18½

39 I made the following purchases at Kane's: one comb @ 50¢, one brush @ $2.50, various cosmetics @ $2.75. The 8% sales tax was 46¢. The total outlay was $6.21 if I don't count the bus fare.   38 19

40 Are you interested in *debating*? If so, we invite you to join our "Debater's Forum." We shall hold an organization meeting on Friday, June 9, at 3:45, in Sequoia Hall, Room #619.   39 19½

41 Channel 8 (WHNC) will produce two 45-minute programs entitled "Here's to Your Health!" Part 1 will be presented at 9 p.m. on May 27; Part 2, at 9 p.m. on May 30. Don't fail to *tune in.*   40 20

14B WORD DIVISION RULES

Words are divided between speech syllables—but not between all speech syllables. To prepare for 14C, study the rules below.

1 MONOSYLLABLES. Never divide a 1-syllable word. A syllable is an uninterrupted utterance (a sound or series of sounds made without pause in the voice). Adding letters does not necessarily add syllables. *Tip, tipped, pin, pinned* are all monosyllables.

2 1-LETTER SYLLABLES. Nothing is gained by dividing a word after an initial or before a final 1-letter syllable. *E-nough, u-nite, cit-y* are 2-syllable words, but they may not be divided on the typewriter. Note: *stu-dio* but not *studi-o*.

3 2-LETTER SYLLABLES (except in narrow columns like these) should preferably not be carried over to a new line. If possible, avoid dividing words like *teach-er, al-so, love-ly*.

4 COMPOUND WORDS (except in narrow columns) may be divided *only* at the hyphen, as in *above-mentioned* (NOT *above-men-tioned*), *self-control* (NOT *self-con-trol*).

5 DOUBLE LETTERS. Divide between them, as in *fel-low, run-ning*—but do not split a word stem: *spell-ing, pass-ing*—NOT *spel-ling, pas-sing*.

6 SUGGEST FULL WORD by showing as much as possible at line end. *Exam-ple* is better than *ex-ample; indi-cate* is better than *in-dicate*—but all are acceptable.

14C TABLE (Word Division)

SS, LMs: pica 20/elite 29; BC–8

Instructions. Type the word in the left-hand column. Pronounce it slowly to yourself and, in the middle column, type the number of **speech** syllables in the word. In the third column type the word again, using hyphens to show all preferable typewriter divisions. First-row example: *consequence* has *three* syllables and is divided as *con-se-quence.*

To learn to listen for pauses in the voice, do **not** use a dictionary before typing. After you finish, check your work with your instructor or with a dictionary. Then retype the table, correcting any errors made the first time. Set LM 2 spaces to the right of the original setting; BC–6.

consequence	three	con-se-quence
self-esteem		
through		
addressed		
dependable		
occurrence		
strongly		
mission		
reinstall		
taxi		
calling		
among		

14D CALL-THE-THROW PRACTICE

SM–1″, SS

As many ½-minute (½′) timings (p. 127) as time permits (see p. 22 for procedures). Consult your PF (Practice Form) for your starting sentence and make PF entry when you finish (see p. 115, footnote **a**).

15 Five-minute timings □ Horizontal centering □ Shift lock □ Letter sequences

15A REVIEW OF SPEECH SYLLABLES (Alphabetic)

Use DS and the procedures of 13C. LMs: pica 16/elite 25; BC–10.

ri-dic-u-lous   ma-jes-tic   Klon-dike

e-quiv-a-lent   re-a-lize   be-tween

self-es-teem   x-ray   fog-horn

PROGRESSIVE NUMBER AND SYMBOL PRACTICE   Series C

Make Practice Form entries according to the instructions on p. 115, footnote **c**.

		WPM in 1'	WPM in 2'
1	Is Kent & Duff, Inc., located at 178 South Street?	10	5
2	Address Elizabeth's mail c/o Jenkins, Apartment #453.	10½	
3	John's coming anniversary (May 20) is his twenty-fifth.	11	5½
4	"I'd like to be an executive secretary," said Gladys Fox.	11½	
5	They paid $5.30, less 6%, for cases of #10 cans of tomatoes.	12	6
6	Our ballpoint pens cost 30¢ each. Matching pencils cost 12½¢.	12½	
7	By the gross (12 dozen or 144), "Nibs" pens @ 9½¢ each are a buy!	13	6½
8	Jones & Company ordered 4 dozen shirts, sizes 15, 15½, 16, and 16½.	13½	
9	Sometimes, footnotes are starred: * for the first, ** for the second.	14	7
10	"We pay 7% dividends; that amounts to $14 on your $200," said the clerk.	14½	
11	The discount on high-cost items should <u>not</u> be raised by more than ¼%.	15	7½

Use the underscore for italics.

		WPM in 1'	WPM in 2'
12	I bought my oil stocks @ 48¼ per share; but the next day they dropped to 46½.	15½	
13	Mr. Clarkson's number is 785-2846 (Extension 907). Call him between 1 and 2:30.	16	8
14	One dress @ $44, another @ $45, and a pair of gloves @ $9½—why that's about $100.	16½	
15	Use the *slant* for: c/o (care of), o/a (on or about), B/L (bill of lading).	17	8½
16	"I'll *never* agree to that plan! I'd rather lose the entire $400!" John said.	17½	
17	The 40-piece silver service (eight 5-piece settings) costs $194; the 30-piece set is $158.	18	9
18	We invested $3,000 in the bonds offered by May & Maxland. This sound investment yields 8¼%.	18½	
19	In Tuesday's *Press,* Hansen & Sons advertised #2 cans of peas @ 35¢ each—usually 41¢.	19	9½
20	"Today's temperature is 67; the humidity is 45%; wind, south at 10-12 mph," said the announcer.	19½	
21	The hotel has 90 double rooms @ $22-$36 daily and 78 suites @ $38-$75. Add 15% as a service charge.	20	10
22	"Oh, yes—let's have our time-check!" said the radio announcer. "It is now EXACTLY 2¼ minutes to eight."	21	10½
23	The sales tax started at 2% in 1946. In 1948, it became 3%—next, it was 4%—and now it's 8%.	22	11
24	Franklin & Beckman announce a sale of women's "Easy-Tread" shoes, sizes 4½ to 9½. The sale will continue ALL WEEK.	23	11½

15B STRAIGHT COPY TIMINGS

From now on, straight copy timings that measure your skill will be the same length as most employment tests (5'). Read and then take Timing 15–1 (next page). Then read and take Timing 15–2. Use WL–70 (pica margins 10–80, elite margins 15–85) and DS. Divide words, using MR key when necessary. (Scoring is described on the next page; how to grade your performance is explained on pp. 158–159.) Enter the average scores for the two timings on your TR (Timing Record).

15C HORIZONTAL CENTERING/SHIFT LOCK FOR SOLID CAPITALS

A A horizontally centered item (such as a heading) has equal side margins. Half the item is left of center; the other half is right of center.

B To find the starting point of any item to be centered horizontally, let the typewriter do the counting by backspacing from center.

HOW TO CENTER HORIZONTALLY

1 Set margins at extreme left and right; clear tab stops.

2 Set tab stop at center (pica 42, elite 51).*

3 Tabulate to center point.

4 Backspace once for each two strokes (letters, spaces, and other characters) in the line to be centered. **Spell** in groups of two and backspace **as** you spell.

    a Disregard an odd or leftover space; do not backspace for it.

5 Start to type where the backspacing ends.

   *There are 102 elite and 85 pica spaces across an 8½" page. The center points are: elite 51 (½ of 102), pica 42 (½ of 85). For all work, be certain to set the paper guide exactly at zero.

TASK 1 Use SS. After backspacing for—but before typing—each of the five items, check your starting point.

	Starting Point	
Item	Pica	Elite
Notice	39	48
Price List	37	46
Programs	38	47
Where to Dine	36	45
Centering	38	47

TASK 2 Center **each** of the items below (DS). To type in solid capital letters, depress the SHIFT LOCK (above left shift key). To release lock, depress either shift key. If you finish with Task 2 early, continue with SP–18, p. 107.

MODERN COLLEGE TYPEWRITING

How to Set Margins

LOCAL WEATHER REPORT

Board of Directors

Horizontal CENTERING Procedures

Rules of Syllabication

15D LETTER SEQUENCES

Read the instructions on p. 118 and start to practice the materials following them. Make PF entry (see p. 115) when you finish.

15E SKILL EVALUATION (Centering)

Your instructor will time you on centering the three lines at the right. Use DS.

Can you complete all three lines in 2 minutes? 1¾, 1½, 1 minute?

For Honest Value

For Prompt, Efficient Service

Call DALLAS CLEANERS

22 The fabric ribbon that is used in many typewriters deposits a heavy ink on the type faces. For clear copy, the keys must be cleaned periodically, using one or another of the available type cleaners. Another method of removing caked ink from the type faces involves setting the ribbon selector in stencil position and then striking each key a number of times—in both upper and lower case—until no impression can be seen. If any ink is still deposited on your paper, that letter or character is not yet clean. Be sure, particularly, to clean the type faces just before you prepare a master for duplication.

23 The bit of cotton that we cut from a spool and deftly thread through the eye of a needle is the product of one of the greatest industries in the world. We must look for it first in the fields of our southern states; or we may trace it to Egypt, where a plant similar to our cotton plant grows. The seeds are sown in February or March, and in ten days the green shoots are up. Before the middle of June plants are well grown and covered with showy yellow or purple flowers. These quickly fall and in their place grows the fruit, containing the seed. Around the seeds are many downy fibers—cotton in its first stage.

24 Ants are social insects, working together, providing food for the community, and raising their young in common. There are three groups of ants: males, females, and workers, which are really undeveloped females. Every community has a queen; often several queens live in the same community without either jealously or rivalry. Each queen lays tiny eggs scarcely visible to the naked eye, dropping them carelessly in the nest's runways. The workers thereupon shift the eggs to warmer, dryer, safer areas. If a disturbance occurs, the busy workers excitedly carry the immature, partly developed larvae to places of greater safety.

25 Of the many species of ants in existence, we are probably most familiar with the small brown ants that throw up particles of earth above their underground burrows. The burrows are elaborately constructed; with chambers, galleries, and connecting runways, built by the ants in an orderly, systematic manner. Other varieties include the carpenter ant, a much larger species. Carpenter ants feed on half-rotten timbers, in which they cut out extensive galleries. They often damage wooden sheds and buildings; a large colony may become very destructive. Still another variety, the leaf-cutting ant, is a threat to agricultural communities.

26 Two thousand years ago there were many pirates operating near Italy. For years these pirates defied the power of Rome. They attacked her coast; they took many of her citizens prisoner and often held them for ransom. Although many ships were sent to hunt them down and destroy them, they always failed in that assignment. Then the task of overcoming the pirates was given to a great Roman, who was to become famous—Julius Caesar. In a single summer he smashed the whole pirate fleet of more than a thousand ships, destroyed the docks which served as their hiding places, pulled down their forts, and captured more than twenty thousand prisoners.

27 At one time Julius Caesar was taken prisoner by pirates. While he was being held for ransom, he observed their methods and discovered the places where they usually hid when they were being pursued. When his ransom had been paid and he was again free, he used this information to track down and destroy the pirates. As a reward, Caesar was given a military post. Here his accomplishments won him rapid promotion. He brought about many popular reforms. At the same time, he was feared and hated by corrupt men who had cheated the State and had misappropriated the people's money. Although he was the idol of the people, he became marked for assassination.

FOR 5-MINUTE TIMINGS ONLY

Use column "a" or "b" at the right of the copy, plus the numbers (+0, +1, +2, +3) *below* the line under the copy, as follows:

If you do NOT complete the copy, use column "a." *Example:* Suppose you typed through *walki* (line 6 of 15–1, below). If so, you typed 15 wpm: 14 wpm (from column "a" alongside your last full line) +1 wpm (because your partial line ends within the +1 range under the copy). If, instead, you had typed through *are* on that line, your speed would be 14 + 2 = 16 wpm.

If you completed the copy and started again, use column "b." *Example:* Suppose you reached *sensa* (line 2 of 15–1, below) the second time around. If so, you typed 30 wpm: 28 wpm (from column "b" alongside your last full line) +2 wpm (since partial line ends within the +2 range under the copy).

FOR TIMINGS OTHER THAN 5 MINUTES

Use the CW (cumulative words column) plus the numbers (from 1 to 14) *above* the long line under the copy, as follows:

3-minute timing. Suppose you reached *The* (line 4 of 15–1, below). If so, you typed 49 words: 42 words (from the CW column alongside your last full line) +7 words (because your partial line *ends* nearest to the 7 *above* the line under the copy). Since wpm = total words typed ÷ time, your wpm = 49 ÷ 3 = 16.3 = 16 wpm.

4-minute timing. If you reach *The* (as in the 3-minute example above), your wpm = 49 ÷ 4 = 12¼ = 12 wpm.

DIFFICULTY MEASURES

Sy or syllabic intensity (average number of speech syllables per dictionary word) and **St** or stroke intensity (average number of typewriter strokes per dictionary word) measure the difficulty of the copy. For business communications, Sy = 1.54 and St = 6.0 are the exact averages, and Sy 1.51 − 1.57 or St 5.7 − 6.3 are within the average range. Lower numbers mean easier copy; higher ones mean more difficult copy.

NOTES
1. Rounding processes make your final speed correct to within ± 1 wpm of an exact score.
2. See inside the front cover for an explanation of identifying and counting errors.
3. Tables 1 and 2, pp. 158–159, explain how to assign a grade to your performance.

15–1 (5 MINUTES)

	GWPM		
	a	b	CW
Try several times, with eyes closed, to touch the tip of your nose	3	28	13
with your fingertip. You never miss because the sensations of motion	5	31	27
and position in your muscles and joints inform you of the distance and	8	34	42
direction of your movements. The muscle sense is called kinesthesis––	11	36	56
a term that has no equivalent in everyday language. All skills involv–	14	39	70
ing movements, such as walking and talking, are based on kinesthesis.	17	42	84
The kinesthetic sense, not the sense of touch, underlies skillful	19	45	97
typing. When muscular sensations instantly tell you, without looking,	22	47	111
whether you have hit the correct key, you are on the road to expertness.	25	50	126

```
   1     2     3     4     5     6     7     8     9    10    11    12    13    14
     +0                      +1                      +2                +3
```

Sy 1.52
St 6.2

15–2 (5 MINUTES)

	GWPM		
	a	b	CW
For many years it was wrongly supposed that the beginning typist	3	27	13
should be required to imitate the expert by keeping eyes on copy. At	5	30	27
the start, you probably found it difficult and sometimes impossible to	8	33	41
do so. Research in many skills, including typewriting, has supplied	11	35	55
the explanation or principle applicable to all of skill learning. The	14	38	69
kinesthetic or muscle sense develops only after some learning has taken	17	41	84
place on the basis of vision. At the start, you must look to learn.	19	44	97
How have you progressed in that regard? With each passing day do	22	47	111
you less frequently watch your fingers and the keyboard?	24	49	122

```
   1     2     3     4     5     6     7     8     9    10    11    12    13    14
     +0                      +1                      +2                +3
```

Sy 1.54
St 6.0

16 Some wild animals change their color with the changing seasons, a method of camouflage. Many others are born into or adopt a background with coloring similar to their own, thereby effectively escaping the notice of possible enemies. For example, a toad may sit stock-still on a mossy stone, where he is scarcely visible. A bat hangs from a beam on the ceiling, resembling a cobweb. Human beings similarly have learned that by coating their faces and hands and dressing in drab clothing, they become very nearly as invisible as the wild creatures.

17 It is well known that straight copy typing is a school training task that does not exist in later life except in some employment tests. No employed typist or personal typist copies from per-fect print without correcting errors. Except for form fill-ins and other fixed-arrangement jobs, most real-life tasks require advance decisions about arranging materials on the page. All of them require that errors be corrected. A number of careful investigations have shown that deciding about arranging materials on the page plays a larger role than stroking skill.

18 Some forms living in water are known to have continued in existence throughout the ages. These tiny organisms, too small to be visible to the naked eye, are revealed under the microscope to consist of only a single cell. At frequent intervals this microscopic cell divides into two new, complete living creatures. This division apparently continues endlessly, so that these single-celled forms may be said to live forever—unless they make a meal for some larger creature. Possibly some one-celled animals alive today have already had a life of over a million years.

19 In the distant South Atlantic there's a small island inhabited by English-speaking people, called the island of Tristan da Cunha. This island, thousands of miles from the nearest mainland, is almost entirely isolated from the outside world. Ships rarely call there, because it has no products that would interest traders. It depends for its foreign mail and imported merchandise on the occasional ship that comes for some special purpose. The appearance of this ship far off in the distance is an exciting event for these simple people, who give those aboard a hearty welcome.

20 The first time we saw the mountain we planned to climb, it was perhaps a hundred miles away. It was very early in the morning. We could see the distant mist beyond, green with the light of the forest in the valley below. Then came ridge after ridge of rolling hills. Beyond them, apparently hung in the blue sky above, rose the mountain itself. As we continued on our way, we temporarily lost sight of it. We did not see it again for several days, because it was always hidden by nearer mountains. As the challenging climb approached, we were filled with excitement and anticipation.

21 When the narrow path we had followed turned suddenly, we saw our mountain again. It looked very forbidding at close quarters, towering above our heads. It took us several days to find a suitable way up. As we climbed ever higher, the air grew steadily thinner and our breathing grew faster and more difficult. In order to become accustomed to the change, we advanced slowly and climbed only about a thousand feet a day. Then we pitched camp and waited until we were adjusted to the new altitude. Gradually our strength returned, and the following day we were able to climb another thousand feet.

16A REVIEW (Alphabetic Table)

LM: pica 14, elite 23; BC–5. DS after centered heading. SS the two rows.

PREFERABLE TYPEWRITER DIVISIONS

ex-actly   quo-ta-tion   ido-lize   tho-rough-ness

be-devil   mas-sive   jackal   aware-ness

16B PROGRESSIVE PRACTICE   Five 1' speed timings, p. 127; SM–1". Make PF entry when finished.

1 The skill building program that begins today starts with speed practice. Accuracy practice follows later.

2 Select from the materials that begin on p. 127 a sentence which, when completed in 1 minute, is 1 wpm more than your average gross wpm on the two 5' timings of Lesson 15.

3 If you finish the sentence—**regardless of errors**—in the next timing, type the next sentence. If you do not finish, repeat the same sentence until you can complete it in 1 minute. Use SS; omit the sentence numbers, but DS between one timing and the next (at the signal "Double down," space down twice).

4 Upon completing today's practice read the rules on p. 126 and enter **your** practice schedule on your Timed Practice form. Then line out (according to Footnote **b,** p. 115) the items at which you succeeded.

16C NEW KEYS   Machine settings: WL–50, SS

Top-row ' and home-row 1
Top-row 1 and !
Home-row '

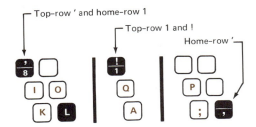

USE ASPOSTROPHE

LOCATE ON YOUR KEYBOARD

Apostrophe: Shift of **8** (**k** finger) OR to right of the **;**

Number 1: **ell** key OR extreme left of top row (**a** finger)

Exclamation point: Apostrophe–backspace–period OR shift of the top-row **1**

Space twice after end-of-sentence **!** Hurry!   It's late!
Space once after within-sentence **!** That's great! wonderful!

a In possessives ('s in singular) (s' in plural)
But note 's in irregular plurals

Add 's to proper names ending in s, except when no additional s is sounded (see lines 5 and 6).

b For plurals of single characters
c In contractions

d To show dimensions in feet
e For minutes when a digit precedes

1 Mary's hat, John's mother, child's play, Jim's pen
2 boys' games, my sons' uncle, grandparents' estates
3 men's work, children's school, women's bridge club

4 St. James's Infirmary, Doris's gloves, Lois's room
5 Charles's dog--but Dickens' novels, Achilles' heel
6 Lois's 18-year-old enjoys reading Hutchins' poems.

7 Mind your p's and q's. Use two r's; count by 8's.
8 I can't. Won't he? Isn't she? I'll buy 8 books.

9 For 8' x 8', read 8 feet by 8 feet. 1' is 1 foot.
10 A 1' timing is a 1-minute timing; 8' is 8 minutes.

. . . . .1. . . . .2. . . . .3. . . . .4. . . . .5. . . . .6. . . . .7. . . . .8. . . . .9. . . .10

9   Autumn has arrived; winter looms ahead. Soon all nature will be asleep, and the land will lie still as if scarcely breathing until spring again awakens the world. This miracle happens so regularly every year that we hardly think of it as wonderful. Yet this sleep of nature followed by this awakening to a new life is truly marvelous. All over the broad land, in countless numbers of plants and trees, this wonderful stirring of the life force produces new, beautiful growths.

10   The first successful typewriter was developed by an American, Christopher Latham Sholes, and was patented a few years after the end of the Civil War. The typewriter revolutionized office operations, and recognition of the enormous market for typewriters led to intense competition among typewriter manufacturers and the establishment, early in this century, of an annual contest for the world's typewriting champion. These contests consisted of an hour of continuous straight copy typing.

11   Legible adult longhand is written at a rate of about one hundred letters per minute. Ordinary typing speeds are about two to three times as fast as longhand rates and range up to more than seven times the speed of longhand. When you remember the other advantages as well, it is simple to see why the typewriter has become the world's primary means of making written records. Consider, for example, the perfect uniformity of typed characters and, consequently, the perfect legibility of typescript.

12   Numbers are more easily recognized accurately when expressed in figures than when spelled out. For that reason, but with certain exceptions, figures are preferred to words in business and technical writing. However, one exception to the preference for figures over words occurs when the sentence begins with a number. Another applies to the numbers from one through ten. Writers often intentionally revise sentences in order to avoid beginning them with a number. Approximate numbers are also spelled out.

13   Beavers are excellent swimmers, as well as tireless workers. With their sharp, powerful teeth, they gnaw off branches and twigs to provide building material and food. They use their little paws very skillfully in handling sticks, mud, and stones to build their dams and to erect burrows leading to them. They build a pond so deep that it does not freeze completely to the bottom, no matter how cold the weather may be. From the water, they dig a tunnel leading to a place of concealment, where they rear their young.

14   Like all professions, the law includes a number of specializations, such as civil law, criminal law, probate law, admiralty law, patent law, etc. Within each of these fields, the kind of work done has so much in common that there has developed over the years a body of legal terms, phrases, sentences, paragraphs, and even whole legal documents that are used again and again in instance after instance. Particular information that fits a particular situation is inserted in blank spaces in these otherwise standard legal papers.

15   Wild animals wage a continual struggle against one another. Only the craftiest or the strongest survive. The weaker animals of the countryside are of necessity masters of disguise and concealment. Nature's creatures of the forest are seldom seen by us mainly because they instinctively sense when and where to hide and because our eyes are not trained for careful observation. At the approach of noisy human beings, instead of dashing about and becoming clearly visible, they stand motionless, relying on the background to conceal them.

Note the variation in spacing after an exclamation point.

11 Jump higher! higher! Yes! we're leaving--at once!
12 Hand it over! Not a chance! Strike three! Stop!
. . . .1. . . .2. . . .3. . . .4. . . .5. . . .6. . . .7. . . .8. . . .9. . . .10

Continue with SP-16, p. 106.

16D TIMING   3', WL-65, DS. Listen for your bell; do **not** copy line for line. TR

	CW
John's father bought 8' sections of lumber at Gage's at 181 Front	13
Street. I'll help him with the 1' x 8' bookcase shelves for his son's	27
room. In a few hours they'll be done--you'll see!	37

. . . .1. . . .2. . . .3. . . .4. . . .5. . . .6. . . .7. . . .8. . . .9. . . .10. . . .11. . . .12. . . .13. . . .14 .

17   4 □ $ □ Typing from print

17A REVIEW
(Alphabet and Symbols)

SM-1": pica 10-75, elite 12-90. Repeat until time for 17B.

> **TYPING FROM PRINT**
>
> Printed matter differs from typed matter and usually cannot be copied line for line. You **must** listen for your bell and act accordingly as **your** line ends.

Ms. Jacquard ordered 18 dozen flags to be sent by railway express. She'll have them quickly—I'll guarantee prompt delivery!

17B PROGRESSIVE PRACTICE   Six to ten 1' timings (pp. 127-130), SM-1". PF

1 Start today's practice according to your PF entries of Lesson 16B. From now on, change between S (speed) and A (accuracy) practice according to **your** PF schedule (the "up 5, down 2" rule). Line out each item on your PF as soon as you succeed at it.

2 Your progress will be rapid at the start. Soon thereafter you'll find that it takes several trials at the same copy until you succeed. Still later, it will take quite a few trials before you succeed. So be patient.

17C NEW KEYS

Machine settings: WL-50, SS

Use **f** finger and anchor **a** finger.

No space after $ or around decimal point.

Top-row stroking technique. Keep fingers well curled, with knuckles (middle joints of fingers) directly over guide keys to reach top row *without arm swing*. Also, with anchor finger in place, raise other fingers slightly to permit easy stroking on top row.

1 .f4f f4f f4f--4 days, 4 weeks old, 4-year-old child
2 f$f f$f f$f--a waste of $4, our bill for $48, $414
3 Your clerk made out a bill for $41 instead of $14.
4 My check for $4.18 may have been lost in the mail.
5 Did Tom pay $84 for that junk? I wouldn't--not I!
6 Never again! A $4 lunch is too rich for my blood.
7 Alex plans to go away quite soon--perhaps June 14.
8 I prefer the $14 hat to the one at $8. Don't you?
9 Hay's Furniture Company charged $414 for the sofa.
10 We can't afford more than $14 for a 4-foot runner.

. . . .1. . . .2. . . .3. . . .4. . . .5. . . .6. . . .7. . . .8. . . .9. . . .10

Make Practice Form entries (see Lessons 59–60E, p. 79; also p. 126; also p. 115, footnote **c**).

WPM
in 2'

1   This is to acknowledge receipt of your posting machine. As soon as we have had a chance to make a careful examination, we shall notify you of the approximate cost of the repair and the time it will take. We shall begin work as soon as we receive your approval. If we find later that the actual cost of materials and labor is below our estimate, we shall give you the benefit of the reduced figure.   40

2   Almost anybody, young or old, who is limber enough can learn to ski. If you enjoy the silence of snowy winter scenery, try cross-country skiing. You should wear light, warm, loose clothing in layers that you can easily strip off. Wear sunglasses and take along a knapsack, food—and good friends. A gliding stride, halfway between walking and running, will keep you comfortable, even on bitterly cold days.   41

3   Large numbers of inexperienced high school graduates are employed for retail sales and office positions. In larger companies, completing a job application form is the first step in screening job applicants. Attentiveness is one of the things measured by the form. Employers expect it to be filled out completely, accurately, and neatly. Omissions, misspellings, and illegible handwriting count against the applicant.   42

4   We are pleased to submit a bid on installing a new heating system in your Harewood plant. The specifications you have outlined are receiving our careful attention. We shall send a representative to inspect the premises shortly and plan to send you our estimate by the end of next week. We can assure you that our materials and workmanship will meet the highest standards and that our installation will fully satisfy your needs.   43

5   The station-to-station telephone rate applies whenever you are willing to speak with anyone who answers at the called telephone. Do not ask the telephone operator for a specific person, department, or extension phone. The person-to-person rate applies whenever you wish to talk only with some one person, department, or extension phone. A conference call permits you to speak with a number of people in different places at the same time.   44

6   In recent years office copying machines have become increasingly common, especially in large offices or when high-quality copies are needed. On such machines a copy can be made in seconds, and high-speed machines turn out many copies very rapidly. For that reason copies are often made by machine, whereas in earlier years, carbon copies were made at the typewriter. The time spent correcting errors on carbons makes machine copies less expensive.   45

7   A person might complain that he is feeling tired when, in reality, he is bored or distracted. The truth is that in mental activities and ones in which little muscular energy is spent, fatigue is a motivational factor. That is, when interest is high, people are highly resistant to fatigue and can work for surprisingly long periods without rest. In light muscular tasks like typewriting, the effects of fatigue are usually on quality, not quantity, of work.   46

8   A vast amount of water flows from rivers into the numerous waterways of the world, apparently forever. Fourteen of the largest rivers alone pour five billion tons of water into the oceans annually. Rivers flow from land to ocean and back again in different form. When we see masses of moving clouds, we are gazing at the constant flow of rivers back into the air. The sun changes water into vapor; vapor rises upward and, falling as rain, renews the ceaseless cycle.   47

11 Men's work pants sold at $14.84 at Warren's store.
12 Green's Lumber Yard sold 8' pine for $1.14 a foot.

....1....2....3....4....5....6....7....8....9....10

Continue with SP–17, p. 106.

17D CENTERING

Center each of the lines at the right; SS, DS, and TS (triple space) as marked.

Time—nearest ¼'. This means your instructor will time you to the nearest ¼ minute.

MODERN COLLEGE TYPEWRITING

DS ———— Leonard J. West

TS ————

SS — Harcourt Brace Jovanovich, Inc.
New York, Chicago, San Francisco, Atlanta

17E SKILL EVALUATION   3' timing, DS, WL–60. First ¶ is alphabetic. TR. Do **not** copy line for line; listen for sound of your bell.

	CW
Jantzen's Hardware is offering for quick sale at $148 Bixby	12
power mowers——a very good buy!	18
That's an item I've always wanted; I'm going to rush downtown	31
right away, before they're all sold.	38

....1....2....3....4....5....6....7....8....9....10....11....12....13.

18 5 □ % □ / □ Vertical centering

Special note. Numbers and symbols are more difficult to type than alphabetic letters. These lessons are intentionally packed with the new keys to give you extra practice.

18A REVIEW (Alphabetic)

SS, SM–1". Repeat if time permits.

The Bellmacker Company rejected the $18.48 per dozen price quotation we gave on boxes of soap. Imagine that!

18B PROGRESSIVE PRACTICE   Six 1' timings (pp. 127–130); SM–1". PF

18C NEW KEYS   Use **f** finger for 5 and % (anchor **a**). Use **;** finger for / (anchor **j**).

WL–50, SS

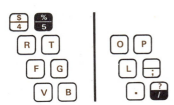

1   f5f f5f f5f 5f; 5 days; a $5 book; $5.85 per dozen

Space once after, not before, %.

2   f%f f%f f%f %f; 5% discount; 15% down; a 4.5% rate

Use / in fractions and dates.

3   ;/; ;/; ;/; a 4/5 share; 5/8 off; August 5 is 8/5.

62   It has sometimes been said that young people are lacking in a sense of purpose. Those of us who have worked with young people would not agree that this statement is correct. Young people very definitely have purposes, but those purposes are not apt to be the same as those of adults.   **57**

63   Consider man's attempts to make written records. The cave man chiseled records on stone. Much later, men wrote with a stick on wet clay. The Chinese were the first to use ink and paper, writing with a brush. Today we use the typewriter, which can turn out work at extremely rapid rates.   **58   29**

64   The paper used for printing paper money in the United States is supplied by a firm that has a secret process for producing a kind of paper that nobody can counterfeit. Only the owner of the mill knows the secret of this process. He received it from his father; he will pass it on to his son.   **59**

65   You may think it strange that the author should think it necessary to tell you how to use an eraser; but you must learn not only how to use it, but how to use it so well that the reader will not notice that it was used. Use a good typewriter eraser for original copies and a soft eraser for carbons.   **60   30**

66   We reduced our stock of merchandise because it appeared likely that there would be a reduction in the cost of some kinds of goods. Our buyers are now able to purchase such goods at lower prices, and we, in turn, can pass these advantages on to our own customers in the form of better value for their money.   **61**

67   Plastic products, which are light and durable, are now being widely used to make articles that were formerly made of glass, bone, metal, wood, and leather. They serve an almost endless variety of needs. Common examples—to list only a few—are buttons, handles, frames, cases, dishes, and ornaments.   **62   31**

68   I have your letter and the map on which you have marked the part of my property which the state plans to acquire in order to widen the present state road. I shall make a careful study of the map so that I may be in a position to talk the matter over with your representative when he comes. Please ask him to phone.   **63**

69   The storm burst upon us with all its fury. It was all we could do to stand up against it. The night was pitch dark and very cold. Deep down below us we could hear the thunder of the surf upon the rocks, but we could find no signs of the vessel for which we had come to search. Perhaps she had already gone to pieces.   **64   32**

70   If you have made an error on the left side of the sheet, move the carriage to the left as far as possible before you begin to erase. If it is on the right side, move to the right. This is to keep the bits of scrap which fall when you erase from dropping into the machine. Like dust, these are a typewriter's worst enemy.   **65**

71   There are several different styles used in listing references at the end of a report. All of them contain three sections showing, in order: author, title, and publication information. Differences among the various styles are found in such matters as punctuation within and between sections, capitalization, and quotation marks.   **66   33**

72   Corrections can be made by typewriting eraser, with specially coated correction tape or strips, or by various white correction fluids painted over the error with a small brush. If you are typing only an original or if copies are to be made by machine, coated correction paper is fastest, but fluids do the best and most permanent job.   **67**

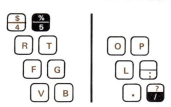

Hyphen is preferred in mixed numbers (8-5/8). The hyphen stands for "and"; it ties the whole number to its fraction. As shown in line 4, a space instead of hyphen (8 5/8), however, is acceptable.

4 Eight and five—eighths is typed as 8–5/8 or 8 5/8.
5 The house has a 5% mortgage. Isn't that rate low?
6 These coats——now on sale at $85——were reduced 15%.
7 Bob realized that a loss of $48——over 15%——is bad.

c/o means "care of."

8 Address the note to John Evans, c/o Quincy's shop.
9 Joe's address is Box 45, c/o Postmaster, New York.

The / is also the division sign: 50/2 means 50 divided by 2.

10 5/5 equals 1; 44/4 equals 11; 48/11 is 4–4/11; 5/8
11 Our discount is 4%——if the invoice is paid by 5/1.

    . . . .1. . . .2. . . .3. . . .4. . . .5. . . .6. . . .7. . . .8. . . .9. . . .10

Continue with SP–18, p. 106.

18D VERTICAL CENTERING   **Remember:** Six vertical lines in single spacing make one inch.

HOW TO CENTER VERTICALLY

1 Count total of typed lines plus any blank lines between typed lines. Count 1 blank line between DS lines, 2 blank lines between TS lines (see Section D, p. 4).

2 Subtract total from 66 lines on a full page or from 33 lines on a ½-page.

3 Divide remainder by 2 (ignore fractions). Add 1 to your answer and space down that number of lines from top edge of paper. (If you do not add 1 line, the top margin will be too narrow.)

4 Use DS or TS to space rapidly all or most of the way down.

Examples: Reach line 19 by 6TS (or 9DS) + 1 SS. Reach line 14 by 7DS or by 5TS, then turn back 1 line. (As in these examples, use DS if your machine does not have a setting for TS; otherwise, use TS.)

5 To save paper, short tasks are often centered on a ½-sheet. For ½-sheet centering, fold paper in half and crease it—but do **not** tear it. Insert whole sheet in typewriter **un**folded. To work on bottom half, space down from crease. With crease as guide after removing paper from typewriter, you can tell visually whether your work is centered. Do Tasks 1 and 2 on the same side of one sheet.

TASK 1 Center on a ½-sheet, vertically and horizontally, the 4 lines of Item 4 of SP–18 (p. 107). DS after lines 1 and 2; SS thereafter.

TASK 2 Center on a ½-sheet the 4 lines of Lesson 17D. In turn, DS, TS, then SS.

18E SKILL EVALUATION (Centering)
Time—nearest ¼'

Center horizontally and vertically on a ½-sheet lines 8–11 of 18C. SS each pair and DS between pairs of lines. Use arithmetic, not backspacing, to determine LM for these 50-space lines: center point minus 50/2. Your time on the 41 words of lines 8–11 starts with paper insertion and includes vertical planning and margin setting. When you finish, continue with SP–18 (p. 107).

19 9 □ 0 □ (□)

19A REVIEW (All Numbers and Symbols Taught)
SS, SM–1"

At $48.15, less 5%, the price is 1/5 less than last month's offer. That's a real bargain!

49   The toughest kind of linen is used to make paper money. It takes about twenty days to finish the process of getting a piece of paper money ready for circulation. The average life of a paper bill is less than two years.   **44 22**

50   You should always try to keep the files in good order. When too much material is placed in one file, it makes it hard to find a specific piece of correspondence or infcrmation. Keep the proper amount of material in each file.   **45**

51   There were dozens of little boys in the main street of the town. If a tourist came near them, they would all start tumbling about like clowns in a circus. Then they would run up to him with palms outstretched, crying for a coin.   **46 23**

52   As you will see in our report, we have enough contracts on hand to keep our plant in full operation for several months to come. We are taking steps to study the means by which our facilities may be fully employed all through the year.   **47**

53   Before underscoring, first type the word or words that are to be underscored. Then, if only a very few letters are involved, backspace to the first letter; otherwise, move the carriage back by hand. Use the shift lock before underscoring.   **48 24**

54   Selecting the right kind of carbon paper to use rests on a number of factors. The choice may depend, among other things, on the number of copies to be made, the kind of machine, the touch of the typist, and the weight of the paper that is used.   **49**

55   Since recent correspondence is always kept in the front of the file, you should start at the back to remove old correspondence. This process is known as transfer, and equipment manufacturers make special cheap cases of cardboard for this material.   **50 25**

56   The iron and steel industry is one of the basic industries of the country, exerting an influence on many others. For this reason, business men and women everywhere follow with keen interest the reports of the large companies that produce iron and steel.   **51**

57   Travel by air has become increasingly popular during recent years. Moreover, the use of airplanes for the purpose of transporting freight is becoming more general. As a result, there has been a steady growth in the volume of business handled by our airlines.   **52 26**

58   Everyone loves to win. It is a good feeling to be on top, to be first in the things we try. Often the prize is not worth the effort, but still we like to win. In life, all can win; there is a place for us and work for us to do. The winner must earn his victory.   **53**

59   Until recent times most of the articles used in daily life were made of raw materials produced by nature. Man merely collected and refined them to suit his purpose. In this age of science, man has developed from these raw products superior materials known as plastics.   **54 27**

60   If, at any time during your typing, you discover that you are making certain types of errors, give special attention to the stroke combinations or words that are causing you difficulty. In addition, immediately retype any incorrect word before continuing with the next word.   **55**

61   Paper money which has been charred black by fire or torn and mutilated may be redeemed. Uncle Sam has an office where workers paste together the remaining parts on sheets of paper. If three-fifths of the original bill can be accounted for, it will be redeemed at face value.   **56 28**

19B STRAIGHT COPY TIMING 5', DS, SM–1". Make TR entry.

	GWPM	
a	b	CW

The skill evaluation paragraphs in these lessons on the numbers — 3 | 26 | 13
and symbols resemble the test timings at the end of the earlier les— 5 | 29 | 26
sons on the alphabet keys; that is, they purposely include in very — 8 | 32 | 40
few lines all or most of the numbers and characters taught thus far. — 11 | 35 | 54
The idea is to check, in little time, all your previous learning. — 14 | 37 | 66

In real—life typing, the numbers and special characters tend to — 16 | 40 | 81
occur less frequently——a sprinkling of them in otherwise alphabetic — 19 | 43 | 95
prose. For that reason some of the ordinary timings from now on will — 22 | 45 | 109
contain a few numbers and, sometimes, symbols. — 24 | 47 | 118

```
    1    2    3    4    5    6    7    8    9   10   11   12   13   14
      +0          |          +1          |          +2          |   +3
```

Sy 1.54
St 5.8

19C NEW KEYS

Fingering. Use **ell** finger for 9 and the left or open parenthesis. Use **;** finger for 0 and the close (right) parenthesis. Anchor **j** and lift other fingers. Keep knuckles over guide keys to minimize swing to top row.

1 lol 191 191 191; 9 times; 19 men, on March 9, a 9—pounder, $19.19
2 ;p; ;0; ;0; ;0; 90/9 equals 10. 10 times 10 equals 100. Buy 90!
3 1(1 1(1 ;););); () Use the ; finger for hyphen (–) and dash (——).
4 General and ex—President Eisenhower was born on October 14, 1890.
5 We shall meet on 4/18 at 10 o'clock, Room 509. Please be prompt!

Spacing is outside (not inside) the parentheses (as in practice lines 6–11).

6 The play opens with Alex (our hero), age 19. At the end he's 50.
7 Inez's signature on business letters is Inez Fox (Mrs. Ivan Fox).
8 Send three boxes (price $9.98 less 10%) to our 14th Street store.
9 Overseas jet airliner service (by BOAC) began on October 4, 1948.

10 Our invoice of 5/9 covers your purchase of 40 cases (as ordered).
11 The balance ($90) was due on 8/10. Won't you mail us your check?

```
. . . .1. . . .2. . . .3. . . .4. . . .5. . . .6. . . .7. . . .8. . . .9. . . .10. . . .11. . . .12. . . .13
```

Continue with SP–19, p. 107.

19D SKILL EVALUATION (Stroking) Contains all letters and symbols taught.

CW

3' timing. Use DS and 1" side margins. WPM = total words ÷ 3. TR–NS. (See note below.)

The Boutique, 948 Jackson Street (corner Mayview), — 10
is offering an extra discount of 10%——1/10 off——on their — 22
$15 ladies' skirts; all sizes. Shop now! Won't you? — 32

```
. . . .1. . . .2. . . .3. . . .4. . . .5. . . .6. . . .7. . . .8. . . .9. . . .10. . . .11.
```

19E PROGRESSIVE PRACTICE

As many 1' timings as time permits (pp. 127–130). PF

Note. Your rate on NS (number and symbol) copy is surely below your rate on ordinary alphabetic copy. To keep track of your progress on NS copy, enter your 19D wpm and errors on the RIGHT side of your timing record. Hereafter, make the entries indicated by the abbreviations TR, TR–NS, PF.

32 Repeated typing of these little paragraphs not only increases your speed on these materials but will add to your rate on new material. 27

33 Fast and fluent typing is not so much a matter of striking the key quickly as it is of releasing each key quickly and moving on to the next key. 28 14

34 We must inform you that we cannot fill your new order until we receive your check to cover the shipment which we sent to you on the first day of May. 29

35 There is always a difference of opinion between the sales and legal departments of the company regarding the procedure for collecting unpaid accounts. 30 15

36 In selecting a place of residence, people usually consider the advantages for their children. They prefer to reside near good schools and near park areas. 31

37 I should appreciate your signing both copies of the contract and returning one to me before next week together with the information form completed in duplicate. 32 16

38 As a rule, we require a deposit of at least half the amount with your first order, since we cannot dispose of the calendars after your name has been printed on them. 33

39 The personnel office has requested that each secretary submit a complete job analysis, which will be kept on file and referred to when hiring new employees for such jobs. 34 17

40 Our wide experience, covering a period of more than thirty years, enables us to give you many helpful suggestions in your selection of books as gifts for children or for adults. 35

41 You are required to type this set of drill lines until you can type the whole group of lines in the time allowed. Give every bit of your spare time to this sort of practice. 36 18

42 There have been many recent complaints about breakage. We believe the reason for this breakage is that the men in the shipping room have not been careful enough in packing merchandise. 37

43 As soon as you can type smoothly and within one minute the lines on which you have been working, you are to proceed to the next set. This set is a little longer than the one you just typed. 38 19

44 Benjamin Franklin was a scientist as well as a statesman. It was he who performed the famous experiment of flying a kite during a thunder storm, proving that lightning is an electrical discharge. 39

45 By the use of this easy program you will not fall into any habit of slow, lazy stroking. You will be trying to raise your stroking rate. You will also be striving for writing that is fluent and even. 40 20

46 By breaking down the atom, man is now able to release more energy than ever before. Whether this discovery of science results in good or evil depends upon the use to which mankind will put this new force. 41

47 We are all familiar with the type of man who will explain to anybody who will listen how to manage the finances of this country, but will then try to borrow a dollar or two to keep him going until next pay day. 42 21

48 There are several ways to build typing skill—not just one way that is correct for all. Each of us must find the right way to type so that maximum growth will come in the quickest time and with the least effort. 43

20A REVIEW Type 19D, preceding page; SM–1″.

20B NEW KEYS

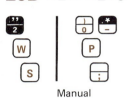
Manual

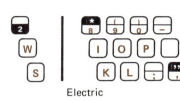
Electric

On most **manuals,** " (quotation mark—or quote, for short) is shift of 2, and * (asterisk or star) is shift of hyphen. On most **electrics,** " is shift of apostrophe (to right of ;), and * is shift of 8. Use WL–50.

For 2, anchor **a,** raise other fingers.

For " on 2, anchor **a,** use **s** finger.
For " on ', anchor **j,** use **;** finger.

For * on –, anchor **j,** use **;** finger.
For * on 8, anchor **;,** use **k** finger.

HOW TO USE QUOTATION MARKS*
(See starred footnote below Rule 8.)

1 Space outside, not inside, " [2, 20].

2 Period always inside " [5, 17].

3 Use , before a short quotation [5, 17] or after one [7]. Comma **inside** close " [6, 7, 8].

4 The unquoted part of an interrupted quotation is surrounded by commas—**no** space before the comma [6].

5 Use ' (single quote) for a quote within a quote [7, 8]. Note .'" at end of sentence 8.

6 The ? and ! are inside the quote when the quoted part is a question or exclamation [9, 10, 19, 26]. Otherwise, they are outside [11, 12].

7 Semicolon always outside " [13].

8 Use " for time in seconds when an Arabic number precedes [14]; also for inches when an Arabic number precedes (read **x** as "by") [15].

⸻

*Numbers in brackets refer to the prac-tice sentences that illustrate the rule. Study the rules and the sentences that illustrate them.

1 sws s2s s2s s2s; a $2 item; a 2' pole; 1's and 2's

2 s"s s"s s"s
   ;"; ;"; ;"; Ed awaited the "Start" or "Go" signal.

3 ;–; ;*; ;*; ;*;
   k*k k*k k*k k*k A 4* rating means a 4–star rating.

4 The asterisk (*) is often used as a footnote sign.

5 The teacher said, "Let's try four 2' timings now."
6 "Don't worry," Ted assured us, "I'll fix it soon."

7 "Sing 'Mandalay' for an encore," Albert was urged.
8 "Don't begin," Fred warned, "until you hear 'Go.'"

9 "Why not?" he asked when they refused to continue.
10 "Gladly!" he exclaimed when they asked him to run.

11 Did they begin on signal when the coach said "Go"?
12 Say "please"! We'll thank you to say "thank you"!

13 Bob said "Gesundheit"; he often uses German words.
14 Take a 20" (20–second) timing, then a 5" time-out.

15 Sid read 21'2" x 9' as 21 feet 2 inches by 9 feet.
16 He knows 5" can mean either 5 inches or 5 seconds.

17 The teacher said, "Let's try two 20" timings now."
18 If we cry "Wolf! Wolf!" too often, nobody listens.

19 "Is this $200, 8% note due in 90 days?" Max asked.
20 Poe's "The Raven" is probably his best–known poem.

21 A few movie critics gave the new film a 4* rating.
22 Sue said the items marked with a * are "Personal."

23 The Latin abbreviation "e.g." means "for example."
24 "Isn't that a $25 item?" Ed asked the sales clerk.

25 She advertised "Brand X," selling at $4, less 1/8.
26 "What a blow!" he cried at the 20% loss of income.

. . . . 1 . . . . 2 . . . . 3 . . . . 4 . . . . 5 . . . . 6 . . . . 7 . . . . 8 . . . . 9 10

Continue with SP–20, p. 107.

PROGRESSIVE PRACTICE Series A (for 1′ timings)   ½′ scoring column for Call-the-Throw Practice only.

Make entries on your Practice Form according to the instructions on p. 115, footnote **b**.

#	Sentence	½′	1′	2′
1	Be sure to pay.	6		
2	She shall not go.	7		
3	They held it for us.	8	4	
4	It should be paid for.	9		
5	Rush the form to the men.	10	5	
6	I have seen all of the men.	11		
7	When both men come, we may go.	12	6	
8	Give the money to the other man.	13		
9	He can keep that much cash on hand.	14	7	
10	They will remain together a long time.	15		
11	He says that they have to go away today.	16	8	
12	Leave your full name with the chief clerk.	17		
13	Take the time to work it out in the best way.	18	9	
14	This makes the third time we have had to return.	19		
15	It is not easy for us to know the right way to go.	20	10	5
16	I shall send you the letter as soon as I have the time.	22	11	
17	If there is one thing I want to do well, it is to typewrite.	24	12	6
18	We shall take the usual discount on the order received last week.	26	13	
19	The head of the firm has just returned from a long tour of inspection.	28	14	7
20	I am sorry to hear that he will be unable to come to the meeting next week.	30	15	
21	There is nothing we can do to help you unless you submit your claims in writing.	32	16	8
22	We hope to hear from you soon about the order we placed with you for five dozen pens.	34	17	
23	If there is something we can do to help, please do not hesitate to call on us at any time.	36	18	9
24	Some of us feel it would not be fair to ask the new men to give such large amounts to the fund.	38	19	
25	When we were here last week, I said I would buy some things if you would charge them to our account.	40	20	10
26	If the weather is quite good tomorrow, it will be a real pleasure to go into the country with them again.	42	21	
27	I can send you a small check for part of the amount due in two weeks and complete the payment late next month.	44	22	11
28	An excellent way to avoid making many mistakes is to begin slowly and pick up speed very gradually as you go along.	46	23	
29	Please inform me as soon as you can of any change in your plans concerning the ship-ment of the goods I ordered from you.	48	24	12
30	Each time you repeat one of these exercises you should get closer to the goal of com-pleting the sentence in the time allowed.	50	25	
31	If you do not rush too fast the first time you try each of these sentences, you will sooner be able to complete it with real ease.	52	26	13

20C SKILL EVALUATION   Contains all letters and symbols taught, except ;.

3' timing. Use DS, SM–1″. TR–NS.
(See **Note** below 19E.)

CW

```
Were the 25 boxes of our No. 10, 4-star (4*) enve-     10
lopes, at $1.90 each, 2% off, sent to Mr. Jack Quayzer,  21
c/o Ed Gill, 28 St. John's Square, marked "Rush!"?       31
. . . .1. . . .2. . . .3. . . .4. . . .5. . .6. . . .7. . . .8. . . .9. . . .10. . . .11
```

20D OPTIONAL PRACTICE   If you did not finish practice lines 1–26, do so now. Then continue with SP–20 (p. 107) or select from SP–16 through SP–19 (pp. 106–107). Or, perhaps your instructor may prefer to conduct several progressive practice timings.

21   7 □ & □ ½ □ ¼ □ Aligning numbers

21A REVIEW   Type 20C; SM–1″.

21B NEW KEYS   The ampersand or "and" sign, &, is used **only** in company names and is **always** preceded and followed by a space.

Raise other fingers and—

For 7 and &, use **j** finger
—anchor ;.

For ½ and ¼, use **;** finger
—anchor **j**.

Reset for WL–65.

Note commas **around** Inc.
(incorporated).

```
1   j7j j7j j7j j&j j&j j&j Jones & Kay at 17th Street

2   ;½; ;½; ;½; ;¼; ;¼; ;¼; a ½-sheet, 2¼ degrees left

3   A "mixed number" is a whole number and a fraction (e.g., 7½, 7¼).
4   The 1-digit numbers (0-9) are called "integers"; 7 is an integer.
5   Fractions can be expressed as decimals--¼ is .25; 170¼ is 170.25.
6   The Jansen & Clapper Company is at 20½ Pell Street, in Manhattan.
7   Dun & Cox, Inc., offers a 2½% (2.5%) discount for payment by 9/7.
8   We paid $78.50 less 4½% ($74.97) to Baines, Jackson, Clarke & Co.
    . . . .1. . . .2. . . .3. . . .4. . . .5. . . .6. . . .7. . . .8. . . .9. . . .10. . . .11. . . .12. . . .13
```

Continue with SP–21, p. 108.

21C PROGRESSIVE PRACTICE   Three to five 1' timings (pp. 127–130); SM–1″. PF

Progressive practice

PROGRESSIVE PRACTICE PROCEDURES

1 As illustrated in the columns below, the Progressive Practice rule is:

Up 5, down 2

You work (1 wpm at a time) for a speed gain of 5 wpm. Then you drop back 2 wpm for accuracy practice. When you can type with good accuracy at your previous best speed, you return to speed practice for another 5 wpm gain—and so on.

Speed rule. Finish the sentence within the time allowed—*regardless of errors.*

Accuracy rule. Same as the speed rule, *plus* make no more than 2 epm (errors per minute).

2 Your first practice is for speed, based on your previous 5' timing speed. Thereafter you practice entirely according to your Progressive Practice performance, without further 5' timings.

3 When you finish your first Progressive Practice session, enter *your* "up 5, down 2" schedule on your Timed Practice Form (see the examples below). Then, line out the items at which you succeeded. Thereafter, line out each item as you succeed at it (see footnote **b,** p. 115).

Ten Sample Practice Schedules
(S = Speed, A = Accuracy)

| 5' wpm = | 9 | | 12 | | 13 | | 14 | | 15 | | 18 | | 22 | | 27 | | 30 | | 34 | |
Start at	10		13		14		15		16		19		23		28		31		35	
	S	A	S	A	S	A	S	A	S	A	S	A	S	A	S	A	S	A	S	A
	10S		13S		14S		15S		16S		19S		23S		28S		31S		35S	
	11S		14S		15S		16S		17S		20S		24S		29S		32S		36S	
	12S		15S		16S		17S		18S		21S		25S		30S		33S		37S	
	13S		16S		17S		18S		19S		22S		26S		31S		34S		38S	
	14S		17S		18S		19S		20S		23S		27S		32S		35S		39S	
		12A		15A		16A		17A		18A		21A		25A		30A		33A		37A
		13A		16A		17A		18A		19A		22A		26A		31A		34A		38A
		14A		17A		18A		19A		20A		23A		27A		32A		35A		39A
	15S		18S		19S		20S		21S		24S		28S		33S		36S		40S	
	16S		19S		20S		21S		22S		25S		29S		34S		37S		41S	
	17S		20S		21S		22S		23S		26S		30S		35S		38S		42S	
	18S		21S		22S		23S		24S		27S		31S		36S		39S		43S	
	19S		22S		23S		24S		25S		28S		32S		37S		40S		44S	
		17A		20A		21A		22A		23A		26A		30A		35A		38A		42A
		18A		21A		22A		23A		24A		27A		31A		36A		39A		43A
		19A		22A		23A		24A		25A		28A		32A		37A		40A		44A
	20S		23S		24S		25S		26S		29S		33S		38S		41S		45S	
	21S		24S		25S		26S		27S		30S		34S		39S		42S		46S	
	22S		25S		26S		27S		28S		31S		35S		40S		43S		47S	
	23S		26S		27S		28S		29S		32S		36S		41S		44S		48S	
	24S		27S		28S		29S		30S		33S		37S		42S		45S		49S	
		22A		25A		26A		27A		28A		31A		35A		40A		43A		47A
		23A		26A		27A		28A		29A		32A		36A		41A		44A		48A
		24A		27A		28A		29A		30A		33A		37A		42A		45A		49A
	25S		28S		29S		30S		31S		34S		38S		43S		46S		50S	
	26S		29S		30S		31S		32S		35S		39S		44S		47S		51S	
	27S		30S		31S		32S		33S		36S		40S		45S		48S		52S	
	28S		31S		32S		33S		34S		37S		41S		46S		49S		53S	
	29S		32S		33S		34S		35S		38S		42S		47S		50S		54S	
		27A		30A		31A		32A		33A		36A		40A		45A		48A		52A
		28A		31A		32A		33A		34A		37A		41A		46A		49A		53A
		29A		32A		33A		34A		35A		38A		42A		47A		50A		54A
	Etc.		Etc.		Etc.		Etc.		Etc.		Etc.		Etc.		Etc.		Etc.		Etc.	

21D TABLE WITH NUMBERS

Center the table on a ½-sheet (33 lines). Set LM 27 spaces left of center; BC–8 (meaning, leave 8 spaces between columns). Set tab stops as you type Row 1 (see Lesson 13C, Task 1, Step 3, p. 24). Thereafter, tabulate from column to column. TS below heading; DS between rows. Keep digits lined up (the 4 of 40¼ under the 5 of 750). **Hint:** Set for SS. After typing the table title and spacing down three times, reset line space regulator for DS. For most tables, do not set for DS until you reach the first row of the table.

Cost, yield, and Maturity Date of Selected Bond Issues			
Endicott Utilities	100 ½	7.5%	1987
City of Hampshire	750	8.4%	1985
Kane & Wills, Inc.	40 ¼	9.2%	1984
Burlington & Co.	290	9.8%	1988

21E SKILL EVALUATION

Contains all letters and symbols taught, except ;. 4', DS, SM–1". TR–NS

	CW
In the Zeeman & Kahner catalog* (page 190), "Emtiko" robes are	13
shown at $28.75, less 4½% for quantity orders—worth the extra cost	26
over the $27¼ price, less 2–7/8%, of Bates & Jenks. Let's order	39
now! Do you agree?	43

. . . . 1 . . . . 2 . . . . 3 . . . . 4 . . . . 5 . . . . 6 . . . . 7 . . . . 8 . . . . 9 . . . . 10 . . . . 11 . . . . 12 . . . . 13 . .

21F OPTIONAL PRACTICE

Continue where you left off last time with stroke refinement practice (p. 121–125) or with letter sequence practice (pp. 118–119). PF

NOTE. In a correctly typed 21D, column 1 begins under the first letter of the heading and column 4 ends under the last letter of the heading. Tables are attractive when their columns are blocked under the table title or heading.

22 6 □ _ (Underscore) □ : (Colon) □ Repeat keys □ Italics

22A REVIEW

Type 21E. SM–1" for 22A, 22C, 22D

22B UNDERSCORING

First type the words to be underscored. Then back up to the starting point—either by backspacing or by pushing back (or returning) the carriage, whichever method is faster. To underscore more than a few letters, lock the shift key—but remember to unlock it afterwards.

REPEAT KEYS

On many electrics, the underscore/hyphen and the backspace keys are "repeat" keys. Holding them down continues the underscoring or backspacing, or creates a dashed line. The space bar, the **x** key, and the period are also repeat keys on many electrics.

ITALICS

When the typist underscores (New Keys), the printer uses italics (*New Keys*). When the printer uses italics, the typist should underscore.

29 g/t

get gate gift thing light guest tongue strong
goat great stage tag stag eight though guilty

The host gently greeted these strange guests.
At length, a telegram came giving great news.

The stranger had an argument with two gentlemen tonight. I thought they'd stage a fight.

30 e/t

get the test tent sent time debt treat except
east eat ate best three west went effort meat

Ted regretted that his efforts were defeated.
They tried to test their strength three ways.

Mr. Roberts intends to settle the rate later.
At present, retail trade is really excellent.

31 z/a

zeal lazy hazy crazy amazed blaze razor waltz
zebras equalize realized czars zigzag analyze

The zebra amazed and dazzled the gazing boys.
I realize his brazen crime must be penalized.

Zelda was hazy about the signs of the Zodiac.
Mr. Taze's zest and zeal dazzle and amaze me.

32 s/c

sick stock close cross select because succeed
secret coast scene scold escapes science case

Scott's sickness causes absences from school.
Consider how Cass secured success in science.

Cal's stock consists of a selection of coats,
suits, and scarves--seconds, at lowest costs.

33 x/c/s

excels excess expects extracts coaxes exceeds
exchanges exercise excerpts lexicons Mexicans

The excited Mexican explained his experience.
Alex expects to be excused from excess taxes.

Axel's experience was scarcely extraordinary.
Coax Mr. Caxton to exchange the box of cards.

34 b/n

bin been bone bean bank knob blank unbendable
beneficial barn bend bond burn numb bun noble

Between you both, nobody obtains any benefit.
In the beginning the bank's business was bad.

Nobody put the new blanket beneath the bench.
A number of brand new cabins belong to Benny.

35 g/b

big grab begins oblong bridge baggage bulging
grumble beg brag obliged budget gamble badges

She was obliged to begin packing the baggage.
Mr. Berg grumbled, but he gave Ben a bargain.

Bogan obliged me by buying a big bag of buns.
Bill's arm bulged from the bite of a big bug.

36 i/k

kit kin skin kind like knit sink think nickel
king wicked kid silk Dick kick stick ink pick

I like to think of Dick as kind and skillful.
Miss King is knitting a skirt for Kip Linker.

I think I could kindle a fire with the sticks
in this kit. I'd like some bricks around it.

37 q/a

equal square quarrel acquire quarter squander
quantity quota acquit quality equator banquet

The quartet was acquainted with that request.
Quakers are quiet people; they shun quarrels.

Al Quan squandered a quarter of the quantity.
The quota Quant acquired equaled his request.

38 t/f

fit flat feet float fault staff affect effect
fruit drift first future effort fat fast fact

In the future make some effort not to forget.
At first he felt that the staff was at fault.

Later he found that the facts were different.
A tariff was on the fleet of fast staff cars.

22C NEW KEYS

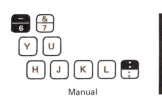

Manual | Electric

Fingering. On manuals, the underscore is the shift of the **6** (use **j** finger); on electrics, the shift of the hyphen (use **;** finger).

For 6, anchor **;**.

For **j** finger _, anchor **;**.
For _ on –, use **;** and anchor **j**.

For **:**, shift and use **;** finger.

Spacing Rule. Space twice after the colon (as in lines 4, 6, 10) and between sentences.

Underscore the titles of books, magazines, and newspapers.

Note, in line 5, the solid underscoring—but not of the end-of-sentence period. In line 11, contrast the separate underscoring of individually emphasized words—but not the spaces or any punctuation.

1 j6j j6j j6j 6 days; a $16 item; a 1/6 portion
2 j_j j_j j_j Buy <u>The New York Times</u>. Say <u>yes</u>.
   ;_; ;_; ;_;
3 ;:; ;:; ;:; 6:15 a.m.; 8:46 p.m.; a 6:1 ratio
4 FOR SALE: a 6-room house at $46,600, 8½%, 25-year mortgage.
5 State the meaning of the expression <u>lock, stock, and barrel</u>.
6 Use the underscore for emphasis, as in: Do <u>not</u> omit commas.
7 His book, <u>Africa Today</u>, was serialized in the <u>New York Post</u>.
8 NO SMOKING and CAUTION signs were hung on the factory walls.
9 Which one gives the greater emphasis: <u>Go away</u>! or GO AWAY!?
10 Note <u>no space</u> after comma in figures: 5,280 feet in a mile.
11 <u>Monsieur</u>, <u>Madame</u>, and <u>Mademoiselle</u> are common French titles.
12 The odds are 6:1 (6 to 1) against rainy weather on Thursday.
13 ABC-TV broadcasts the news on Channel 6 at 11:15 each night.

. . . . 1 . . . . 2 . . . . 3 . . . . 4 . . . . 5 . . . . 6 . . . . 7 . . . . 8 . . . . 9 . . . . 10 . . . . 11 12

Continue with SP–22. p. 108.

22D VERTICAL CENTERING (Table)

Time—nearest ¼′

LM: pica 10, elite 19; BC–5. Use ½-sheet; TS after heading, DS between rows. Can you finish the 37 words in 3–4 minutes?

MEMORABLE   DATES

Christopher
^*Columbus lands in the New World*   *October 12, 1492*
The Pilgrims land at Plymouth   *December 21, 1620*
Declaration of Independence signed   *July 4, 1776*

22E SKILL EVALUATION   Contains all keys taught, except **;** and *****. 4′, DS, SM–1″. TR–NS

	GWPM		
	a	b	CW
Jack Diaz wired Max Quigley as follows: "Effective 8/16 our	3	16	12
discount on items over $25 will be increased to <u>10%</u> (from 6%)."	7	20	26
On April 29, Evans & Clark stock closed at 147½—UP 2¼ from	10	23	39
last month's high! Isn't that an all-time record for that stock?	13	26	52
		4′	

1   2   3   4   5   6   7   8   9   10   11   12   13
+0   +1   +2   +3

19 c/v

cave carve curve voice clever active advances
cover covet advice vacant services vice civil

I have a clever plan to cover a vacation job.
He is convinced Civil Service has advantages.

Victor advocated the advice received from Dr.
Vincent Carver. He soon recovered his voice.

20 g/h

hog hang high cough ought thing hedge changed
graph thought ghost might laugh gash huge hug

The sight of the hungry hogs frightened Hugh.
At length, something seemed to change things.

Gus thought the strange sights might frighten
the child, but Gail just laughed and laughed.

21 y/t

try they truly lately fifty payment yacht toy
daytime today yeasts youth type yet sty stays

Tony may buy toys of this type for the party.
Stu can try to type the thirty letters today.

Daytime flights leave Tuesdays and Saturdays.
My typists type at sixty, maybe seventy, wpm.

22 s/w

was west wish snow wise sweet swing Wednesday
waste whose shower swallow saw ways swim show

We saw Les wear his new sweater on Wednesday.
Was it wise of Wes to waste the sweet sauces?

Mr. West saw the wet snow and wasted no time.
I showed slow and swift ways to sweep floors.

23 d/k

desk duck duke dike liked drink remark killed
joked dusk desk skid kind dark packed thanked

Dick kindly remarked that he liked Ed's work.
He thanked Ed for undertaking so hard a task.

Stars sparkled in the dark as Vicky awakened.
Derek linked arms with the kind, joking Duke.

24 f/r

for from fire fear first after forget forward
scarf refer future efforts far firm four fair

I prefer to wait for him to confirm my offer.
At first, the forty boys refused to pay fare.

In the future, my firm will make every effort
to refer offers. Why not forgive and forget?

25 p/o

top post open poet hope prove copper probable
power poem pot spot soap possible people pour

It is probably proper to oppose your opinion.
I hope the program we provide proves popular.

Stop hoping for the impossible to happen. It
isn't in your power to improve the operation.

26 j/h

John josh jihads Jewish Joseph Joshua Johnson
jackhammer Judah mahjong Jonah Johanssen Hajj

Joshua joyfully joined Joseph with his banjo.
A jar of hot juice was jerked out of my hand.

Just a short while ago, Jack had a job with a
jeweler as junior salesman. He left in June.

27 r/u

rub four hour rule outer upper refuse trouble
route under rug rust urge require return sure

Avoid the rush hour by returning before four.
Under the circumstances, refuse our products.

I urge the return of unwrapped rug purchases.
Our customers are sure to require urgent aid.

28 s/e

set lose send else step steel seven necessary
possesses lease sweet same size easy seem use

The senator's desire to serve seemed sincere.
James sees it is advisable to sell his house.

To win success in this business, it is necessary to establish a name for honest services.

23A REVIEW   Use 22D. SM–1″ throughout Lesson 23

23B NEW KEYS

Top-row ¢ and @ | Home-row ¢ and @

New key notes.   On manual machines, ¢ and @ are to the right of the semicolon; @ is the shift of the ¢. On electrics, @ is the shift of the 2, and ¢ is the shift of the 6.

Practice the drills in lines 1–2 below that apply to your keyboard. Then read the notes at the left below.

For **;** finger ¢, anchor **j**.
For **j** finger ¢, anchor **;**.

For **;** finger @, anchor **j**.
For **s** finger @, anchor **a**.

For **3**, use **d** finger and anchor **a**.
For **#**, use **d** finger and anchor **a**.

¢ is used only for amounts of less than $1; 5¢ is preferred to $.05.

is used only with Arabic numbers. It means "number" when it precedes and "pound" when it follows a number.

@ is used only when quoting prices, typically unit prices on invoices.

ABBREVIATIONS

Some abbreviations are typed all in small letters, others in solid caps—sometimes with periods, sometimes without. Small-letter abbreviations should be typed without spaces; capital-letter abbreviations are sometimes spaced, sometimes not. Study the examples in ¶s 11–17.

The Latin abbreviation *i.e.* means "that is."

The Latin abbreviation *e.g.* means "for example."

The Latin abbreviation *viz.* means "namely."

Note the comma after the Latin abbreviations—just as if the words for which they stand had been spelled out.

1
```
;¢;  ;¢;  ;¢;    a 6¢ stamp; a 9¢ candy bar; 5¢
j¢j  j¢j  j¢j
```

2
```
;@;  ;@;  ;@;    two @ 6¢ each; a dozen @ $1.48
s@s  s@s  s@s
```

3 `d3d  d3d  d3d  add 3; a 3-day pass; two @ $30`

4 `d#d  d#d  d#d  20# paper; order #3; check #85`

5 `We can offer you #3 pens @ 29¢ each (ball point).`

6 `Airmail letters to France cost 31¢ (per ½ ounce).`

7 `Invoice #584 showed: "20# paper @ $3.60 a ream."`

8 `Their check #179,528 is in the amount of $603.94.`

9 `Buy 10# nails @ 4¢ and #9 brushes @ $13.20 a doz.`

10 `Check #283 covers order #67 for #2 brushes @ 98¢.`

11
```
    Always use per (not a) in expressions of rate,
as in:  wpm (words per minute), ppm (parts per mil-
lion), rpm (revolutions per minute), mph (miles per
hour), cps (cycles per second).
```

12
```
    United States is abbreviated as "U.S." or as
"U. S."; but USIA is the United States Information
Agency.  The modern tendency is to close up abbre-
viations, without periods (e.g., UNESCO, FBI, ICC),
especially in government agencies.
```

13
```
    AA (i.e., American Airlines) flight #16 leaves
at 11:30 a.m. from JFK (John F. Kennedy) Airport.
```

14
```
    The underscore is used to indicate italics;
(e.g., the f finger, two r's in embarrass).
```

15
```
    The Low Countries (viz., Holland and Belgium)
are on the North Sea, across from England.
```

16
```
    Five abbreviations from the Latin are often
used in formal English writing:  (1) etc., (2) i.e.,
(3) e.g., (4) et al., and (5) viz.  The abbreviation
"et al." means and others.
```

`. . . . .1. . . .2. . . .3. . . .4. . . .5. . . 6. . . .7. . . .8. . .9. . . .10. . .`

Continue with SP–23, p. 108.

23C SKILL EVALUATION

SM–1″; TR–NS

4′ timing on practice lines 5–10 above. Each full textbook line contains 10 words. Use DS and type all lines as one ¶. On a partially typed line, count strokes and divide by 5 to get words.

9 w/e

ewe few when wide week knew well women answer
jewels write dew new slew west owed wire wise

When the wedding was over, the two flew west.
When I went to work, few moments were wasted.

I waited twenty minutes for you on Wednesday.
Then I went to work. Where were you, Walter?

10 d/e

red deed dear held dread ended denied demands
dew dent heard mend grade made danced endured

Edna decided on a different method of debate.
Fred disliked Della's attitude toward Daniel.

Edwards delayed paying his debts. Such delay
was dangerous. His credit standing suffered.

11 o/l

oil soil lose below towel could people pillow
fellow lovely old bold coal color noble world

Old people must make allowances for children.
Local boys should be allowed only some tools.

An omelet and a roll could be a meal for Lon;
he is allowed to eat only plain, simple food.

12 f/g

fig gift golf fang forge forget figure forgot
grief Graf flying refuge frog fog frugal flag

Finding a refuge, the fugitive felt grateful.
Fay forgot the figures, but Greg forgave her.

Flo has a gift for Mr. Graf--four golf balls.
After Fred left, Guy agreed to follow Friday.

13 i/u

unit unite music issue until insure beautiful
introduce ruin unfit juries using quilt guild

The figures I submitted are quite sufficient.
The musician inquired about the guitar price.

I issued instructions about disposing of your
business. Its equipment will suit our buyer.

14 a/e

ate eat seat meat east fade eaten state early
quake wear sea tea cage made eager waste year

I knew the reason Bella acted in that manner.
Because of great fear, his heart beat faster.

Alex was certainly an eager beaver. He began
early on Wednesday and wasted no time at all.

15 k/l

kill milk lark walk cloak skill black quickly
Brooklyn chalk lake look clock luck lock like

Black chalk shouldn't be used on blackboards.
Looking at the clock, Cal walked off quickly.

Kelly won the weekly contest, partly as a result of skill but also with remarkable pluck.

16 c/d

cad duck cold crowd decay acted ascend direct
decide clad code could scold cried doctor cod

An excited crowd called his fall no accident.
Dan's doctor scolded Dick but cured his cold.

Before deciding on direct discussion a candid
consideration of my credit code is conducted.

17 u/y

buy busy July bury fully young subway country
journey supply lucky truly ugly jury your you

The young boy made a journey south last July.
Surely! you could buy a supply--if you hurry.

You are young; you could be busy and usefully
employed in this county year in and year out.

18 f/d

fed feed fled food draft field friend forward
offered fad fade defend filed fraud defy deaf

Frieda was afraid she had offended my friend.
I was frightened, as I faced a difficult job.

Fred confided to my friend that he definitely
favored a defense of fraud and offered funds.

24A REVIEW

Practice the ¶ below in preparation for a 4' timing; DS, SM–1". Listen for sound of bell. TR–NS

	a	b	CW

    The expression 2/15, n/30 means: "Deduct 2% if you pay within 15 days; — 4 19 14

pay the net amount within 30 days"; e.g., for 100 #2 pencils @ 5¢ each, pay- — 8 23 31

ment within 15 days would be $4.90 (i.e., $5, less 10¢); for payment within — 12 27 46

16–30 days after delivery, the amount due is the full $5, without discount. — 16 31 63

4'

    +0   +1   +2   +3   +4

24B PROGRESSIVE NS (Number and Symbol) PRACTICE

Five 1' speed timings.

Select from Series C (pp. 135–137) the item which, when completed in 1', is 1 wpm more than your speed on 24A. Apply the usual rules for progressive practice (see p. 126): "Up 5, down 2"; i.e., up 5 wpm—**not** 5 sentences or paragraphs. When you finish today, enter **your** schedule on your PF (see p. 115).

24C VERTICAL CENTERING

Although your stroking skill is as yet quite modest, you are gradually reaching the point at which the typing part of any task will be just routine. The greater part of many typing tasks is deciding what to do—planning the work before typing. Skill in planning is easily worth quite a few wpm in stroking speed.

Do not type Tasks 1–3. Just do the arithmetic for determining the distance from the top edge to the first line of typing. Plan **and** type Task 4.

Materials in DS require twice the number of typed lines, minus one (e.g., 10 DS lines use 20 − 1 = 19 lines of space).

TASK 1 Plan the 4 lines of 24A, in DS, centered on a ½-sheet.

TASK 2 Plan the copy for 15–1 (p. 27), headed KINESTHESIS. TS after the heading and DS the lines. Center on a full sheet.

TASK 3 Plan the table of Task 1 of 15C (p. 26). DS after column headings, then SS. Center on a ½-sheet.

TASK 4 Plan **and** type the 3-line ¶ of 19D (p. 32), DS on a ½-sheet. Head it SKILL EVALUATION, then TS. Use WL–55.

24D OPTIONAL PRACTICE

Continue with stroke refinement (pp. 121–125) or letter sequences (pp. 118–119) until it is time for 24E.

24E SKILL EVALUATION

5', DS, SM–1". TR–NS

Contains all letters and characters except * and ;. Your performance will provide a standard against which to compare your NS (number and symbol) proficiency at later stages of training. Underscore the italicized word.

	a	b	CW

    Make invoice #749 read: "6 doz. men's white shirts @ $5.28 each." — 3 17 14

Our usual terms of 1/15, n/30 apply. — 4 19 21

    During the week of June 3–7, our TOWN ANNEX will feature a special — 7 22 35

15% markdown sale on Quiner & Sloan muslin sheets (81" x 104"). They — 11 25 53

will sell at $5.42—a saving of 96¢! Visit our Bargain Basement for other — 14 28 68

½-off and ¼-off items, won't you? — 15 29 73

5'

    +0   +1   +2   +3

The most common keystroking error consists of striking the key alongside (or just above or below) the desired key. Sometimes, the opposite hand is used (*d* for *k*). Such errors are the most frequent because the reach toward any key is little different from the reach toward an adjacent key. To master the small differences in motions toward adjacent and other substituted keys, it is helpful to practice on materials that focus on the mis-struck keys.

The materials that follow cover the most common substitution errors, applied to the 26 letters of the alphabet in rank order of frequency of errors. Practice on them will help to "refine" your stroking motions and should result in fewer stroking errors.

Type at a snappy rate; don't dawdle. If you should make a mistake—and sense it immediately—retype the word and continue with the next word.

Practice these materials in your spare time, continuing each time where you left off the time before. Enter on your Practice Form the proper starting point for your next practice (see footnote **f**, p. 115).

For timing purposes, each line in drills 1–38 contains 9 words (45 strokes). Each line on p. 121 contains 15 words (75 strokes).

1 r/t

rift trim dart fret crate start rather terror
trial create raft thrift tray stir trust trip

Bert trapped three terrible tigers in Africa.
Mr. Tarkenton is greatly troubled at present.

Roberta had neither the time nor the material
to write separate letters to her two sisters.

2 m/n

mend menu amen name mount human number demand
normal omen moment mink demon moan month numb

Norma was misinformed and made many mistakes.
Annamarie Thomson mentioned many eminent men.

Martin examined the statement you made Monday
morning. It is of minimum importance to him.

3 o/i

soil toil Iowa into point tonic notice polite
obtain voice iota coin avoid office omit riot

Victor soiled his hands working on the radio.
Who is coming tonight? I hope to get action.

To avoid serious objections, I must obtain an
official opinion on the petition Olin issued.

4 a/s

ask sea fast also stamp stand escape separate
aisle sat raise sap answer stay pleasant same

Was the message sent to A. Davison's address?
Ask James Lassaman for a satisfactory sample.

When the class reaches the stairs, the leader
has to step aside, so that the rest can pass.

5 e/i

ice side file chief write knife direct office
indeed exist desire like prize wise their lie

She expressed gratitude for their efficiency.
Our office tries to give service if required.

We desire to be efficient and polite in deal-
ing with clients. Elise has certainly tried.

6 s/d

aids soda send dress deeds deals speed ladies
solid sound stand dense does side showed desk

The ladies said the old desks should be sold.
He said her misdeeds destroyed sound demands.

Sandy intends to travel to distant lands. He
promised he would send cards to your friends.

7 r/e

dear year fare every never eager serve regard
there their heard true erase earn either were

Read and return the record of their earnings.
Edgar heard you are eager to restore service.

No matter what occurs later, I shall remember
my troubles forever. They were a sore trial.

8 v/b

verb brave bravely believe vegetable valuable
above everybody vibrate bevel overbear brevet

I believe the job you described is available.
We have established a Better Business Bureau.

David believes in being available whenever we
are very busy. Vic values his able services.

25A TYPING A DATE

To develop skill at tabulating and at typing numbers (especially the year), set 1-inch LM and tab stops at 40, 70 (elite) or 35, 55 (pica) and type 3 SS rows of today's date in 3 columns, as at the right.

```
October 14, 1977     October 14, 1977     October 14, 1977
October 14, 1977     October 14, 1977     October 14, 1977
October 14, 1977     October 14, 1977     October 14, 1977
```

25B ADDRESSING ENVELOPES

1 Of the many sizes of envelopes the two most widely used are (a) the Legal—or No. 10—envelope (9½″ x 4⅛″), shown below, and (b) the Commercial—or No. 6¾—envelope (6½″ x 3⅝″). Examine their details.

2 The writer's name is often typed above a printed return address, as shown on the Legal envelope. Female titles (Miss, Ms., Mrs.) are included; male titles are omitted.

3 Notations to the postal authorities (e.g., AIRMAIL) are typed in solid caps or rubber-stamped a TS below the postage stamp

—or an airmail envelope may be used instead. Notations to the addressee (e.g., HOLD FOR ARRIVAL) are typed a TS below the return address.

4 Start the address 1–2 lines below center, ½–1 inch left of center, depending on the length of the longest address line.

5 On envelopes your instructor will collect, always type your name in the return address position.

6 **Now** read 25C (next page) for the information it contains.

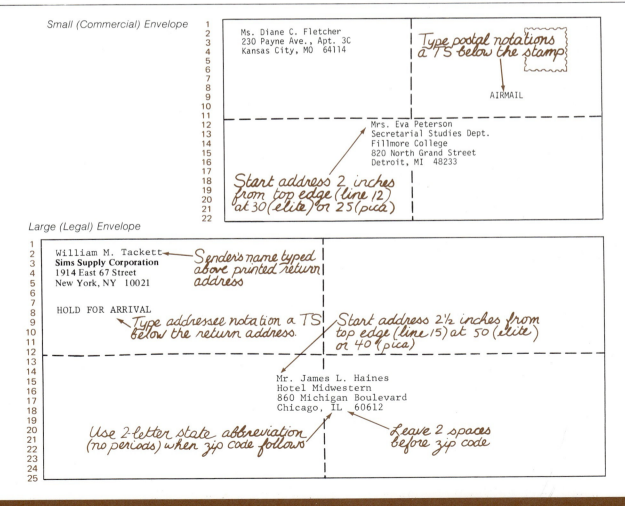

Small (Commercial) Envelope

Ms. Diane C. Fletcher
230 Payne Ave., Apt. 3C
Kansas City, MO 64114

Type postal notations a TS below the stamp

AIRMAIL

Mrs. Eva Peterson
Secretarial Studies Dept.
Fillmore College
820 North Grand Street
Detroit, MI 48233

Start address 2 inches from top edge (line 12) at 30 (elite) or 25 (pica)

Large (Legal) Envelope

William M. Tackett
Sims Supply Corporation
1914 East 67 Street
New York, NY 10021

Sender's name typed above printed return address

HOLD FOR ARRIVAL

Type addressee notation a TS below the return address.

Start address 2½ inches from top edge (line 15) at 50 (elite) or 40 (pica)

Mr. James L. Haines
Hotel Midwestern
860 Michigan Boulevard
Chicago, IL 60612

Use 2-letter state abbreviation (no periods) when zip code follows

Leave 2 spaces before zip code

The explanation at the top of the next page also applies to the materials on this page. Each line, including a carriage return, contains fifteen 5-stroke words.

```
    . . . .1. . . .2. . . .3. . . .4. . . .5. . . .6. . . .7. . . .8. . . .9. . . .10. . . .11. . . .12. . . .13. . . .14. . . .15
```

r/t	1	Try to rotate the truck tires at intervals. The three tradesmen returned.
m/n	2	For a nominal sum we can maintain a money account in the name of many men.
o/i	3	We are going to obtain action tonight. Omit the notations. Avoid a riot.
a/s	4	A sample sent to our latest address will satisfy us. Ask Sam to stand up.
e/i	5	Indeed, efficient service is their chief consideration. Itemize receipts.
s/d	6	Doris insisted on sending fine dress goods to the ladies. Sid sold cards.
r/e	7	Their recent remarks were regarded as nearer the truth. We earn a reward.
v/b	8	The battery described above was believed best. Everybody behaved bravely.
w/e	9	Where were the new sweaters we wanted on Wednesday? She knew a few words.
d/e	10	Edna developed a different method of dealing with delays. End the danger.
o/l	11	That fellow has the only large allowance of the lot. Would olive oils do?
f/g	12	Do not again forget to give the gift to Mr. Ferguson. Gus forgot fatigue.
i/u	13	The alumni inquired into the failure of the businesses. Submit the issue.
a/e	14	To our great amazement each steamer disappeared in the haze. Ed ate meat.
k/l	15	It was a lucky tackle. He has workable skill. Talk quickly. Lack chalk.
c/d	16	She decided the accident was due to December weather. I could catch cold.
u/y	17	Mr. Burney usually goes south via Yuma on his July journey. Buy it today.
f/d	18	He offered to defend the man who fled because he was afraid. Fred fasted.

```
    . . . .1. . . .2. . . .3. . . .4. . . .5. . . .6. . . .7. . . .8. . . .9. . . .10. . . .11. . . .12. . . .13. . . .14. . . .15
```

c/v	19	The convict's voice convinced the club of his conversion. I crave advice.
g/h	20	Go through Bathgate. Mr. Hagman bought a huge foghorn. She might charge.
y/t	21	Try to buy the toy before Tuesday. They have yet to stay. Anthony types.
s/w	22	I wish to leave for the West on Wednesday. I sewed the washed sweatshirt.
d/k	23	Kidder liked the kind Duke who drank and joked. Dick skidded on the dock.
f/r	24	I offered further information to Frank after father confirmed our efforts.
p/o	25	I suppose he will probably oppose our opinion of the option. Open a shop.
j/h	26	June and July, in his judgment, are too hot. John just bought a huge jug.
r/u	27	As a rule, we urged Ruth to return all purchases turned down by customers.
s/e	28	I sincerely desire to serve you. Please rest. These steps are necessary.
g/t	29	The great gift is to see things in the right light. Mr. Gertz forgot him.
e/t	30	He sent the receipt with return postage guaranteed. Get the debt settled.
z/a	31	She was amazed at his zest and zeal. We realize he is lazy. Buy a razor.
s/c	32	The case was closed because of sickness. The science class was a success.
x/c/s	33	Cissy coaxes him to exchange six exact copies. Pay extra. Excuse excess.
b/n	34	Bind it with ribbon. Nobody put the blanket beneath the bench. Brand it.
g/b	35	Beggars began to grab the baggage. Bragging is disagreeable. Egbert sat.
i/k	36	We think that kind of man is wicked. Dick likes to pick up skill quickly.
q/a	37	The quartet quarreled over quaint music. Quality and quantity were equal.
t/f	38	In fact, the high tariff had a further, fatal effect on trade and traffic.

```
    . . . .1. . . .2. . . .3. . . .4. . . .5. . . .6. . . .7. . . .8. . . .9. . . .10. . . .11. . . .12. . . .13. . . .14. . . .15
```

TASK 1 Type your name and home address in the return address position and address one small and one large envelope to Mr. Harris (see below TASK 5). Set LM at the beginning point of the address, as stated in the model (use the margin release key for the return address position). On the small envelope space down 4TS (or 6DS) from the top edge to line 12; then reset for SS. On the large envelope space down 5TS (or 7DS + 1SS) from the top edge; then reset for SS.

TASK 2 Using the completed **small** envelope of Task 1, practice (at least 6–10 times) each of two methods of quickly reaching the first address line without counting:

a Use strong flip or two of the cylinder knob. Learn how much force it takes to reach the line.

b Pull forward ratchet release and swiftly **roll** the envelope to the first address line. Then instantly lock the release.

Fix in your mind a picture of the distance from the top edge to the first address line. The expert does not stop to count lines.

TASK 3 Address **small** envelopes to addresses 1–3 of SP–25, p. 109. Omit return address and set LM at beginning of address. Visually check appearance of each envelope after you address it; also, compare it with the model. Can you finish all three envelopes in 3–5 minutes?

TASK 4 Use the completed **large** envelope of Task 1 and practice the two quick insertion methods of Task 2.

TASK 5 Address **large** envelopes to addresses 4–6 of SP–25, p. 109. Set LM and check afterwards, as in Task 3. Can you finish in 3–5 minutes?

```
Mr. John R. Harris
56 Ward Avenue
Rumson, NJ  07760
```

25C STRAIGHT COPY TIMING Listen for your bell; underscore the italicized word on the last line.

5', DS, SM–1". TR

	GWPM		
	a	**b**	**CW**

The address style on postcards and envelopes is aimed at correct machine sorting of mail. The OCR (Optical Character Reader) scans addresses from left to right, starting one-half inch from the bottom edge of the envelope or card, reading upward line by line, stopping at a blank line. It is therefore important to single space addresses. Otherwise, the OCR will reject the envelope for later manual inspection, thus delaying delivery.

At 2-letter SOLID CAPS state abbreviation (without periods)—followed by 2 spaces—precedes the zip code. If, for whatever reason, no zip code is available, write the state name in full or use the longer abbreviation (e.g., Michigan or Mich., *not* MI).

a	b	CW
3	31	13
6	34	28
9	37	43
12	40	58
15	43	73
18	46	88
20	48	102
23	51	116
26	54	131
28	56	139

Sy 1.58
St 5.9

+0	+1	+2	+3

25D CAPITALIZATION PRACTICE

Use the Capitalization Drills on p. 120 for optional practice when time permits. Read the instructions on that page and start that practice now. Make PF entry when you finish (see instructions on p. 115).

PF, TR, AND TR–NS ENTRIES From now on, whether or not the abbreviations are given, make an entry on your PF (Practice Form) for (1) Progressive Practice, (2) Progressive NS Practice, (3) Stroke Refinement, (4) Letter Sequences, (5) Capitalization, and (6) Keyboard Practice. Also, make a TR entry for 5' straight copy timings and a TR–NS entry for 5' number and symbol timings.

CAPITALIZATION PRACTICE

1 These materials provide intensive practice in shifting for capital letters. Practice at them will improve your skill and be especially helpful to those who often type beheaded capitals or have other shift key difficulties. Each line requires the use of the shift key at least seven times, and the 32 sentences require a total of 264 uses of the shift key.

2 Type at a snappy rate—don't dawdle. If you make a mistake —and sense it immediately—retype the word and go on to the next word.

3 Each line (plus carriage return) contains 15 five-stroke words. The dotted word-count lines make it convenient to use the copy for timing purposes.

4 Enter on your Practice Form your starting point for your next practice (see footnote **g**, p. 115).

```
. . . . 1 . . . . 2 . . . . 3 . . . . 4 . . . . 5 . . . . 6 . . . . 7 . . . . 8 . . . . 9 . . . 10 . . . 11 . . . 12 . . . 13 . . . 14 . . . 15
```

1 The American Plastic Company, Inc., has offices in New York and St. Louis.
2 Mr. Hardy, Director of Public Relations for Koch & Co., is very competent.

3 Thomas mailed an order for drugs to Manders Drug Service, Washington, D.C.
4 The Cooperative Labor League of Fort Haven was reorganized last September.

5 Our salesman, Mr. Ott, will be in Baton Rouge, Louisiana, in June or July.
6 The International Flower Show opens Thursday at Gardinia on Monroe Square.

7 In June, Betty Carroll and Myra Shields took a trip to the Virgin Islands.
8 The Queen Bess sailed on Sunday, June 6, and arrived on Wednesday, June 9.

9 Mr. and Mrs. Martin Lane have three sons: Martin Jr., Kenneth, and David.
10 The Polk Museum of Fine Arts is showing some old Charlie Chaplin pictures.

11 The Park Cinema's attraction this week is "Panama City," with Fred Fields.
12 The Phoenix Suns will play the Hawks at Madison Square Garden on Thursday.

13 The Hayden Planetarium, Central Park West, has a new show: "The Heavens."
14 Whenever Mr. Flint goes to St. Paul, he stays at the Thomas Dorsett Hotel.

15 Have you seen Mrs. Levitt? Yes, I met her at the Bridge Club on Saturday.
16 The Hawaii Visitors Bureau, Honolulu, invites you to this Golden Paradise.

```
. . . . 1 . . . . 2 . . . . 3 . . . . 4 . . . . 5 . . . . 6 . . . . 7 . . . . 8 . . . . 9 . . . 10 . . . 11 . . . 12 . . . 13 . . . 14 . . . 15
```

17 Blunt Bros., New York, and Hudson Co., Los Angeles, sell Robin Hood coats.
18 Carol and Sue enjoy the story of Little Red Riding Hood and of Cinderella.

19 If I need more information, I'll call the World Travel Bureau on Thursday.
20 The Robinson Gallery of Fine Arts will have a Renoir exhibit in September.

21 Santa Claus is called St. Nicholas and Kriss Kringle by European children.
22 Leon F. Garland, President of Essex College, presided at Friday's meeting.

23 Professor Wilde's talk was entitled "A History of American Party Systems."
24 Joseph wrote to Mr. Finch, Chairman of the Board, Van Dyke Clothiers, Inc.

25 For your vacation, visit the Shady Nook Health Club at Pinewood, New York.
26 The Ponderosa Life Insurance Society paid John a $44 dividend in November.

27 The Little Theater presented Shakespeare's "Romeo and Juliet" last Monday.
28 Mr. and Mrs. Theodore Lang have an account at the Southside National Bank.

29 Clark, Loeb & Company have branches in New York, Chicago, and Los Angeles.
30 McCray's Television Shop will have a sale Wednesday, Thursday, and Friday.

31 A TV program opening in May is called "News and Views of American Voters."
32 The firm of Pierce & Raft, Inc., is known in London as Pierce & Raft, Ltd.

```
. . . . 1 . . . . 2 . . . . 3 . . . . 4 . . . . 5 . . . . 6 . . . . 7 . . . . 8 . . . . 9 . . . 10 . . . 11 . . . 12 . . . 13 . . . 14 . . . 15
```

26A REVIEW

Type the date (as in 25A). Then continue with Stroke Refinement or Letter Sequences until it is time for 26B. Make proper PF entry.

26B POSTAL CARDS

1 Read the postal card at the right.

2 Date ends at right margin; side margins are 2–3 spaces.

3 To make room for another 2–4 lines in the message;

    a Use 1-space side margins.

    b Put both salutation and date on line 2 (or 1) and start message on line 4 (or 3).

    c Use TS, not 4SS, from closing to department.

Note that paragraphs are often blocked at left margin, not indented.

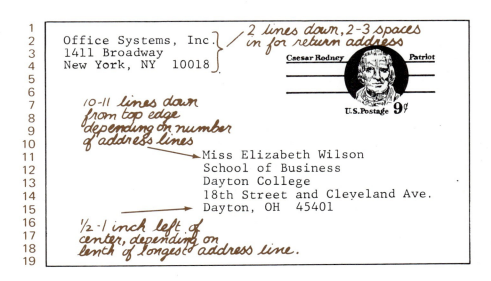

```
 1
 2    Colon after salutation,        Backspace    Current date
 3                                   (1 for 1) from
 4    Dear Miss Wilson:   DS         right margin
 5                        DS
 6    Postal card size (5½" x 3¾") ordinarily permits a
 7    message of up to 7-10 lines.
 8                        DS
 9    Note DS between each section and the next--but 4SS
10    between the closing (Very truly yours) and the de-
11    partment (or title or typed signature) of the send-
12    er--for longhand signing.
13                        DS
14                                   Very truly yours,  Comma
15    Set tab stop at                                   optional
16    approximate center:  <4SS   Arthur R. Drake
17    30(elite),25(pica)
18                                   Customer Service Dept.
19
```

4 Start the address 11 lines below the top edge (6–7 lines below return address, 4–5 lines below the stamp). Type it ½–1 inch left of approximate center (elite 25, pica 20).

TASK 1 Type the message of the model postal card, but send the card to yourself at your home address from your typing instructor at your school address (see inside the front cover for state abbreviations). Type instructor's full name 4SS below the closing.

TASK 2 Type the message and address sides of cards 1–2 (SP–26, p. 110). If you finish before it is time for 26C, continue with Nos. 3–5, then with Stroke Refinement or Letter Sequences.

```
 1
 2    Office Systems, Inc.    2 lines down, 2-3 spaces
 3    1411 Broadway           in for return address
 4    New York, NY  10018
 5                                 Caesar Rodney   Patriot
 6
 7    10-11 lines down
 8    from top edge                  U.S.Postage 9¢
 9    depending on number
10    of address lines
11                     Miss Elizabeth Wilson
12                     School of Business
13                     Dayton College
14                     18th Street and Cleveland Ave.
15                     Dayton, OH  45401
16    ½-1 inch left of
17    center, depending on
18    length of longest address line.
19
```

26C SKILL EVALUATION

Time—nearest ¼ ′

Can you complete the message and address sides (with return address) of card No. 6 (SP–26, p. 110), totaling 66 (5-stroke) words, in 5 minutes?

-m jam, submit, acme, admit, hem, Kaufman, fragment, freshman, dim, blackmail, calm, summer, unmask, come, topmost, army, dismay, utmost, dumb, sawmill, axmen, symbol, jazzman

-n fan, abnormal, picnic, kidney, tent, deafness, ignore, technique, dine, unknown, illness, condemn, inner, done, hypnosis, earn, snake, witness, aunt, Dubrovnik, gowns, laxness, shyness

-o aorta, about, scorn, adopt, neon, afoot, rigor, shove, ratio, job, beckon, alone, demote, tenor, food, sport, wrote, sow, stood, quote, evoke, sword, exotic, young, razor

-p lap, subparagraph, Macphail, handpainted, keep, halfpenny, magpie, ashpit, sip, inkpot, Alpine, damp, unpack, drop, apple, harp, spy, output, cup, Cowper, expose, Egypt

-q aqua, subquality, acquire, headquarters, request, earthquake, liquor, catafalque, kumquat, banquet, eloquent, parquet, square, bouquet, exquisite

-r jar, abrupt, across, draw, terror, afraid, agree, three, firm, Jr., Akron, ballroom, Mr., enrage, form, April, hurry, misread, betray, curl, chevron, dowry, xray, lyric, Ezra

-s lash, absent, tactics, nods, does, cliffs, lags, laughs, risk, packs, also, yams, answer, cost, lapse, arson, missile, itself, rush, revs, bows, flax-seed, says, buzzsaw

-t path, obtain, actor, width, lets, often, pigtail, ought, with, blacktop, salt, boomtown, pants, moth, empty, qt., partly, mostly, attend, cut, Vt., growth, extra, daytime, Aztec

-u haul, suburb, acute, reduce, feud, fur, argue, shut, triumph, injury, skull, plus, amuse, snub, doubt, spun, quit, true, surf, stun, vacuum, vulgar, swum, exult, Yukon, azure

-v pave, obvious, adverb, never, Nashville, five, Rockville, solve, circum-vent, envy, dove, serve, Louisville, outvote, souvenir, flivver, Bronxville, Sayville, rendezvous

-w law, subway, dwell, jewel, halfwit, dogwood, pathway, handiwork, awkward, always, Cromwell, inward, vow, upward, overwhelm, swung, between, Kuwait, glowworm, Maxwell, byword, zwieback

-x coax, exit, fix, calx, anxious, boxy, Marx, luxury, Exxon, Styx

-y pay, ruby, lacy, body, keys, clarify, energy, shyly, lucky, flyer, roomy, many, joyful, happy, pry, asylum, duty, guy, ivy, lawyer, oxygen, lazy

-z amaze, subzone, eczema, adze, sneeze, zigzag, size, blitzkrieg, Balzac, frenzy, dozen, Leipzig, Tarzan, Szechuan, waltz, fuze, frowzy, analyze, dizzy

27A PREPARATION   Type the date. (See 25A, p. 39.)

27B PLANNING A TABLE

HOW TO DETERMINE TAB STOP SETTINGS

1 Intercolumn space (the space between columns) is measured from the end of the longest item in a column to the beginning of the next column.

2 If the longest item in any column is not the first item, follow the steps at the right.

a From LM, strike space bar once for each letter and space in the longest item in column 1. Do **not** type the item.

b Continue to space for the number of spaces to be left between columns 1 and 2. Then set a tab stop.

c Continue to space through the longest item in each remaining column, plus BC (between-column) spacing. Set tab stop at beginning of each column as you reach it.

d Return to LM; then type and tabulate from column to column.

TASK 1 Center the table at the right on a ½-sheet. TS after the heading and DS the rows. Set LM 25 spaces left of center; BC–10.

1 From LM, space through *South America,* plus another 10 spaces, and set tab stop.

2 Then space through *Kilimanjaro,* plus 10 spaces, and set tab stop.

3 Follow with Step **d,** above.

TASK 2 Retype the table of Task 1 with LM 23 spaces left of center and BC–8. Remember to clear previous tab stops. Can you finish in 3–5 minutes, including setting the new LM and new tab stops?   **Time—nearest ¼′**

CONTINENTAL MOUNTAIN PEAKS

Asia		Everest		29,028
South America	10 spaces	Aconcagua	10 spaces	22,834
North America		McKinley		20,320
Africa		Kilimanjaro		19,340
Europe		Mont Blanc		15,771

27C WORD DIVISION (Additional Rules)

---

1 Medial means "in the middle." Medial 1-letter syllables are preferably typed before—not after—the hyphen. *Equiva-lent* is better than *equiv-alent; ridicu-lous* is better than *ridic-ulous.* It is also preferable to keep the 2-syllable endings *able, ible, ical,* as a unit, as in *teach-able.*

2 Divide between consecutive 1-letter syllables (at the diagonal), as in: *grad-u I a-tion, hu-mil-i I a-tion, con-cil-i I a-tory.*

3 Do not divide contractions even though they may contain more than one speech syllable: *wouldn't, isn't.*

4 Divide **within** a part of a proper name (Wil-son, An-der-son).

Avoid dividing numbers, dates, abbreviations, and between parts of a proper name. If division is necessary, divide as shown below.

Acceptable	Undesirable
Frank H. Thompson	Frank H. Thompson
April 23, 1977	April 23, 1977
Decem-ber 8, 1976	a $234, 108 deficit

Type the expressions below, using a hyphen at permissible division points and a diagonal (slant) to show what may be carried over to the next line without a hyphen.

Examples
Sey-mour L. / Rich-ards
De-cem-ber 8, / 1976

Benjamin R. Cromwell   shouldn't   January 3, 1958   idiocy   162,048,537

27D PROGRESSIVE or OPTIONAL PRACTICE   As many Progressive Practice 1′ timings as time permits or as much Optional Practice as time permits; PF

LETTER SEQUENCES

The lines of words below contain all the two-letter combinations in the language that occur in nontechnical words judged to be familiar to a literate adult—plus occasional proper names. The lines thereby provide practice at all the keyboard reaches involved in typing nontechnical materials.

Practice the words at your highest possible speed, one after the other, including the comma. If you stumble on a word, repeat it as many times as necessary until you can type it smoothly then continue with the next word. Enter on your Practice Form your starting point for your next practice (see footnote **e**, p. 115).

-a bazaar, abate, scan, day, meal, afar, again, that, dial, ajar, skate, clad, smart, snail, roam, span, Aqaba, moral, message, stall, dual, evade, swam, exact, payable, plaza

-b labor, rubber, Macbeth, standby, rebate, offbeat, ragbag, flashback, fib, backbone, Albert, lamb, unbend, lob, raspberry, barber, passbook, football, scrub, jawbone, oxblood, maybe, Uzbek

-c lacy, subcommittee, account, grandchild, neck, offcast, dogcart, ash-can, pick, cockcrow, balcony, armchair, lance, lock, mapcase, arc, mascot, match, duck, showcase, excess, cycle

-d lady, rubdown, Macduff, saddle, led, serfdom, kingdom, withdraw, kid, breakdown, old, Camden, end, odd, trapdoor, lord, Tuesday, outdoor, rude, Blvd., crowd, hydrant, Mazda

-e Caesar, label, ace, idea, keel, offer, aged, she, diet, reject, faked, sled, amend, sneer, poem, ape, free, asset, ate, fuel, love, owed, oxen, layer, size

-f loaf, subfloor, Macfarlane, goldfish, left, effort, bagful, faithful, lift, breakfast, half, harmful, unfit, sofa, helpful, wharf, misfit, outfit, muff, awful, Oxford, playful

-g lag, subgroup, McGovern, lodge, leg, Afghan, logger, flashgun, fig, blackguard, bulge, Irmgard, angle, jog, stopgap, argue, misgiving, outgo, mug, lawgiver, taxgather, playground

-h Utah, subhead, ache, childhood, behave, offhand, dough, withhold, hardihood, backhand, girlhood, farmhouse, inhale, John, sphere, perhaps, fish, other, Uhlan, anywhere, exhibit, boyhood, Muzhik

-i mail, abide, decide, edit, rein, office, agile, thin, Hawaii, jig, akin, slit, amid, tonic, toil, spice, Iraqi, trim, aside, stiff, suit, avid, switch, exit, buying, sizing

-j major, object, adjust, reject, fjord, logjam, highjack, Fiji, Hajji, blackjack, killjoy, circumjacent, enjoy, project, flapjack, Marjorie, disjointed, bootjack, hallelujah

-k make, lambkin, lucky, handkerchief, seek, Kafka, Bangkok, Oshkosh, like, bookkeeper, talk, bank, joke, napkin, lark, task, Atkins, duke, hawk, dyke, whizkid

-l fall, able, enclose, ladle, felt, rifle, eagle, richly, sill, tackle, rally, harmless, unlit, fold, ample, girl, asleep, atlas, dull, Vladimir, crawl, axle, shyly, puzzle

28A REVIEW Type today's date 9 times (3 rows and 3 columns, as in 25A).

Do the remainder of this lesson as an INFORMAL TEST, using it as review and preparation for formal testing in Lessons 29–30 that end the first six weeks of this course. Work from one item to the next without pause. Your instructor will tell you your completion time to the nearest ½-minute. If you want to score your speed in wpm, divide your completion time into 197, the total of 5-stroke words in Lesson 28, made up as follows: small envelope (23 words), large envelope (33 words), postal card (78 words), centering (18 words), table (45 words).

Time—nearest ½'

28B ENVELOPES   One small and one large envelope

| Small | From: | Anson & Dill | 1620 Elder Drive | Shreveport, LA 71102 |
| | To: | Mr. William Benson | 2064 Pine Lane | Montgomery, AL 36104 |

Large	From:	Stein Office Supply Co.	406 Adams Street	Chicago, IL 60614
	To:	Mrs. Walter L. Rand, Head	Business Education Dept.	
		Grant College	740 Yale Avenue	Chicago, IL 60607

28C POSTAL CARD

Use today's date and the address and return address of the small envelope of 28B. Type the message side as follows:

Dear Mr. Benson: Thank you for your order for 60 cases of #2½ cans of peeled tomatoes, WHITE STAR brand. (¶) We expect to ship your order on Friday, October 18, and you should receive it no later than Monday, October 21. Very truly yours, Retail Sales Dept.

28D CENTERING

Center each line horizontally and the group of lines vertically on top ½ of full sheet. Use the vertical spacing shown in parentheses.

PHOENIX THEATER (SS) Actors' Fund Benefit (DS) HAMLET (DS) Starring (SS) Richard Burton

28E TABLE / WORD DIVISION

Use bottom ½ of same sheet used in 28D.

Note. Do not use a dictionary before typing.

Center vertically on ½-sheet. Use as heading: SPEECH SYL-LABLES AND TYPEWRITER DIVISIONS. TS after heading and DS the rows. Set LM 20 spaces left of center and set tab stops to leave 4 spaces between columns. In column 1, type the words listed at the right. In column 2, type the number of **speech** syllables in each word. In column 3, type each word and insert hyphens to show all preferable typewriter divisions; e.g., for the word *interest-ing,* you would type:

identification
currency
drummed
misspelling
violinist
healthy
running

interesting   4   in-ter-est-ing

28F OPTIONAL PRACTICE

Continue on a practice sheet with Stroke Refinement (pp. 121–125) or Letter Sequences (pp. 118–119). PF

Note. In a correctly typed 28E, column 1 begins under the first letter of the heading and column 3 ends under the last letter of the heading.

37 Write these numbers in one column: $9\frac{1}{2}$, $5\frac{1}{4}$, and 6-7/8. What's their total?
38 The price of Style #84 jacket, size 13, is $30; sizes over 40 are 10% more.

39 "The very _idea_!" said Quill. "I won't pay 25¢ extra for wrapping!"
40 Fiske & Glass are having a sale (the first this year) of fur-trimmed coats.

41 "This meat is marked 2-3/4 lbs.; the scale shows $2\frac{1}{2}$!" complained Mrs. Judd.
42 She added: "At 96¢ a pound, that makes quite some difference, doesn't it?"

43 Barton & Co. carry this glove (style #17) @ $9.50, but only in small sizes.
44 At $8\frac{1}{4}$% discounts on coats, we _know_ we'll do a land-office business.

45 We admit boys and girls (age 6 to 14)--yearly charges, $750; books are $38.
46 We expect a committee's report, entitled "Civil Justice," in a _week_.

47 Problem #9: What is $\frac{1}{2}$ of 72? $\frac{1}{4}$ of 56? 50% of 8; of 108? Answer quickly!
48 Our magazine, _Pro_, costs 95¢ each issue; annual subscription, $10.80.

49 Foamy omelet: 4 egg yolks, $\frac{1}{4}$ tsp. salt, $2\frac{1}{2}$ tbsp. of milk, 4 beaten whites.
50 Pamphlet #167 (issued 9/73 by Sullivan & Baxter) is entitled "Fertilizers."

51 Copies cost 35¢ each--$3.36 per dozen; _20%_ discount in that quantity.
52 What's the telephone number of Tucker & Josephson, 89 Grove Street? Hurry!

53 Box #114 ($2\frac{1}{2}$' by $1\frac{1}{4}$') holds blankets and quilts. At 20% off, it's only $3.
54 One-bedroom apartments at Parklawn, 1760 Grand Street, rent at $99 to $185.

55 I _rush_ ordered; they sent: 1 doz. cups @ $14, 1 doz. saucers @ $9.
56 Does J. & W. Vincent's catalog list "Day-by-Day Recipes" at 98¢? I'll see.

57 After a month's practice, I reduced the running time from $4\frac{1}{2}$ to $4\frac{1}{4}$ minutes.
58 I wrote: "Address my mail c/o Row & Martin, 76 East 9 Street, Room #1281."

59 My hourly pay ($7.85) is 5% more than his. _Why_? Our jobs are alike.
60 I left very early--not quite 10:30; I had only 10¢, and I had to walk home.

61 I bought a 32-oz. can of apple juice @ 75¢ and a box of strawberries @ 98¢.
62 "It's 8:40--time to start! Who's coming?" said Jerry quietly; and he left.

63 Our order #470 (dated 9/1) for 2 chairs @ $35 hasn't been filled. Why not?
64 Davy & Kahn's $5\frac{1}{4}$% bonds sell _below_ par; they yield $6\frac{1}{2}$% to 6-3/4%.

65 "It's 8 o'clock--I must leave by 8:30! I'll go in $\frac{1}{2}$ or $\frac{1}{4}$ hour," said John.
66 Stan needs 15 calories per pound daily; for 150-pounders, 2,250 (150 x 15).

67 Suite #416 rents at $195; #417 is 8% _more_--$210.60. Which is best?
68 Ken bought six 15¢ pencils at Rosenzweig & Quarles' stationery store today.

69 You'll find McQueen & Kurtz's advertisement on page 48--exceptional values!
70 "Sale today _only_--70 suits $\frac{1}{4}$ to $\frac{1}{2}$ off," said Mr. Jay (the manager).

71 R & C stock was quoted at 94; it rose 10-7/8 points after the news at 9:30.
72 Plate #36 is marked $1.25. Wasn't it always priced @ 98¢? Why 25¢ higher?

73 This month's cash surrender value--Policy #9416 (issued 9/6/73)--is $7,350.
74 John's mark in his civics test was 82%. _Is_ that better than last week?

75 A prisoner pleaded: "_Not_ guilty!" I requested an extension of time.
76 Vaughan & Crane sent me these 98¢ gloves in size $6\frac{1}{2}$; I had ordered size $6\frac{1}{4}$.

29-30A PREPARATION   2' on 13A, p. 23

29-30B STRAIGHT COPY TIMINGS   Read each piece of copy before typing. Enter average speed and errors on TR.

5', DS, SM–1"

GWPM a	b	CW
3	34	13
5	37	27
8	39	41
11	42	55
14	45	69
17	48	83
19	51	97
22	53	111
24	56	122
27	58	135
30	61	149
31	62	156
Sy 1.54		
St 6.0		

For many years it had been wrongly supposed that various types of special drill materials are useful for developing typing accuracy. Instead, research has shown that striking the right key depends upon controlling the time intervals between motions, on stroking at the right speed. Again contrary to conventional belief, the right speed for accurate work is not a slow, careful speed, but one that differs little from your normal, comfortable rate. The established principle for all motor skills is that any large difference from one's normal rate has harmful effects on the movement and increases errors.

For accurate work, do not hurry—but do now slow down to a crawl either. If many errors result, the typing rate was either too fast or too slow—instead of just right.

+0   +1   +2   +3

GWPM a	b	CW
3	35	13
6	38	28
8	41	42
11	44	56
14	47	70
15	47	75
18	50	88
20	53	102
23	56	116
26	59	130
29	61	144
32	64	159
32	65	162
Sy 1.54		
St 6.0		

Another important research finding about learning to type is that there is no tendency for speed and accuracy to go together. Typists at all levels of accuracy may be found at all levels of speed. This means that the two aspects of performance are based on different underlying factors. Therefore, it is not possible to practice toward both objectives at the same time.

The skill building program in this book is based on the research findings. You practice for speed until you have attained a substantial gain—with little regard for errors. Then you change to accuracy practice at a slower speed. If you have practiced with understanding and with high motivation toward gaining skill, your test performance at an unhurried rate will have an acceptable level of accuracy and be faster than it was before.

+0   +1   +2   +3

Optional practice

KEYBOARD PRACTICE

Each line contains 75 strokes (15 words), and each group of four lines covers the entire keyboard, except for the asterisk. Enter on your Practice Form your starting point for your next practice (see footnote **g,** p. 115).

```
. . . .1. . . .2. . . .3. . . .4. . . .5. . . .6. . . .7. . . .8. . . .9. . . .10. . . .11. . . .12. . . .13. . . .14. . . .15
```

1 I'll shortly deposit my spare cash at the X & Z Savings Bank (a/c #36,804).
2 Lemonade: $1\frac{1}{2}$ cups lemon juice; $1\frac{1}{4}$ cups sugar; 4-3/4 cups water; stir well.

3 Frank Roque said, "One gross pencils @ 95¢ a dozen--2% off--that's $11.17."
4 "What's the charge?" asked the driver. "Not speeding! At 30 miles?"

5 Jo spent 75% of her week's allowance on sweets (candy and ice cream).
6 The manager of Bendix & Holtzman announced: "This equipment cost $83,000."

7 The postage on the package Jim mailed to Zone #12 was 94¢--nearly a dollar!
8 I need two boards $6\frac{1}{4}$ or $6\frac{1}{2}$ feet long; 8-3/4 inches wide. Do you have them?

9 James used 3-3/4 lbs. of grass seed @ 49¢ and $1\frac{1}{4}$ lbs. of clover seed @ 79¢.
10 Has Mrs. Saxe (age 75) really received $1,500 in May dividend checks?

11 "A dozen #2 cans cost $6.50; this #$2\frac{1}{2}$ size costs 20% more," said the clerk.
12 Come to Blay & Company's "Get Acquainted!" sale--date: Wednesday, April 8.

13 Check #1439 for $200, issued to Squire & Katz, date: 6/27, is outstanding.
14 I've reduced prices on fall coats: all at least 20%; some up to 50%.

15 "Who's ringing?" asked Dad. "Answer the bell! Then get me two 8¢ stamps."
16 Mr. Knox's income (since retirement) is only $\frac{1}{4}$ to $\frac{1}{2}$ of his previous income.

17 Forward Jack's mail, c/o Quinby & Merz, P.O. Box 721, Tampa, Florida 33608.
18 We enclose dividend #9, 50¢ a share (formerly 40¢)--a 25% jump.

```
. . . .1. . . .2. . . .3. . . .4. . . .5. . . .6. . . .7. . . .8. . . .9. . . .10. . . .11. . . .12. . . .13. . . .14. . . .15
```

19 Shirley used $\frac{1}{2}$ cup oil and $\frac{1}{4}$ cup vinegar in this dressing. Do you like it?
20 The clerk added: "These mats sell @ $1.25 each; but four cost only $4.50."

21 "The size $6\frac{1}{4}$ glove isn't an exact fit--too tight; I'll try $6\frac{1}{2}$," said Cindy.
22 The meeting began at 7:30 (or perhaps a little later); it broke up at 9:45.

23 Asquith & Jones report they added 30% new space at a cost of over $128,000.
24 What a bargain! The #312 wire @ $10.45 a reel is a giveaway, isn't it?

25 This year Jaffe & Gay's sales went to $98,300 (16% over last year's).
26 The book's title is "Justice for Elizabeth"; cost, $7.45--plus the 60¢ tax.

27 Question #8 is as follows: What do $2\frac{1}{4}$ pounds of pears @ $47\frac{1}{2}$¢ a pound cost?
28 Twelve months (52 weeks) make a year. Then don't 4-1/3 weeks make a month?

29 This meeting of Walzer & Co.'s directors may last $4\frac{1}{4}$ to $4\frac{1}{2}$ hours (or more).
30 The manager stated: "We'll make 6 broadcasts; #1 today; #2-#6 next month."

31 What's the quotation on Jordan stock? It's very high--50-3/8--up 9 points!
32 His are priced @ 75¢ each, $7.50 a dozen--that's over a 10% discount.

33 The announcement read: "Lask & Frazer, Inc., have just opened Branch #24."
34 Pint jars sell for 89¢; quart jars for $1.65. Save 13¢ by getting a quart.

35 What's the life expectancy of Mrs. May Sherwood (aged 70)? About 15 years?
36 Interest rates are rising: They were $6\frac{1}{4}$%; later $7\frac{1}{2}$%; and now 8-3/4%.

```
. . . .1. . . .2. . . .3. . . .4. . . .5. . . .6. . . .7. . . .8. . . .9. . . .10. . . .11. . . .12. . . .13. . . .14. . . .15
```

29– ENVELOPE
30C 78 words
Address a large envelope **from** Mrs. Rand **to** the Stein Company (see 28B).

29– CENTERING
30D 30 words
Type item 7 of SP–18 (p. 107). Center each line horizontally and the group of lines vertically on a ½-sheet. DS after line 3 and after line 5; SS other lines.

29–30 Two-day test or review: Part 2 (Number and symbol timing ▫ Postal card ▫ Table)

29– PREPARATION   2' on 24E, p. 38.
30E

F-G-H are a continuation of the test.

29– NUMBER AND SYMBOL TIMING (Alphabetic)   5', DS, SM–1". TR–NS
30F

	GWPM		
	a	b	CW
Toxner & Squire's accident insurance policy costs only $2.55 a month	3	14	14
(just 8½¢ a day). Isn't the protection it gives well worth that amount—	6	18	30
and more? Miss Jane Betz writes: "I have your check for $139 in payment	9	21	45
of my claim on policy #4760. Many thanks for your promptness."	12	23	58

+0	+1	+2	+3

Time on G and H—nearest ¼'

29– POSTAL CARD
30G 74 words
Type the message and address sides (including return address) of card #7 of SP–26, p. 110.

29– TABLE
30H 32 words
Center the table below vertically on a ½-sheet. Set LM 18 spaces left of center, BC–8. TS after the heading, DS the rows.

SOME POSTAL ABBREVIATIONS

Massachusetts	Mass.	MA
Michigan	Mich.	MI
Minnesota	Minn.	MN
Mississippi	Miss.	MS
Missouri	Mo.	MO
Montana	Mont.	MT

Practice forms

There are eight types of practice materials—used at intervals in this book—in which your starting point in any lesson depends on your performance the previous time the materials were used. Rather than relying on your memory to identify the proper starting point each time, use the Practice Forms provided. In this way, you also will have a continuous record of your progress.

Of the eight types of materials, four are timed; the remaining four are for untimed optional practice. How to make entries on your Practice Forms is explained in the footnotes. (Also, see pp. 128 and 136.)

Staple the forms into the other side of the same file folder containing your Timing Record (see p. 7).

Timed Practice Form

Call-the-Throw[a]	Progressive Practice (1')[b]		Progressive Practice (2')[c]		Progressive NS Practice[c]		Paced Practice[d]	
1' wpm = _11_ Start at _12_	5' wpm = _12_ Start at _13_		5' wpm = _26_ Start at _27_		5' wpm = _14_ Start at _15_		5' wpm = _22_ Start at _24_	
Next Trial	Schedule		Schedule		Schedule		Schedule	
	S	A	S	A	S	A	S	A
#11	~~13S~~		~~27S~~		~~15S~~		~~24S~~	
#15	~~14S~~		~~28S~~		~~16S~~		~~26S~~	
	~~15S~~		~~29S~~		~~17S~~		~~28S~~	
	~~16S~~		30S		18S			26A
	17S		31S		19S			28A
		15A		29A		17A	30S	

[a]**CALL-THE-THROW** shows 11 wpm as the previous 1' timing speed and a start at call-the-throw practice at 12 wpm. The final success during the first practice session was at 15 wpm (Sentence #10); so the "next trial" (at 16 wpm) will be on Sentence **#11.** Beginning with **#11** at the second practice session, the final success during that session was at 19 wpm (#14); so the "next trial" will be on Sentence **#15.**

[b]**PROGRESSIVE PRACTICE (1')** shows 12 wpm as the previous 5' timing speed and a start at progressive speed practice at 13 wpm. As each item on the schedule is successfully typed, the item is lined out. In the illustration, the student suc-ceeded from **13S** through **16S** (S for speed) and should start next time at **17S.**

[c]**PROGRESSIVE PRACTICE (2') AND PROGRESSIVE NS PRACTICE** use the procedures described in Footnote **b.**

[d]**PACED PRACTICE** shows 22 wpm as the previous 5' timing speed and a start at paced practice (for speed) at 24 wpm **(24S).** As each item on the schedule is successfully typed, the item is lined out. In the illustration, the student succeeded from **24S** through **26A** and should start next time at **28A** (**A** for accuracy).

Untimed Practice Form (Optional)

Letter Sequences[e]	Stroke Refinement[f]	Capitalization[g]	Keyboard Practice[g]
Next Item	Next Item	Next Item	Next Item
c	L-8	#6	#5
f	L-15	#9	#9
	D-32(3)		

[e]**Letter sequence practice** shows that the student completed practice at **a** and **b** and should begin next time with **c.** The second entry means that the drills for **c, d,** and **e** were completed; so begin next time with **f.**

[f]**Stroke refinement practice** shows that the student completed Line 7 and should begin next time with **L-8** (Line 8). The second entry shows that lines 8–14 were completed; so next practice begins with **L-15.** The third entry means that the second line of Drill 32 was completed; so begin next time with **D32(3)**—the third line of Drill 32.

[g]**Capitalization and Keyboard Practice** entries are like those for the first two Stroke Refinement entries (see Footnote **f**). Show the line number to begin with next time.

Continue on a practice page with one or more of the following: Stroke Refinement (pp. 121–125), Letter Sequences (pp. 118–119), Capitalization (p. 120), Keyboard Practice (pp. 116–117).

Notice that different amounts of the four types of special practice materials are supplied. Choose among them with the objective of finishing all four **once** (generally by taking turns at them) before you begin any of the four a second time.

Remember to enter on your Practice Form the starting point for **next** practice.

From now on, whenever time is available (at the end of the period and whenever you finish a piece of work before it is time to start the next part of the lesson), do Optional Practice.

31 Paced practice □ Table versus prose

31A PREPARATION   Type the date, as usual.

31B PACED PRACTICE   Three 3–3½ minute timings (pp. 139–155).

1 The ideas behind Paced Practice are explained in the 60-wpm materials on p. 155. Read those materials **now.**

2 Select from the materials that begin on p. 139 those at the next even-numbered speed above your speed on the timing of Lesson 25. When STOP is called, if you are within 5 strokes on either side of the exact place in the copy—regardless of errors—in the next timing, proceed to the next higher speed. If you are more than 5 strokes away, repeat the same copy until you succeed.

3 To help you get the feel of adjusting your typing rate to time

announcements, a few short paced timings (30 seconds to 1 minute) will be given first. The three formal timings (3–3½ minutes) will follow.

Note. You will never be told in advance how long each timing is to be.

After you finish today's practice, read the Paced Practice rules on p. 138 and enter **your** practice schedule on your Timed Practice Form. Then line out (according to footnote **d,** p. 115) the items at which you succeeded.

31C TABLE VERSUS PROSE

Using 1-inch side margins, type the information given in the table of 27B in sentence form in 1 paragraph. Model the 5 sentences (1 for each row of the table) on these:

```
         Asia's tallest peak is Mt. Everest, at 29,028 feet.
     South America's tallest peak . . . (and so on).
```

Compare the length of time it takes you to identify from your typed paragraph and then from the table of 27B: the name of the tallest mountain in Europe, the height of Mt. Kilimanjaro, the location of Mt. McKinley. Do you see how efficient tabular presentation is for the reader?

31D TABLE

Add, as column 4 to the table of 29–30H, the capital cities listed at the right of this ¶. Set LM 26 spaces left of center, BC–6. Use the same vertical spacing as in 29–30H and center the table on a ½-sheet. List the cities in pencil on scrap paper to avoid having to turn back and forth between pages: Work from p. 45 plus your penciled list.

Boston
Lansing
St. Paul
Jackson
Jefferson City
Helena

1 Terrell & Moore, Inc., 508 Seventh Avenue, Baltimore, MD 21212. Gentlemen: We have studied the specifications you sent us for the electrical work on the building you are constructing on Candlewood Avenue and appreciate the opportunity to bid on the work. (¶) In accordance with the options contained in your specifications, we are enclosing two sets of figures representing our bid for handling the electrical installation as your subcontractor. We shall of course be pleased to answer any questions you may have. Sincerely yours, J. H. Watt, Vice-President

2 Mrs. Ella Ingersoll, Office Manager, Coveney & Co., 42 Arbor Street, Kansas City, MO 64106. Dear Mrs. Ingersoll: In response to your request for samples of designs for new letterhead stationery for Coveney & Co., we are enclosing four designs different in various aspects of typography and layout. We are confident that, among them, you will find one you like especially. (¶) We look forward to hearing from you. Sincerely yours, Peter H. Gannett, Sales Manager

3 Mr. Edward Kenilworth, Manager, Hale's Market, 603 Regent Place, Bayonne, NJ 07002. Dear Mr. Kenilworth: Yesterday our truckman delivered to your store several dozen cases of canned goods. Later in the day he found that a case of Burgundy peaches, addressed to Cling & Dill, was missing. To locate the missing case, we are writing to all the places where he had made deliveries earlier in the day. (¶) We should be most appreciative if you would check the delivery made to you on the chance that it includes the missing case. If so, please phone us collect. Very truly yours, Brian Lask, Head, Shipping Department.

4 Mrs. Frances H. Munter, Office Manager, Craig & Co., Inc., 432 Decatur Avenue, Roanoke, VA 24017. Dear Mrs. Munter: Our trucks will arrive in three days to begin transferring your office furniture to your new facilities. In order to make this move an efficient one, we suggest you observe the following procedures. (¶) Make certain that all file cabinets have been locked, all desk drawers emptied, and all items not to be moved by truck flagged with the yellow tags provided by Mason Van Lines. Very truly yours, William Gresov, Manager

5 Mr. Lee Tolson, Manager, Claremont Stationers, 18 Oak Avenue, Scranton, PA 18502. Dear Mr. Tolson: We are able to ship to you at this time only part of the merchandise listed on your Purchase Order No. 77-1833. Within the week you may expect to receive 4 dozen reams of the Mainland paper, #814; the 20 dozen kraft paper wrappers; and the 4,000 sheets of multiplex forms. (¶) However, we have such a heavy backlog of orders for 20# Duramate paper that it will be four weeks before we can supply you with it. If you can use a slightly lighter weight of paper that many of our customers often substitute for Duramate (samples enclosed), we can make immediate shipment. (¶) Please let us know your wishes. Very truly yours, GIROUX PAPER SUPPLIES, J. L. Wall

6 Mrs. Isabelle Miles, Business Manager, Cromwell Publications, 877 Whitehall Place, St. Louis, MO 63108. Dear Isabelle Regarding your request for promotion and sales reports, 279,000 copies of *Weekend* magazine have been sold during the period April 30 to May 31. I think we will have a clearer indication of sales potential in September, however, and I will send you a breakdown of sales by states at that time (¶) Regarding promotion, in addition to our ad in *Holiday,* a prepublication, full-color, two-page ad appeared in the January 1976 (winter) issue of *The American Tourist;* and, upon publication of our first issue, a one-page ad was placed in the March 1976 issue of *Innocents Abroad.* (¶) I will let you know what further advertising is planned for *Weekend* when we complete our projected advertising schedule for the coming year. Sincerely Sandra Osborne, Head, Promotions Department

7 Mr. Victor Hammel, Fay & McPherson, 199 Beekman Street, New York, NY 10011. Dear Mr. Hammel: We have completed our initial archaeological survey of the Helderberg area, according to the mapping of four quadrants divided into nine sections each we agreed upon last month. (¶) In Sections S-8, W-7, W-9, and E-2, there were random finds of stone implements or pottery fragments belonging to various tribes of the northwestern Iroquois. In Section W-4 there was a major find of iron implements of the Onandaga tribe. (¶) We shall send you a detailed report next week, incorporating our recommendations for further excavation and site preservation. Very truly yours; John Cunningham, Engineer

32 Table placement by backspacing

32A PREPARATION   Type today's date, as usual.

32B PACED PRACTICE   Two timings of 3½–4 minutes each (pp. 139–155). PF

Start today's practice according to your PF entries for Lesson 31B. From now on, change between S (speed) and A (accuracy) practice according to your PF schedule for paced practice. Line out each item on your PF as you succeed at it.

Progress is rapid at the start (if you carefully adjust your stroking rate). Later, it will take several trials at the same copy before you succeed. Still later, it will take quite a few trials. So be patient.

32C TABLE PLACEMENT BY BACKSPACING

Just as you can center a line horizontally by backspacing from center once for each two characters and spaces, you can locate the left margin of a table by backspacing (1 for 2) for the total of the longest items in the columns, plus between-column space.

BACKSPACING TO FIND LEFT MARGIN OF TABLE

1 Set side margins to extreme left and right; clear all tab stops; move carriage to center (pica 42, elite 51).

2 Identify the longest item in each column.

3 Backspace in two steps: first for the typed matter, then for intercolumn space, as follows:

a From center, backspace (1 for 2) for the total of the longest items in each column as if they were all on **one** line to be centered—**excluding** between-column space. For the table of 27B you would backspace for groups of **two** as follows:

h space

South AmericaKilimanjaro29,028

b Continue to backspace for half of all intercolumn space (½ of 10 + 10 in a 3-column table using 10 spaces between columns, ½ of 6 + 6 + 6 in a 4-column table using 6 spaces between columns).*

4 Set left margin.

*Instead of backspacing for half of all intercolumn space, you might prefer to subtract half the total of those spaces from the point on the scale at which the backspacing for the typed matter ends (e.g., 6 + 6 + 6 = 18; ½ of 18 = 9).

TASK 1 Speed in determining table placement can contribute more to skill than speed in keystroking. How rapidly can you backspace to locate the LM for the "longest items" in the examples at the right (a–d)? Do not type them; just backspace and, after each one, check your LM with the correct LM (see below at right).

a 2 cols. (BC–12):   Amount   Discount

b 3 cols. (BC–7): [BC = 2 × 7 = 14, and 14/2 = 7]
Debating Team   March 30   Program

c 4 cols. (BC–6): [BC = 3 × 6 = 18, and 18/2 = 9]
California   Los Angeles   Sacramento   Pacific

d 5 cols. (BC–7): Student Date Speed Errors Grade

TASK 2 Type Table 31D, using BC–10. Center vertically on a ½-sheet, including the heading. Can you finish in less than 5 minutes?

CORRECT LM

	Pica	Elite		Pica	Elite
a	29	38	c	14	23
b	21	30	d	15	24

For additional practice at backspacing for the left margin, see SP–32, p. 111.

LESSON 47 Short Business Letters

INSTRUCTIONS Date about 3½ inches from top of page; SMs: WL–45. Alternate blocked ¶s/open punctuation; indented ¶s/mixed punctuation. Use moving dateline.

1 Mrs. Alex Shaffer, 72 Willow Road, Topeka, KS 66607.

Dear Mrs. Shaffer: Before our new salesroom at 1417 Blake Street opens to the public on Monday, May 23, we plan to have a private showing for our regular customers on Monday, May 16, from 10 a.m. to 1 p.m. A number of our new home appliances that are sure to interest you will be on display. (¶) Won't you please join us at the private showing and then be our guest at luncheon? Very truly yours, Donald P. Hawke.

2 President, Samuel Gross & Company, 449 Rowley Street, Jackson, MS 39204.

Gentlemen: Perhaps it was the rush of the holiday season, but you forgot to mail us your check for $127.75, which was due November 30. (¶) During the past five years you have always had an outstanding credit rating with Pylon Corporation, and we know you will want to maintain it in the future. (¶) Please send us your check as soon as possible. Very truly yours, PYLON CORPORATION, Bruce Williamson, Credit Dept.

3 Mrs. Julia LaRoche, 1616 Otway Avenue, Lansing, MI 48906

Dear Mrs. LaRoche: We are sorry, but we are no longer able to provide home demonstrations of our electrical appliances. The cost, both in labor and transportation, has become prohibitive. However, the vacuum cleaner you are interested in buying is on display in our showroom at 26 Meade Street. A salesperson is always available to demonstrate the use of the appliance and to answer any questions you may have about it. Yours very truly, Marvin K. Trotter, Customer Service Dept.

4 Mr. Thomas Cabanis, 189 Duchamp St., New York, NY 10009.

Dear Mr. Cabanis: We have received your letter of May 31, asking us to cancel your insurance policy. Naturally, we shall comply with your request, but may we point out that if you later decide to take out another policy, a new physical examination will be required. And, of course, your premiums may be higher. (¶) If, upon reconsideration, you decide to keep your policy in force, please notify us before June 15. Yours very truly, DARWIN INSURANCE CO., Robert Huxley, Regional Manager

5 Beaumont, Inc., 28 Brunswick Plaza, New York, NY 10016

Gentlemen: Last July, at your preview of fall fashions in New York, you displayed a large, full-color poster advertising your new "Sirocco" raincoats. This new line has proven to be so popular that we have decided to use this poster as part of our window display next month. (¶) Would you therefore please send us two copies of this poster at your earliest convenience. Sincerely yours, GORING & HOWE, James Devon, Advertising Dept.

6 Morton Richards & Sons, 97 Exchange Boulevard, Brockton, MA 02408

Gentlemen: When we placed our order three weeks ago for brass fixtures, you assured us that we could expect delivery within ten days. We now have your letter suggesting a substitution of stainless steel fixtures in order to expedite shipment. Because we feel that the stainless steel fixtures will not blend well with the general background of our offices, we cannot agree to such a substitution. (¶) Please proceed promptly with our original order. Very truly yours, Christopher J. Merrow, Office Manager

7 Wilkinson Record Co., 1217 Sheridan Circle, Brockton, MA 02408

Gentlemen: Your delivery of September 19 was accompanied by your invoice #18924, charging us for 25 copies of "Breathless," recorded by The Last Gasps, your catalog #48760-2. However, your carton contained only 15 copies of the record. (¶) Please ship the remaining 10 records by November 23. If you cannot make delivery by then, please credit us for the amount of the shortage. Very truly yours, BOB'S RECORDS, Bob Kalfine, Manager

8 Vincent E. Costello, 1823 Shortlands Street, Tacoma, WA 98465

Dear Mr. Costello: A mutual friend, Mr. Lester Bush, told us that you are planning a trip to Hawaii this fall and suggested that we tell you how we made his Hawaiian vacation more enjoyable. We not only handled his airline reservations and arranged his hotel accommodations, but planned his sightseeing trips, too—all at no extra cost. (¶) For the vacation of a lifetime, phone us at 273-5986, or drop in at one of our offices. Yours very truly, TACKETT TRAVEL AGENCY, Mary Okada, Travel Agent

33A KEYBOARD PRACTICE   Contains all letters, numbers, symbols.

Today's quotation on J & Z was 25¼--10% higher than Monday!
Will his old papers fit into a #18 folder, size 9¼ by 14½ inches?
My invoice read: "3½ boxes erasers @ 70¢; 6 boxes pencils @ $1."
The asterisk or star (*) is frequently used to signal a footnote.

. . . . 1 . . . 2 . . . 3 . . . 4 . . . 5 . . . 6 . . . 7 . . . 8 . . . 9 . . . 10 . . . 11 . . . 12 . . . 13

33B PACED PRACTICE   Two 4½–5 minute timings (pp. 139–155). PF

33C TABLE   Center the table below on a ½-sheet by backspace method of 32C; BC–5.

An odd letter will be left over after backspacing for the typed matter. That odd letter, plus a total of 15 intercolumn spaces (3 x 5), makes 16 spaces to be accounted for—by backspacing 8 more times. If you threw away the odd letter in the typed matter and then took half of 15 as 7, your table would not be exactly centered. **Question:** How much space should be left after the heading? between the rows?

Be careful with longhand or printed tables. The item in each column that looks longest to the eye may **not** contain the most letters. Check carefully; if necessary, count letters.
Can you finish the 42-word table below in 5–6 minutes? If you finish early, determine new LM: (1) with last row omitted and using BC–4; then (2) with first row omitted, using BC–5.

CLUB MEETINGS—WEEK OF OCTOBER 3

Economics Club	Thursday	Room 319	Mr. Montgomery
Glee Club	Tuesday	Auditorium	Mr. Farrell
Mathematics Club	Monday	Room 258	Mrs. Conway
French Club	Wednesday	Room 407	Ms. Lowery

33D PLANNING A TABLE   DS between tasks.

Speed and correctness in determining placement—not actual keystroking—are the heart of table typing. In Tasks 1–3, after backspacing for each task, check the correctness of your LM and tab stops by typing the longest items from **each** column all on one row. For example, in the table of 33C you would type *Mathematics Club, Wednesday, Auditorium, Mr. Montgomery* —using BC–5—on one line. A look at your completed typing will show whether LM = RM and if there is equal space between columns.

Do not loaf over the backspacing. Spell rapidly by two's and backspace equally rapidly.

TASK 1   Backspace for the longest items of the table in 33C and type all four longest items on 1 line, using BC–5.

LM Check (for centers at elite 51, pica 42): Elite 19, Pica 10.

TASK 2   Repeat the procedures of Task 1, using BC–4 and omitting the last row of the table of 33C. Longest items now are: Mathematics Club, Thursday, Auditorium, Mr. Montgomery.

LM Check: Elite 21, Pica 12.

TASK 3   Omit column 4 (the faculty sponsors); BC–10. Longest items are: Mathematics Club, Wednesday, Auditorium.

LM Check: Elite 24, Pica 15.

33E PROGRESSIVE PRACTICE   As many 1′ timings as time permits (pp. 127–130). PF

LESSON 44 Personal-Business Letters

INSTRUCTIONS Assume yourself or another member of your family to be the writer of these letters, using your home address. Use ½-sheet for letters 1–4; full sheet for letters 5–8; moving date line in all letters. Alternate between blocked ¶s/open punctuation and indented ¶s/mixed punctuation.

1 To: Madison Community Theatre, 881 Jasper Street, Madison, WI 53706
Ladies and Gentlemen: Please send me tickets for two orchestra seats for your performance of *Private Lives* on Friday, December 16. Charge the tickets ($15) to my American Express credit card, No. 3691 041826 14092. Yours very truly,

2 To: Bernstein & Howard, 1537 Pierce Street, Cleveland, OH 44112
Gentlemen: I have last year's edition of your sales catalog. If you have a more recent edition, I should appreciate your sending me a copy. Very truly yours,

3 To: Guarantee Bank & Trust, 931 Baker Street, Chicago IL 60616
Gentlemen: Three weeks ago I sent you a $1,000 coupon bond, #1-44664, of the Gilmore Paper Company. I sent the bond by registered mail, and I have a return receipt for it. I asked you to exchange my bond for a registered bond of equivalent value. (¶) Please inform me when I may expect delivery of the registered bond. Very truly yours,

4 To: Great Lakes Insurance Co., 1779 Aspen Street, Lansing, MI 48909
Gentlemen: In this morning's mail I received my health insurance policy #H-38895, which you sent me in response to my application for insurance and payment of the initial premium. The identification card mentioned in the accompanying letter, however, was not enclosed. (¶) Please send me my identification card as soon as possible. Yours very truly,

5 To: Personnel Office, Wheeler Insurance Co., 4398 North Cedar St., Philadelphia, PA 19112
Gentlemen: I am interested in securing a summer position with a view to permanent, full-time employment after graduation from Cranston Community College next year. (¶) I am majoring in Secretarial Studies and have an overall average of A−. I am doing particularly well in Typewriting and in Business Communications. (¶) Until June 12, I shall be available after 1:30 p.m. daily, and then full time from June 12 to September 12, when the fall term begins. (¶) May I come in for an interview? My home telephone number is 743-9483. Sincerely yours,

6 To: Ohrmann's, P.O. Box 701, Paramus, NJ 07652.
Gentlemen: Your statement of November 2 covering my charge account #59-1445893 shows a debit balance of $35.41. However, the statement does not show a credit for $18.50 for merchandise returned to you as damaged three weeks earlier (under credit invoice #139501). Please send me a corrected statement. Very truly yours,

7 To: Mr. Michael Di Servio, Agent, State Farm Insurance Co., 38 Prince Street, Decatur, IL 62512.
Dear Mr. Di Servio: In about a month I expect to discontinue use of my automobile for business purposes. Since it will thereafter be used only for local driving, my annual mileage will be greatly reduced, qualifying me for a lower insurance premium. I am also considering other changes in my automobile insurance coverage. (¶) Could you meet with me at my home any evening next week after 7 p.m. to discuss the changes with me? I will phone you in a day or two to arrange the appointment. Very truly yours,

8 To: Ms. Sally Berman, Social Services Department, Community Hospital, 430 Aspinwall Blvd., Duluth, MN 55806.
Dear Ms. Berman: In connection with the transfer of my mother [fill in a name here] from your hospital to the Carter Rehabilitation Center, the Center has informed me that they have not yet received from you their Form No. L-1614, which they sent to you ten days ago. (¶) Since admission of the patient for rehabilitation therapy awaits only receipt of the form, I should be appreciative if you would complete the form promptly and send it to the Admissions Office of the Center. Sincerely yours,

34A KEYBOARD PRACTICE   Type lines 1–2, p. 116. Each four lines includes entire keyboard.

34B STRAIGHT COPY TIMING   5′, DS, SM–1″. TR. Read before you type.

	GWPM		
	a	b	CW
	3	33	13
	5	36	27
	8	39	41
	11	42	55
	14	45	69
	17	48	83
	19	50	97
	21	52	107
	24	55	120
	27	58	134
	30	61	148
	31	62	154

The importance of skill in table typing has been strongly established in a number of investigations. In one that examined junior or clerical typists, it was discovered that table typing consumed ten percent of their time—about half a day a week. Among personal typists, it ranked seventh among students and eighth among adults. In another survey (of all employed typists in the State of Washington), typing tables was tied for fourth in a rank ordering of tasks according to the number of employed typists who performed the task.

Still other studies showed that planning skill greatly outweighs stroking skill in table typing and, for that matter, in most real-life typing tasks. Rapid and correct advance planning—not fast keystroking—is what counts most of all.

Sy 1.54
St 6.1

+0   +1   +2   +3

34C COLUMN HEADINGS

1 Occasionally, table content is clear without column headings (called "heads," for short). More often, descriptive column heads are helpful or necessary.

2 Column heads are always centered in relation to their columns, usually underscored, and always followed by 1 blank line.

3 To center a shorter column head over a longer column item below the head (as in the *Time* column):

a From beginning of column, space forward (1 for 2) for the longest item beneath the head. (To find the midpoint of any item from its starting point, forward space 1 for 2.)

b Backspace (1 for 2) for the head.

c Type the head where the backspacing ends.

4 To find tab stop setting for a shorter column under a longer head (as in the *Radio Station* column):

a From beginning of head, space forward (1 for 2) to its midpoint. (Forward spacing 1 for 2 for *Radio Station* will bring you to the midpoint of that head.)

b Backspace (1 for 2) for the longest item beneath the head.

c Set tab stop for column where backspacing ends.

5 For centering purposes, consider the column head as part of the column. Notice, below, what intervals are separated by 5 spaces.

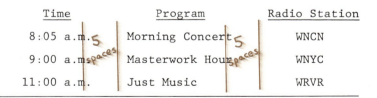

Time	Program	Radio Station
8:05 a.m.	Morning Concert	WNCN
9:00 a.m.	Masterwork Hour	WNYC
11:00 a.m.	Just Music	WRVR

Center the above table horizontally, as follows:

a Set LM by backspacing (1 for 2) from center for longest items: *11:00 a.m.* + *Morning Concert* + *Radio Station* + 10 intercolumn spaces (2 × 5).

b Space forward (1 for 1) through *11:00 a.m.* + 5 spaces and set tab stop. Space (1 for 1) through *Morning Concert* + 5 spaces and type and underscore *Radio Station*.

c Return to LM (on same line) and follow ¶3 above to center

and type *Time*. Then tabulate to column 2 and center and type its heading by the same process.

d Move to the R of *Radio Station* and follow ¶4 above to locate and set tab stop for column 3.

e Set for DS and type the rows of the table. Remember to align digits in column 1; i.e., space forward once before typing *8:05 a.m.* (and *9:00 a.m.*).

LESSON 32 Table Placement

INSTRUCTIONS Follow the procedures of Lessons 32C and 33C (pp. 47–48).

1 2 cols. (BC–10):   Benjamin Marshall   Attorney-at-Law

2 3 cols. (BC–6):   Saturday   Arts and Crafts   Mrs. Kellerman

3 4 cols. (BC–5):   Massachusetts   Capital City   Population   (Sq. Miles)

4 5 cols. (BC–5):   Class   Speed   Errors   Time   Grade

5 3 cols. (BC–6):   Clerical   Stenographers   Typists

6 4 cols. (BC–4):   Letters   Tables   Manuscripts   Business Forms

7 2 cols. (BC–12):   S. S. Leonardo Da Vinci   September 15

8 3 cols. (BC–5):   John C. Dutton & Co.   Boston, Mass.   Insurance brokers

9 4 cols. (BC–6):   Patio table   Regular Price   Sales Price   Discount

LESSON 42 Personal Notes   Alternate between blocked ¶s/open punctuation and indented ¶s/mixed punctuation.

1 Dear Mrs. Abrams, What a lovely weekend—thank you! It was good of you to invite Peggy's friends to your beach house. We all had a great time and we're grateful to you. Sincerely,

2 Dear Leonard, My cousin, Jan Sims, will be visiting me next weekend. Could you come to dinner on Saturday, April 23, at 8 p.m.? I know Jan will enjoy meeting you. Love,

3 Dear Aunt Mary, You should hear the compliments I've been getting on the sweater you knitted for me for my birthday! It fits perfectly. Thank you very much. Love,

4 Dear Jan and Bob and Sally and Matt, Needless to say, it's no fun being in the hospital, but your visit and your beautiful flowers have cheered me up a lot. (¶) Thank you very much for both. Love,

5 Dear Sally, I was so sorry to hear of your uncle's death. What a sad loss for you and your family. Please extend my deepest sympathy to your mother and father and Terry. Love,

6 Dear Martha, Greg told me you have been accepted by the state university law school—congratulations! I knew you could do it, and I know you will make a terrific lawyer. Love,

7 Dear Jimmy, My little brother isn't so little anymore! I wish I could be with you on your tenth birthday, but I have so much schoolwork to do that I can't break away. When I get home next month, I promise we'll have our own celebration. (¶) Happy birthday! Love,

35A KEYBOARD PRACTICE Type lines 3–4, p. 116.

35B TABLES WITH COLUMN HEADS Save time in table typing: When you first reach the horizontal point at which the longest item in a column is to begin, type it if it is the column head. If, instead, it is an item below the head, set a tab stop for it.

TASK 1 Center, horizontally only, the table of 34C; transpose (reverse the order of) columns 2 and 3; use BC–8.

TASK 2 Center, horizontally only, the table at the right; BC–10.

Class	Present	Absent
Typewriting	28	3
Shorthand	24	1

35C OUTLINE PROCEDURES

1 A topical outline displays the main topics and subtopics of a longer presentation in a manner that reveals the structure or organization of the material.

2 Though all six of the levels shown at the right are rarely needed, two additional levels (1 and a) may be shown by underscoring. Set a tab stop at each new level when you first reach it.

3 At the right, 1 space follows the period after each identifying letter or number, but 2 spaces may also be used. Omit period after close parenthesis.

4 Usually SS successive 1-line items at the same level. DS between one level and another, especially in a short outline.

5 Block runover lines, as in (a), or indent them 2–3 spaces.

6 Do not use a period after the topics unless they are in sentence form.

```
    I. Typewriters

        A. Sales

            1. Standard machines

                a. Electrics

                    (1) To schools

                        (a) High schools
                            in the East
```

TASK 1 Set LM 20 spaces left of center and tab stops as needed. Center heading on line 10 and TS after it. Use MR key and backspace once to type Roman II. (Roman I is capital letter I.) SS between 1-line items at the same level; as marked below, DS between one level and another. Space once, not twice, after the period following each identifying number or letter. Leave paper in machine when you finish. Can you finish in 5–6 minutes?

```
                THE STUDY OF FILING
TS_____

DS_____  I. Introduction
              A. Purpose of filing
DS_____     B. History of filing
DS_____  II. Filing equipment
DS_____     A. Types of files
DS_____        1. Flat and vertical files
DS_____            a. Flat files
                        (1) Spindle
                        (2) Shannon
                        (3) Box
DS_____              (4) Loose-sheet drawer
DS_____           b. Vertical files
DS_____              (1) Cabinets
                            (a) Vertical units
```

TASK 2 Continue typing on the same sheet the following handwritten section of the Task 1 outline. Can you complete it in 4–5 minutes?

```
                (b) Horizontal units
                (c) Solid cabinets
            (2) Drawer sizes
        2. Visible files
        3. Transfer files
    B. Contents of the filing cabinets
        1. Guides
            a. materials
            b. Tab cuts and sizes
            c. Divisions
        2. Folders
            a. Purposes
                (1) Individual
                (2) Miscellaneous
```

1 [From] Michael Plymouth, 156 Clairmont Ave., Utica, NY 13509
[To] Dr. Seymour Saltzman, 731 Albany Place, Utica, NY 13508
Dear Dr. Saltzman: Please note that I have moved *from* 1849 Elm Street *to* 156 Clairmont Avenue. My new telephone number is 756-1004. Very truly yours, Michael Plymouth

2 [From] Metcalfe Glass Co., 1992 LaSalle Road, Flint, MI 48508
[To] Collins Housewares, 1712 Malvern Drive, Flint, MI 48511
Gentlemen: The glassware you inquired about will be ready for shipment on Tuesday, May 14, and should reach you the next day. Yours very truly, Shipping Dept.

3 [From] Richardson Cleaners, Inc., 888 Dekker Street, Austin, TX 78707
[To] Mrs. Craig Nadel, 2577 Brookside Street, Austin, TX 78709
Dear Mrs. Nadel: Your rugs will be delivered to your home on Thursday morning, August 27. If you expect to be away, please arrange for someone to accept delivery at your home. Yours very truly, Manager

4 [From] Ronald A. Sisk, 28 Hardy Street, Joplin, MO 64801
[To] Mrs. Lester Snyder, 1217 Melville Avenue, Joplin, MO 64801
Dear Mrs. Snyder: Your electric clock has been repaired. You may pick it up any day (except Sunday) between 9 a.m. and 5 p.m. Yours very truly, Ronald A. Sisk

5 [From] Roberta Donahue, 679 Mountain View Rd., St. Paul, MN 55115
[To] Mrs. Sally Gledhill, 74 Hamilton Boulevard, St. Paul, MN 55115
Dear Mrs. Gledhill: The Executive Board will meet on Sunday, July 11, at 3 p.m. (¶) Please bring your records and be prepared to read the minutes of the previous meeting. Sincerely yours, Roberta Donahue

6 [From] John S. Robertson, 259 Jefferson Avenue, Cleveland, OH 44117
[To] Ms. Denise Montag, 549 Beechwood Street, Cleveland, OH 44112
Dear Ms. Montag: Please note that the time of the next meeting of the Citizenship Club has been changed to 8 p.m. The date and place remain the same. Yours sincerely, John S. Robertson

7 [From] Service Department, St. James Auto Sales, 1197 Polk Avenue, Akron, OH 44305
[To] Mr. J. A. Wendling, 1409 Tanglewood Street, Akron, OH 44306
Dear Sir: Now that you have driven your new car for about six months, we suggest that you bring it in for a checkup. We are open weekdays from 9 a.m. until 5 p.m. and on Saturdays until noon. Very truly yours, Service Department

8 [From] Lori Keenan, 1775 Plantation Avenue, Santa Clara, CA 95060
[To] Ress & Company, 1521 Bay Street, San Francisco, CA 94102
Gentlemen: Would you please send me a copy of your Annual Report. I am not a shareholder, but I should like to use your report as material for my term paper in an Economics course. Thank you. Sincerely yours, Lori Keenan

36A STROKE REFINEMENT   Type lines 1–3, p. 121.

36B COMPARISON PRACTICE   DS, SM–1″. 3′ or 4′ timing. If you begin the copy a second time, compute speed from CW column.

Do **not** enter "Comparison Practice" scores on your TR. Instead, compare your performance on these paragraphs of below-average difficulty with your most recent TR scores and also with your best speed at paced and at progressive practice. Notice that different practice emphases, materials, and timing lengths lead to different scores.

	GWPM	
3′	4′	CW
3	2	10
7	5	21
10	8	31
14	10	41
17	13	51
20	15	61
21	16	64
25	19	74
28	21	84
31	24	94
35	26	105
38	29	114

The station-to-station rate applies when you are willing to speak with anyone who answers at the called telephone. Do not ask the telephone operator for a specific person, department, or extension phone.

The person-to-person rate applies when you wish to talk only with some one person, department, or extension phone.

A conference call permits you to talk with a number of people in different places at the same time.

Most calls can be made collect if the person you call agrees to pay the charge. But be sure to tell the operator when you wish to place such a call.

```
3′  +0  |        +1      |      +2      |      +3      | +4
4′  +0      |       +1          |       +2      |   +3
```

36C MANUSCRIPT IN OUTLINE FORM

A formal outline (like the one of Lesson 35C) is not a very frequent activity. But quite a bit of typing (e.g., a table of contents or instructions 1–5 of 34C) is done in outline form, including some manuscripts or reports that contain step-by-step instructions or details.

Using WL–60 and DS between items, retype the ¶s of 36B in outline form. Type the outline heading, LONG DISTANCE CALLS, on line 21. Number these ¶ headings in turn as 1, 2, 3, 4: Station-to-station calls, Person-to-person calls, Conference calls, Collect calls. Leave 1 space after the period following the number. Type each ¶ at level **a** under its numbered heading, like this: Time—nearest ¼′

```
1. Station-to-station calls
   a. The station-to-station rate applies when you are will-
      ing to speak . . . .
```

36D BACKSPACING FOR TABLE LEFT MARGIN   Use the items of SP–32, p. 111.
or
TIMED PRACTICE   As many Paced or Progressive or Progressive NS timings as time permits. PF

NOTE. To aid you at the start, a diagonal is used to show the end of each line in the first 12 addresses. Do not type the diagonal. Starting with No. 13, diagonals are not shown, and you should omit the commas that separate the address lines.

1 Miss Lydia T. Sobel / 308 Ingraham Street / Tulsa, OK 74115

2 Dr. Louis F. Swarthmore / 709 West Tenth Street / Duluth, MN 55809

3 The Tudor Appliance Co. / 719 Canal Street / New York, NY 10014

4 Ms. Roberta Willis / 254 Central Avenue / San Diego, CA 92116

5 Dr. Don L. Kane / Empire Furniture Co. / 52 Kings Street / Omaha, NB 68118

6 Ingersoll Metal Corp. / 57 Murray Avenue / Dale, IN 47523

7 Mr. Fred Kent, President / Modern Gas Ranges, Inc. / 301 Court Street / Dallas, TX 75212

8 Mr. David B. Carroll / c/o Mr. John Bates / 1305 Queen Building / 191 Oak Street / Yonkers, NY 10708

9 Mr. Paul Anderson / Purchasing Department / Lord & Gale, Inc. / 67 Farley Street / Providence, RI 02908

10 Mr. Everett P. Wunderlich / Manager, Repair Service / Judson Auto Sales / 15 Dale Avenue / Akron, OH 44305

11 Mr. James Mill, Manager / Investment Services / First National Bank / 1108 Raynor Street / Grand Rapids, MI 49522

12 Mrs. Ellen Traynor / Riverside Arms, Apt. 32C / 3406 Front Street / Boston, MA 02109

13 Mr. Roger T. Quarles, Chairman of the Board, Parson Brokerage Company, 193 Exchange Place, Shreveport, LA 71106

14 The Weyman Fuel & Coal Co., 1601 Pontiac Building, 465 Mitchell Avenue, Portland, OR 97227

15 Mr. Henry L. Carstairs, President and General Manager, The American Air Conditioning Co., 149 Jackson Avenue, Niles, KS 67471

16 Mr. Lawrence F. Kane, Treasurer, Wilkins, Bell & Denton, 400 Lyman Street, Boston, MA 02115

17 Messrs. Robert and Allan Davidson, 603 Barnes Avenue, Clinton, IA 52732

18 Ms. Barbara Lester, Littleton Furs, Inc., 721 McKibbin Street, Scranton, PA 18543

19 Prof. Kenneth Morgan, Head, Political Science Department, Draper College, Milwaukee, WI 53202

20 Mr. Seymour T. Harrington, Building Materials Division, Apex Contracting Company, 830 Garfield Street, Bergen, NJ 07311

37A LETTER SEQUENCES   Type the sequences for **a** and **b**, p. 118.

37B ROUGH DRAFTS AND PROOFREADERS' MARKS

1 Copy that shows corrections to be made is called rough draft. Much work comes to the typist in that form.

2 Always read a rough draft before typing it—to insure that all corrections are understood.

3 Correction symbols (called proofreaders' marks) are inserted in the copy. When there is no room to enter the corrections within the copy, they are shown in the margins and are accompanied by symbols, as illustrated below.

4 Simple corrections are often marked by crossing out, circles, arrows, and in other obvious ways—without using formal symbols (as in the last illustration below).

Symbol and Meaning	Edited	Retyped
⌒ Close up	to ad vertise it	to advertise it
ℓ or ℨ Delete (omit, remove)	We now thiink	We think
∼ Transpose	tr We never can aks	We can never ask
/ Small letter (lower case)	l.c. our Spring sales	our spring sales
∧ (Caret) insert*	∨ ∧ Its very, very hot. today	It's very, very hot today.
# Space	to the OR to the	to the
◯ Spell out	sp Ship ④ gals.	Ship four gallons.
] Move to the right	We wish to call your attention	We wish to call your attention
[Move to the left	[to the matter.	to the matter.
≡ Capitalize (upper case)	u.c. on march 2	on March 2
¶ Paragraph	¶ We think he won the prize. third	We think he won the third prize.
stet Let it stand; do not delete. [Note stet in margin and dots under the deletion.]	stet a full carriage throw	a full carriage throw
◯ Change punctuation to period.	Try it, you'll like it.	Try it. You'll like it.
*Punctuation goes inside a (marginal) caret. Invert that caret (like this: ∨) for marks that go above the line (apostrophe, quote).	¶ We believe he will come now in February to visit us. ∨ Well go skating. ice	We now believe he will visit us in February. We'll go ice skating.

TASK 1 Read the sentences below in preparation for a timing (nearest ¼′); LM: pica ½″, elite 1″. When corrected, each sentence, including its number, contains 15 five-stroke words; for wpm for each completion time, see the scoring table at left below.

TASK 1

Min.	wpm	Min.	wpm
¾	80	3	20
1	60	3¼	18
1¼	48	3½	17
1½	40	3¾	16
1¾	34	4	15
2	30	4¼	14
2¼	27	4½	13
2½	24	4¾	13
2¾	22	5	12
60 words			

1. Have you just decided to advertise our sale for Spring of dresses in the Tribune?

2. Under seperate cover, a supply of our report forms has been sent to him. new out

3. "Its a pity," she said, "to dissapoint the little boy on his birthday".

4. The wisest thing to do, provided you agree, is to arrange now for payment. best

10   TV Model 108 sells for $129; Model 209 (color) is priced at $492.
11   My 4* items (Special Sale) were listed between $20.80 and $92.50.
12   Don't "Wintering" and "Spring" appear in his book (1952 edition)?

....1....2....3....4....5....6....7....8....9....10....11....12....13

LESSON 21 7 & ½ ¼

1   Either ¼ or 1/4 is typed to represent the fraction one-quarter.
2   The fraction one-half is written on the typewriter as ½ or 1/2.
3   M & B recommend a 1½-ton air conditioner in a 27¼-inch cabinet.

4   Joe ran a mile in 4½ minutes last year; now he takes 4¼ minutes.
5   Our firm name is Hale & Russell, but we're usually called H & R.
6   Dorothy sent Mrs. Walker a pair of size 7½ gloves instead of 7¼.

7   There's a sale of half-size dresses (12½-16½) at Jaffe & Rand's.
8   Donald's hat size is 7¼, not 7½. Do Kay & Marx carry all sizes?
9   My stock in Orr & Fox showed a "high" of 79½ and a "low" of 77¼.

10   Harvey & Lowe offer 3½-room apartments at $175; 4½ rooms at $220.
11   Simon & Wald are featuring their $10 hats at $7.75 on October 17.
12   We bought 7 more prints at Manson & Clay's--we now have about 70.

....1....2....3....4....5....6....7....8....9....10....11....12....13

LESSON 22 6 _ :

1   The 1960 census showed <u>Illinois</u> with a population of 10,081,158.
2   I missed the <u>early</u> train. The next one doesn't leave till 6:15.
3   Our hospital plan covers you <u>for a lifetime</u>--not just to age 65.

4   Unless they can make delivery <u>at once</u>, cancel our order of 6/26.
5   The banker's property was sold to <u>Kenney & Brothers</u> for $65,690.
6   Dave's coal bin at 164 East 61 Street has a capacity of 6½ tons.

7   Use the slant in fractions; for example: 5/6, 6/7, 6-4/7, 6-8/9.
8   Men, women and children were in a ratio of 10:7:6 (10 to 7 to 6).
9   America's <u>Declaration of Independence</u> was signed on July 4, 1776.

10   Joel, who is only 9, won the contest by catching a 6½-pound fish.
11   Mark, the runner-up, caught a 6¼-pound fish. He is 16 years old.
12   SPECIAL SALE NOTICE: Discounts of 6% to all who buy before 6/16!

....1....2....3....4....5....6....7....8....9....10....11....12....13

LESSON 23 3 # ¢ @

1   Some strokes (for instance: <u>q</u>, <u>z</u>, @, ") use the weaker fingers.
2   A typing speed of <u>30 wpm</u> (i.e., 30 words per minute) is passing.
3   Enclosed are deposit books for accounts #3063, #3739, and #5323.

4   Which is best: "It is 3 am," "It is 3 a.m.," or "It is 3 a. m."?
5   The following check is lost: #638, <u>payee</u> Rowe & Co., amount $93.
6   Joe's grocery store sells #2 cans of soup @ 30¢, @ 39¢, or @ 45¢.

7   Our #73 ringbinder comes in smooth cowhide in several colors
8   (charcoal, ginger, and red). It has 1½-inch rings in either 2 or
9   3 removable-ring style. It sells @ $4.96; 90-sheet fillers, 38¢.

10   Our 17-jewel Gothamite watch (Model #3) is <u>guaranteed</u> water-
11   proof--that is, so long as the crystal is not broken and the case
12   was not opened. You can have one for only $139.50, plus 10% tax.

....1....2....3....4....5....6....7....8....9....10....11....12....13

Min.	wpm	Min.	wpm
1¼	66	3¾	22
1½	55	4	21
1¾	47	4¼	20
2	42	4½	18
2¼	37	4¾	17
2½	33	5	17
2¾	30	5¼	16
3	28	5½	15
3¼	26	5¾	14
3½	24	6	14

TASK 2

83 words

Some people prefer elite type; others prefer pica type. Elite type is more widely used for the very good reason that it saves space. Every 12 pages in pica would take 10 pages in elite type. In 28 double-spaced lines on a manuscript page, using 1-inch side margins, elite type provides about 60-70 more words on the page; a 400-word business letter fits on 1 page in elite, but takes 2 pages in pica.

37C PACED or PROGRESSIVE PRACTICE

As many paced timings of about 5 minutes or progressive practice timings of 1 minute as time permits. PF

38 Rough draft table (unequal intercolumns) □ Typing numbers in columns

38A CAPITALIZATION PRACTICE

Type lines 1–3, p. 120.

38B TABLE

Not all tables require equal spacing between columns. When some columns are more closely related than others, the spacing between columns varies. In the table below, the first three columns are more closely related to each other than they are to the last two columns.

The circled numbers show the spacing to be used between columns. When you finish backspacing for the sum of the longest items in each column, continue to backspace—or subtract from the stopping point for the typed matter—for half the total of intercolumn space (half of 4 + 4 + 8 + 4).

Center vertically and horizontally on a full sheet (66 lines). Use proper spacing after the heading and between rows.

```
Postal Abbreviations and zip Codes in Capital Cities

Alabama     (4)  Ala.  (4)  AL  (8)  Montgomery  (4)  36104
Alaska           Alas.      AK         Juneau           99801
Arizona          Ariz.      AZ         Phenix           85026
Arkansas         Ark.       AR         Little Rock      72210
California        Calif.    CA         Sacramento       95801
Colorado         Col.       CO         Hartford         06101
Connecticut      Conn.      CT         Denver           80202
Delaware         Del.       DE         Dover            19901
```

Continue on a practice sheet with 38C until the class is ready for a timing on it.

LESSON 18 Horizontal and Vertical Centering

1 Martin Company
Lansing Boulevard
Columbus, Ohio

2 General Appliance Service, Inc.
REPAIRS
On All Makes of Vacuum Cleaners
and Home Appliances

3 ARTISTIC DRAPERY SERVICE
Custom-Made Draperies
Drapery Rods Installed
Drapes Hung
Curtains and Drapes Cleaned

4 Acme Auto Sales and Service
SALES—SERVICE—PARTS
Used Cars Bought and Sold
Expert Service Guaranteed

5 Regal Car Company
PRIVATE LIMOUSINE SERVICE
Trips to Mountains—Door to Door
Prompt, Courteous Service
Low Rates

6 CLEARVIEW WINDOW CLEANERS
Professional Work Guaranteed
No less than six windows cleaned
Top and bottom, inside and out
Special Rates for Long-Term Contracts

7 Dr. Harold Snyder
Dr. Carl J. Hurlander
Dr. William Gallagher
Announce their association
For the practice of medicine
at
The Templeton Medical Center

LESSON 19 9 0 ( )

1   A round trip ticket from 49th Street to the terminal costs $4.90.
2   Thursday's forecast (for Friday) was of temperatures of 80 to 90.
3   Franz's policy ($5 a week) covers hospital and/or doctor's bills.

4   Mr. Rice owes us $209. He will pay $100 today ($109 next month).
5   Someone (I've forgotten who) gave us permission to use Room 1095.
6   We can't pay you $450 by 10/8. Will you accept this 90-day note?

7   We'll accept a 90-day note with 5% interest. That is reasonable.
8   Dr. Clark's fee for an office visit is $9 ($15 for a house call).
9   During this period (4/1-4/10), the investment yielded 15% profit.

10   A check for $19.50 (enclosed) is in payment of invoice dated 8/9.
11   Call Al's Fix-it Shop daily (except Sunday) between 9 and 10 a.m.
12   Mr. David Danzig built a $49,500 home on the lot (90 x 100 feet).

```
. . . . 1 . . . . 2 . . . . 3 . . . . 4 . . . . 5 . . . . 6 . . . . 7 . . . . 8 . . . . 9 . . . .10. . . .11. . . .12. . . .13
```

LESSON 20 2 " *

1   The asterisk (*) is often used to bring attention to a footnote.
2   "Elementary!" said the detective. "It's as simple as 2 plus 2."
3   "Go back at once!" he cried. "There's no danger--if you hurry."

4   "Send copies marked 'Personal' to our 12 officers," said Richard.
4   The 12 figures marked * in the manager's report represent losses.
6   "Oh, of course!" said Viola's mother. "How could I ever forget?"

7   Four 20" (20-second) tests were followed by a 1' (1-minute) rest.
8   Roberta is 5'2" (5 feet 2 inches) tall--2" taller than Elizabeth.
9   There's a discount of 20% on 200 copies (or more) of "Starlight."

```
. . . . 1 . . . . 2 . . . . 3 . . . . 4 . . . . 5 . . . . 6 . . . . 7 . . . . 8 . . . . 9 . . . .10. . . .11. . . .12. . . .13
```

Continued on the next page

38C COMPARISON PRACTICE 3' or 4' timing, DS, SM–1". Read before you type.

Few people can compose or prepare a finished piece of writing in one trial. Therefore, much office work is first typed from rough materials in draft form, corrected in longhand, and then retyped.

In a study of the sources of the copy used by clerical typists, it was found that about half was in longhand or in mixed type and longhand. Another investigation showed that many of the most common personal typing tasks also involve draft work. In a survey covering all office employees in the State of Washington, rough draft work was tied for fourth place for frequency among all office workers who use a typewriter; and it was tied for first place among stenographers and secretaries.

	3'	4'	CW
	4	3	13
	9	7	27
	13	10	39
	17	13	52
	22	17	67
	27	20	80
	31	24	94
	36	27	109
	41	31	123
	45	34	137
	46	35	138

```
3'  +0        +1          +2          +3          +4      +5
4'    +0          +1            +2              +3
```

38D TYPING NUMBERS IN COLUMNS

Line up digits as if they were a column of figures to be added. After tabulating to starting point for longest item in column, space forward for shorter items.

Type the columns at the right. (LM 15 spaces left of center, tab stops 4 left and 5 right of center.) Note the abbreviations for *noon* and *midnight*.

825	2	1:00 p.m.
4,206	10	10:30 a.m.
739	$1\frac{1}{2}$	4:15 p.m.
96	$3\frac{1}{4}$	12:00 n.
3,657	14	6:45 p.m.
2	$\frac{1}{2}$	12:00 m.

39 Rough draft table

39A KEYBOARD PRACTICE Type lines 5–6, p. 116.

39B STRAIGHT COPY TIMING 5', DS, SM–1". TR

What would life be like with no electric power? It is not necessary to leave that question to the imagination. In much of the Northeast, late in the afternoon of November 9, 1965, transportation by subway, radio and TV, and industries run by electricity all stopped. The greatest power failure in history had taken place.

A group of highly skilled technical experts searched for days before finding the source of the failure that left most of the Northeast and parts of Canada in the dark. One out of every four persons in this country was affected. The area hardest hit was metropolitan New York. More than half a million people were trapped in subways and elevators. Traffic, left without its controlling stoplights, crawled out of the city. Luckily, the moon was full; the sky was clear; and the New Jersey cities across the Hudson River still had their electrical power.

GWPM		
a	b	CW
3	38	13
5	41	27
8	44	41
11	46	55
13	48	65
16	51	78
18	54	92
21	57	107
24	60	121
27	62	135
30	65	149
33	68	163
35	71	177
Sy 1.54		
St 5.8		

```
+0          +1              +2          +3
```

LESSON 16 1 8 ' !

1   We need you--you need us! Let's cooperate and help one another!
2   Don't pay 18 cents each for those pencils--they're not worth it!
3   We ordered 18 quilts. We received only 11. What's the trouble?

4   I'm afraid Jim's a ne'er-do-well; he's already given up 18 jobs.
5   He's my half brother--he's my father's son, but not my mother's.
6   Tom's letter was dated May 8, but it wasn't mailed until May 18.

7   What a day November 18 was! It rained--it poured--and it poured!
8   The accident occurred on June 1. I didn't return until August 8.
9   Les's new house has 18 rooms. It's as big as a palace, isn't it?

10   Isn't he ready? It's time to leave--it's long past five o'clock!
11   We have boys' clothing; but we won't have men's wear until May 8.
12   It's impossible! You're mistaken! We checked twice--exactly 88!

    ....1....2....3....4....5....6....7....8....9....10....11....12....13

LESSON 17 4 $

1   This picture has a 4-inch frame. Framed, it costs just $18.48.
2   Dr. O'Shea moved from 414 Sixth Avenue to 184 East 48th Street.
3   Orchestra tickets, with tax, are $8.41--$4 more than I brought!

4   Quentin asked $48. My maximum offer is $44. What's a mere $4?
5   Mary will be 14 on June 8. Mary's brother is only 4, isn't he?
6   The boy's jackets were reduced from $18 to $14--a $4 reduction.

7   Isn't Mr. Kramer's rent very high--$184 a month? I pay $48 less.
8   The men's pay was raised from $4.18 to $4.84 an hour as of May 1.
9   Let's see--at $1.48 each, what will 148 bags cost? That's a lot!

10   The boys in Mr. O'Neil's class first marched by 4's, then by 8's.
11   The girls' hats varied in price from $4 to $18. Ann's costs $14.
12   Mrs. O'Hara's gas bill is $4.41. Mine is more than $8.40--a lot!

    ....1....2....3....4....5....6....7....8....9....10....11....12....13

LESSON 18 5 % /

1   It's now 5 p.m.--time for her medicine! Jo's finished 4/5 of it.
2   I pay Fred 5% interest--that's a fair rate. I'll send $8 on 5/1.
3   John Fell's profit is $845. That's 4/5 or 80% of his investment!

4   Dick's sales declined about 15% during the quarter beginning 4/1.
5   My test mark was 85%; that's very good--isn't it? Tom's was 54%.
6   Mr. Rusk's discount is 5%--I can get 15%! That's 15 cents on $1.

7   Our Paris models--now selling from $85 to $185--were reduced 15%.
8   What's 15% of $5? What's 5%? What's 1/5 of $8? Answer quickly!
9   The note was sent to Mr. J. Gay, c/o Quentin's Warehouse, Room 5.

10   The rent's $154--that's exactly 45% of my salary. It's too much!
11   Max's salary is $145. He spends 85% and saves 15%. That's wise!
12   Discounts of 15% and 5% were taken on the rugs listed at $185.45.

    ....1....2....3....4....5....6....7....8....9....10....11....12....13

Continued on the next page.

39C TABLE   In a money column, the $ sign appears only alongside the first item and the total at the bottom (if any)—not with amounts in between. To save typing time, type the $ sign in the right space according to your table plan, but set the tab stop one space to the right of the sign.

TASK 1 Set LM 13 spaces left of center; BC–10. Copy the columns at right, as follows: space through (without typing) *Regency sofa,* space 10 more times, type $, set tab stop. Return to LM and type all rows.

Lamp	$ 46
Easy chair	129
Regency sofa	350
	$525

blank line here ←

TASK 2 Center the table vertically and horizontally on a ½-sheet. Note the instructions for vertical spacing, as well as the circled numbers showing intercolumn spacing. "Sp" in the margin alongside a circled abbreviation means that it is to be spelled in full. Note also that the $ sign is 1 space to the left of the **longest** money entry.

Quarterly 2↓ PENSIONS PAID TO RETIRED EMPLOYEES   (SP)
— DS —

— TS —   Ludlow Chemical (Corp.)

#___	*Name*	*Amount*		*Name*	*Amount*
	Edith T. Burnham	③ $1,100	⑥	Philip Lustig	③ $ 825
DS	Joseph R. Clarke	800		Alice T. Manning	900
the rows	Albert A. Edington	1,000		John Miracolo	700
	Dora Farrell	7̶6̶0̶		Otto R. Peterson	1,000
	Milton C. Garner	800		Henry P. Stillwell	900

39D PROGRESSIVE NS PRACTICE   As many 1′ timings as time permits (pp. 135–137). PF

40 Rough draft corrections

40A STROKE REFINEMENT   Type lines 4–6, p. 121.

40B NS TIMING   5′, DS, SM–1″. TR–NS

	GWPM		
	a	b	CW
Join your friends at BARDO'S RESTAURANT, 2648 Broadway (telephone	3	16	13
436-5970). Our motto is: "Food at Its *Best.*" Meals are served daily	6	19	29
from 7 a.m. to 10:30 p.m. Breakfasts are priced from 85¢ to $2; table	9	22	43
d'hote luncheons, from $1.95 to $4.25; dinners, from $3.75 to $10.50.	11	25	57
Try our #3 breakfast tomorrow—just 95¢!	13	26	65

5′

+0	+1	+2	+3

13 Just relax. I shall inquire about the experiment.
14 Mr. Waxman was well equipped for the job, Barbara.
15 Answer the question. Explain the basis of habits.

16 Just quietly do your best. Stop offering excuses.
17 I doubt whether we can exchange the damaged quilt.
18 Albert expects to be too busy to answer questions.

19 I am quite sure the boys took an express to Luxor.
20 I cannot acquire luxuries. Taxes are responsible.
21 Bobby is quite exhausted by this experience, Jack.

22 You frequently express doubts about my experience.
23 The Drixman building is about a quarter mile away.
24 The box was not quite beyond repair. He fixed it.

25 I can supply the extra quantity that Bob requests.
26 Stop by the exquisite exhibit of quaint porcelain.
27 His requirements extend beyond our ability to pay.

. . . . 1 . . . . 2 . . . . 3 . . . . 4 . . . . 5 . . . . 6 . . . . 7 . . . . 8 . . . . 9 10

LESSON 9   V   Z   ?

1 Do you realize the value of his advice? I wonder.
2 I recognize your improvement. Do I criticize you?
3 Will Hazel and Evan leave for the Canal Zone soon?

4 Why did you authorize delivery? That puzzles him.
5 Above all, must we recognize the value of honesty?
6 Have you included zip code numbers? I believe so.

7 Do all good citizens believe in and love our land?
8 Will Evans give me a dozen boxes in various sizes?
9 Is it below zero? I am very cold. I feel frozen.

10 How do you like my magazine? I have it delivered.
11 Who has authorized delivery of the bronze fixture?
12 Is this outlet provided for using electric razors?

13 I have emphasized the hazard involved, have I not?
14 When did Mr. Lopez move from Venezuela to Arizona?
15 David lives in Beverly Hills. Did Liza visit him?

16 Do you realize how much work I have every day, Vy?
17 Was that Evelyn? I believe Dexter recognized her.
18 Did Queen Elizabeth or Queen Victoria live longer?

19 Dickens was called Boz. Have you read his novels?
20 Do several of you expect to travel to New Zealand?
21 This razor blade is very sharp. Have you used it?

22 Have you gone to the bazaar? Is it worth a visit?
23 Hazel has never requested a favor before, has she?
24 Have we analyzed the trouble? Do we recognize it?

25 Will Mrs. Rizzo visit Brazil on her next vacation?
26 What evidence did Elizabeth Vail seize in advance?
27 Does division by ten involve removing a zero, Vic?

. . . . 1 . . . . 2 . . . . 3 . . . . 4 . . . . 5 . . . . 6 . . . . 7 . . . . 8 . . . . 9 10

40C ROUGH DRAFT CORRECTIONS

TASK 1 Read before you type.

1 I have just sent you under separate cover, an additional supply of our revised report forms.

2 If ~~your supply is~~ these are not insufficient, let me know, please.

3 Fill one out for every call you make, and send it to the New York Office.

TASK 2 Read the ¶s below (50 words) in preparation for a timing (nearest ¼'). Use WL–60 (LM 30 spaces left of center). For wpm for each completion time, see table at the left below.

TASK 2			
Min.	wpm	Min.	wpm
¾	67	3	17
1	50	3¼	15
1¼	40	3½	14
1½	33	3¾	13
1¾	29	4	12
2	25	4¼	11
2¼	22	4½	11
2½	20	4¾	10
2¾	18	5	10

By special delivery mail, we have just sent you a supply of our new report forms.

No ¶ If your ~~supply is insufficient~~ need more, let me know, please be to you and additional copies will be sent. ¶ A form should be filled out for every call you make and sent ot the New York Office.

40D COMPARISON PRACTICE
Practice the copy in preparation for a 4' timing. Read before you type. DS, SM–1"

	GWPM	
	a	b	CW

The straight copy test timings you take from time to time are designed to measure your stroking skill under the artificial conditions of copying from perfect print, without correcting errors. Under such conditions, it is easy to fall into the trap of supposing that a typist merely copies what she or he sees. Nothing could be further from the truth. As the materials of 40C should make apparent, paying attention to corrections is what counts; the keystroking is mere mechanics.

GWPM values:
a	b	CW
3	27	13
7	31	27
10	34	40
14	38	54
17	41	68
21	45	82
24	48	96

4'

+0   +1   +2   +3

40E PACED or PROGRESSIVE PRACTICE
As many timings as time permits. PF

pp. 139–155 or 127–130

1. Yesterday the weather was as warm as a spring day.
2. If anything goes wrong, I know the fault was mine.
3. Twice a year Godfrey Waygo and his family go away.

4. We are fully aware of the many dangers facing you.
5. I suggest you go today. We will follow on Monday.
6. I must go downtown Wednesday morning. Come along.

7. Mary has enough money to pay what her mother owes.
8. If anything should go wrong, they would try again.
9. You thought that Gladys was ready to go Wednesday.

10. We are going to reply. We are not ready just yet.
11. My company supplies pure orange juice twice a day.
12. Mr. Gary has something to show you. Just ask him.

13. I know why the judge agreed. He knows I am right.
14. When Mr. Wray gets here tomorrow, show him a copy.
15. All the goods will go forward within a day or two.

16. We are always happy to make any necessary changes.
17. Perhaps we ought to know who manages your company.
18. Spring was mild last year, and the summer was hot.

19. As Mr. Gwynn suggested, we always use your system.
20. The weather was good. We went on a trip Thursday.
21. As Young suggests, the Wagly system might succeed.

22. On Sunday, Monday, and Tuesday, we shall go there.
23. Gwynn should make the journey without great delay.
24. Sy was careless; he crossed against the red light.

25. As you know, I am looking forward to your company.
26. Four green lights were swaying wildly in the wind.
27. William G. Yong was greeted with joy when he came.

. . . . 1 . . . . 2 . . . . 3 . . . . 4 . . . . 5 . . . . 6 . . . . 7 . . . . 8 . . . . 9 10

1. I find your inquiries are disturbing. Just relax.
2. The next time Alex requests help for a job, agree.
3. I explained why we quarreled. Bob will excuse me.

4. He expects to submit a request for a cut in taxes.
5. The bank examiners brought up some more questions.
6. We shall probably require a number of extra boxes.

7. The mixture can quickly be changed to liquid form.
8. Robert now requires complete quiet and relaxation.
9. These extra bottles can hold six quarts of liquid.

10. The opinion of the expert made acquittal possible.
11. Because of expert defense, the jury acquitted him.
12. My taxes may be quite high, but they must be paid.

. . . . 1 . . . . 2 . . . . 3 . . . . 4 . . . . 5 . . . . 6 . . . . 7 . . . . 8 . . . . 9 10

Continued on the next page

41A CENTERING WITHIN TABLE COLUMNS

Spacing methods are efficient for finding (a) the left margin of a table and (b) the starting point of the longest item in each column —whether it is the CH (column heading) or an item below the CH. But there is a much faster and safer method for (c) centering CHs in relation to their columns, illustrated here.

Spell *C-o-u-r-s-e* as you point with your pencil, in turn, to the *C-h-e-m-i-s* of *Chemistry 35*. Then count 1-2-3-4-5-6 as you point, in turn, to *t-r-y-space-3-5*. $6 \div 2 = 3$ (blank spaces on each side of *Course*). Start *Course* over the fourth letter, *m,* of *Chemistry 35*. That is, from the starting point of *Chemistry 35*,

space forward three times before typing *Course*. In the same manner, set a tab stop for *Becker* under the *s* of *Instructor*.

Course

Chemistry 35
English 18

```
Course123456
Chemistry 35
```

Instructor

Kane
Becker

```
Instructor
Becker1234
```

Center the table horizontally only; BC–6. **After** typing all CHs, set LM where the names of column 1 begin.

Instructor

Abrams
Baker
Connor

Course

History 106
Philosophy 212
English 307

Section

3
1
4

41B MANUSCRIPT IN OUTLINE FORM

Use top and side margins of 1 inch; SS within and DS between items. Set a tab stop for each level when you first reach it; space in twice to type I and once to type II. Align each section as shown: Do **not** bring lines after the first one in each item out to the left margin. Read before you type.

HORIZONTAL TABLE PLACEMENT BY SPACING AND COUNTING METHODS

I. Identifying the longest item in each column

   A. Be careful with longhand or printed matter. If there is any doubt, count letter by letter and space by space.

   B. The CH (column heading) is part of the column. If the CH is longer than any item below it, consider the CH as the longest item.

II. Finding the starting point for column 1

   A. Backspace from center (1 for 2) in two stages:

      1. First, for the longest item in each column, one after the other, exclusive of BC (between-column) space;

      2. Next, for half of all BC space—or subtract half of all BC space from the point at which the backspacing for the typed matter ends.

         a. If there is an odd letter left over after backspacing for the typed matter, add it to the total of BC space before carrying out Step IIA2.

   B. After completing all backspacing, if the CH is the longest item in column 1, type it. Otherwise, set the LM (left margin) and wait until later to type the CH.

III. Setting up later columns

   A. As you reach (by forward spacing 1 for 1) the beginning point of each additional column, type the CH if it is the longest item; otherwise, set a tab stop.

   B. When you have either typed the CH or set a tab stop for each additional column, go back and set missing tab stops or type missing CHs by the counting method described in 41A.

      1. For money columns, set the tab stop one space after the $ sign.

      2. Later, when you tabulate to these columns, backspace once before typing the $ sign.

13 If the offer is rejected, Elliot has another idea.
14 The first, second, and third seats are taken, Joe.
15 As Charles has noted, the conditions are too hard.

16 Knock at the door, as Dr. Otis closed it too soon.
17 As I indicated, neither Locke nor Connor can join.
18 Look at the clock, Jackson; see if it is too late.

19 Honor Dick, Cal, and Scott for their heroic deeds.
20 He told the children stories of fact, not fiction.
21 The totals differ. There is, Con feels, an error.

22 His store, said Eric, honors all her credit cards.
23 Joe Colston, his friend, said he can assist Scott.
24 Alice, Oscar, and Flo Corockson left for Colorado.

. . . . 1 . . . . 2 . . . . 3 . . . . 4 . . . . 5 . . . . 6 . . . . 7 . . . . 8 . . . . 9 10

LESSON 6   P   U   M

1 Mother and father sometimes drop in as a surprise.
2 In our opinion, it is much too soon to make plans.
3 At the moment, it is difficult to understand Paul.

4 Speak to Mr. Pace. He must use some other method.
5 Mr. Parkhurst spent the summer in Portland, Maine.
6 I complained. As a result, Tom reduced the price.

7 The shop should open soon, perhaps in ten minutes.
8 This project means success or failure to the firm.
9 Continue to send information. Much depends on it.

10 Al is in a position to help. Please count on him.
11 James Madison and James Monroe are famous men, Pa.
12 Mrs. Prout has left for the Appalachian Mountains.

13 Please read this note from Ed. Mr. Murat sent it.
14 Stu honors the name of President Thomas Jefferson.
15 Mrs. Plump has too little control of her children.

16 At a time like this, I must take complete control.
17 At present, this house is open to all our friends.
18 As Tom noticed, computers are used in this office.

19 Our decision came as a complete surprise to Maude.
20 The accident happened an hour or more after lunch.
21 Mr. Samuel hopes to run for some important office.

22 Our success appears to depend on Mr. Paul M. Muir.
23 Baume plans to spend March and April in Chihuahua.
24 After June, do not count on Paul. He cannot come.

25 Mack accepted the picture. I painted it in Spain.
26 Peter Palmer is out. He should return in an hour.
27 His sudden punishment seems uppermost in his mind.

. . . . 1 . . . . 2 . . . . 3 . . . . 4 . . . . 5 . . . . 6 . . . . 7 . . . . 8 . . . . 9 10

42 Personal notes

42A LETTER SEQUENCES   Type the sequences for **c** and **d**, p. 118.

42B PERSONAL NOTES

1 A personal note is an informal communication, such as a "Thank you" note, a social invitation, or a letter to a friend.

2 Stationery for personal notes is often printed with the name and address of the writer and comes in many sizes—often ½-sheet size. It is usually used with long edge vertical (5½" wide and 8½" long)—as illustrated in the model—but long edge horizontal is sometimes used.

3 A personal note includes: (1) date, (2) salutation (followed by a comma), (3) message or body, (4) complimentary closing ("close" or "closing" for short), and (5) longhand signature.

¶s may be indented 5 spaces (as in the model) or blocked at the LM (see the model in Lesson 43).

On a ½-sheet of paper with long edge vertical, date, closing, and typed signature (if any) start at round-number midpoint: pica 25, elite 30. With long edge horizontal, use exact center: pica 42, elite 51.

4 If not printed, the writer's address may be typed above the date (see next page), or it may be omitted if the writer's address is known by the addressee.

5 On a ½-sheet of paper with long edge vertical, use 1" side margins (pica 10–45, elite 12–54) and 1"–3" top and bottom margins, depending on length of message. Judge message length before typing to make distance from date (or address) to top of page approximately equal to distance from signature to bottom of page.

With long edge horizontal, use top and side margins of 1 inch.

Use the current date in all work.

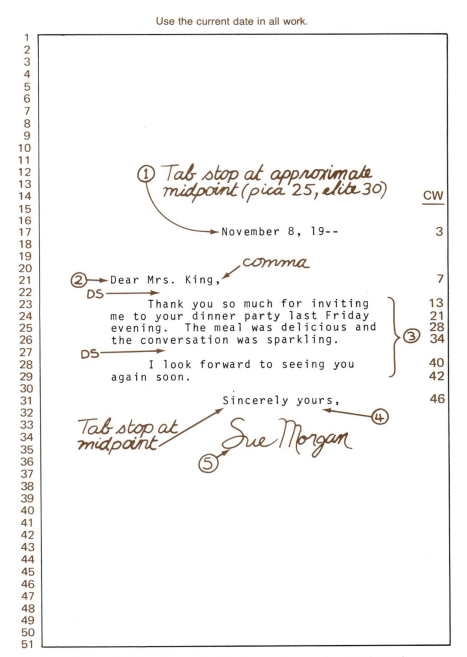

TASK 1 Copy the model letter (½-sheet, long edge vertical), but sign your own name. Can you finish in less than 5 minutes, starting with paper insertion?

TASK 2 Try again, this time with long edge horizontal.

19   she thanked their father; a little later than that
20   trained seals; this is a final trial; half as hard
21   the first and the third aisles; a different island

`....1....2....3....4....5....6....7....8....9....10`

LESSON 4   SHIFT KEY   PERIOD

1   Frank is in Iran. Katherine said Iran is in Asia.
2   I shall thank Edith. I find she is a real friend.
3   Take a letter. Address it to Dr. Kenneth Hearner.

4   I take a keen interest in Ted. He is in Arkansas.
5   St. Helena is an island. I shall sail here first.
6   Dr. Lane is in Atlanta. He has transferred there.

7   I asked Dr. Linn if Janet is ill. He said she is.
8   It is dark. He is afraid the Flint train is late.
9   Dr. Hess left late. He said he sent Fred instead.

10   Dr. Jaffe said that Seth is ill. He needs a rest.
11   Dr. Kane left. He thinks his illness is a trifle.
12   Edna Janke attended the tea. She had a red dress.

13   Dr. Harland likes Sardinia. He has settled there.
14   I like Kenneth Frankler. His ideas are different.
15   Here is the letter I started. Let Jeff finish it.

16   At first Jan fasted. Then she drank a little tea.
17   Frank left at three. Irene left a little earlier.
18   Stan Dane finds rest a treat. He is indeed tired.

19   I tried hard. I find he learned little after all.
20   Here is a list. I shall finish the details later.
21   The rain fell. It is rather dark here after nine.

22   All these skirts are finished. Start the dresses.
23   Lester J. Fieldson and Frieda Kreller are related.
24   Their train starts at East Sanders Street at nine.

`....1....2....3....4....5....6....7....8....9....10`

LESSON 5   O   C   COMMA

1   As it is not cold, Richard need not take his coat.
2   He calls the child either Elinor, Nell, or Nellie.
3   The front door is closed, and so is the side door.

4   The store had the coat in red, not in soft colors.
4   Neither Dick, Joan, nor Clare joined in the dance.
6   Clean the dishes, knife, and fork. Stand in line.

7   If he is free this afternoon, I can see John then.
8   Jackson is not far off. The station is near, too.
9   In the accident, the front cars ran off the track.

10   Therefore, local trains often ran on these tracks.
11   In fact, the corner store had no increase in rent.
12   The case is closed. Hereafter, Dan has no credit.

`....1....2....3....4....5....6....7....8....9....10`

Continued on the next page

TASK 3 [Long edge vertical] **Dear** [first name of a friend of yours at another college], This is one of the first letters I've ever typed. How's that for just two months in a typing class! I'll be able to type my term papers pretty soon. (¶) How are things at your school? Can we get together soon? Yours,

TASK 4 [Long edge vertical] **Dear** [your first name], I'm still pecking away with two fingers. Maybe I'd better take a typing course! (¶) I'm enjoying college a great deal. It certainly is different from high school. (¶) I'll write again soon when I have more time. You do the same. Yours,

If time permits, continue with SP–42, p. 111.

43 Personal-business letters □ Folding for envelope insertion

43A CAPITALIZATION PRACTICE   Type lines 4–6, p. 120.

43B PERSONAL-BUSINESS LETTERS

1 A personal-business letter is one from an individual to a business or other organization —on a business, rather than a personal, matter.

2 In contrast to the personal note (Lesson 42), the model at the right shows: (1) return address of sender just above the date, (2) inside address corresponding to envelope address, (3) colon after salutation, and (4) typed signature below longhand signature. Comma after the closing may be omitted, but only if the colon following the salutation is omitted as well.

3 ¶s may either be blocked (as in the model) or indented (see the model in Lesson 42).

4 Selection of top and bottom margins depends on length of message.

TASK 1 Copy the model letter on a ½-sheet, long edge vertical. Use SM–1″. Can you finish in less than 5 minutes, starting with paper insertion?

TASK 2 Try again, this time with long edge horizontal (top and side margins of 1″).

Question. Can you see why ½-sheets are best used with long edge vertical? With long edge horizontal, if the message has more than 2–3 lines, top and bottom margins fall below the 1″ minimum.

TASK 3 (Long edge vertical) Retype the letter, adding the following new paragraph.

Our science club is building a telescope. The information contained in your brochure will be helpful.

Question. By how much should the date be raised because of the added paragraph? **Answer.** By one-half the number of lines added to the message, including the extra line between paragraphs.

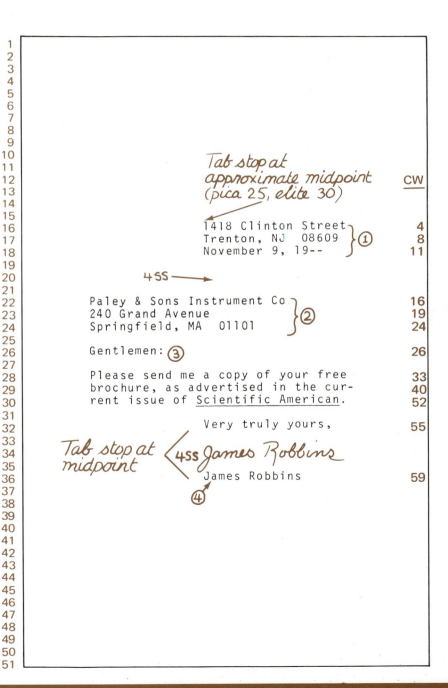

Tab stop at approximate midpoint (pica 25, elite 30)

		CW
1418 Clinton Street		4
Trenton, NJ 08609 ①		8
November 9, 19--		11
4 SS →		
Paley & Sons Instrument Co.		16
240 Grand Avenue ②		19
Springfield, MA 01101		24
Gentlemen: ③		26
Please send me a copy of your free		33
brochure, as advertised in the cur-		40
rent issue of Scientific American.		52
Very truly yours,		55
4 SS James Robbins		
James Robbins		59

Tab stop at midpoint

④

Supplementary practice

LESSON 2 A S D F J K L ; E T N

1 all attend; a faded leaf; a flat fee; land and sea
2 as fast as a jet; settle a fee; a sale; a keen lad
3 taste tea; sealed fast; led a fleet; fell defeated

4 felt safe; a flask leaks; and set a date; an atlas
5 take a taste; takes tea; take a test; least tested
6 attend a tea; attends a feast; needs a lease dated

7 need a desk; sell a sled; tell a tale; lend a tent
8 feels tense; a fatal fall; felt defeat; talk sense
9 a tenant leased an estate; a fast jet; steel tanks

10 sat at a lake; sand and a sea; seek an end at last
11 fell ten feet; sank a fleet; a needle; sat at ease
12 needs talent; a talented staff; settled a flat fee

13 ate ten dates; tasted dates; a ladle; a fatal jest
14 a defeated fleet; saddle a steed; seek a fast deal
15 at a slant; added as a defense; all deans attended

16 at stake; net assets; assets at stake; sets a date
17 all else; a stated date; needs a sled; a fast lane
18 a jet landed; a fatal talk; attend a sale; a lease

19 a talented lad; a lean steak; steal a lead; a deal
20 a flank steak; lank and lean; at a slant; an ankle
21 a fleet at sea; a dead end; need skates and a sled

    . . . .1. . . .2. . . .3. . . .4. . . .5. . . .6. . . .7. . . .8. . . .9. . . .10

LESSON 3 R I H

1 rather far; terrified at first; has his train fare
2 an earlier letter; read this letter; far different
3 he and she are related; had a real treat; this jar

4 he has a hard heart; her heart is tender; heard it
5 she had an earlier start than he did; in dire need
6 started a fire there; left after the rest; in jail

7 thanked the art dealer; think their rates are fair
8 here in the street; an ideal friend; jeered at her
9 shall settle it all later; tried harder; after all

10 near at hand; learned all the details; rather kind
11 his kind interest; find dear friends; kind hearted
12 indeed a fine idea; the fire started near his desk

13 nine hits and three strikes; he hit it rather hard
14 the end is near; a sad end indeed; this free trial
15 an address that is rather far east; a little knife

16 her father is here; after the trial; learn a trade
17 terrified at the risk; shake hands; finished ninth
18 a head start; take an interest; is farther distant

    . . . .1. . . .2. . . .3. . . .4. . . .5. . . .6. . . .7. . . .8. . . .9. . . .10

Continued on the next page

TASK 4 Address a small envelope for the letter, including return address.

TASK 5 Examine the illustrations and read the instructions on p. 157 for folding ½-sheet letters for insertion into envelopes. Then fold the letters for Tasks 2 and 3 and insert each one separately into the envelope for Task 4. Can you then take out each letter by its uncovered edge so that it unfolds easily?

44 Personal-business letters

44A KEYBOARD PRACTICE   Type lines 7–8, p. 116.

44B STRAIGHT COPY TIMINGS   5', DS, SM–1". Underscore the italicized expressions. Enter average scores on TR. Read before you type.

	GWPM a	b	CW

Beginners at the typewriter think and type letter by letter. With more practice, they get skillful at the letter combinations in the words that occur very frequently in our language. That is, they begin to be able to stroke these common letter combinations or sequences in little chains. They no longer have to pay conscious attention to each letter in the sequence. The first chains are for 2-letter sequences, such as *th, he, nd, an.* Later, 3-letter chains appear, such as *the, ing, tio.* Occasionally, even longer chains develop. Sometimes these chained combinations form words. More often, they are parts of words. Apart from a modest handful of very short and highly common words typed as words, all stroking—even among experts—consists of a mixture of chained and single-stroke responses for portions of words. An easy sequence like *th* is readily chained; an awkward one like *az* resists chaining.

GWPM a	b	CW
3	41	13
6	44	28
8	47	42
11	50	56
14	52	71
17	55	85
21	59	106
24	62	120
27	65	134
30	68	148
33	71	163
35	74	177
38	76	191
	Sy 1.52	
	St 6.2	

+0   +1   +2   +3

It is clear that the ease of making the motions required to type a letter combination mostly determines the sequences that can be easily chained, to wit: those motions that can be brought sufficiently close together in time. When a series of motions is made rapidly, the muscular sensations that arise from one motion trigger off the next one. An instance is walking: The sensations in one leg as you complete a step trigger off the movement of the other leg. This and thousands of other skilled movements are done as chained responses, without awareness of the separate motions that make up the series. Indeed, a response chain is defined as one based on muscular sensations—on kinesthetic cues. Because the chained responses that characterize high skill result from reduced time intervals between motions, much practice ought to be done at fast rates. Accuracy practice should be done separately, at a slower rate.

GWPM a	b	CW
3	40	13
5	43	27
8	45	42
11	48	56
14	51	70
17	54	84
20	57	99
23	60	113
25	62	127
28	65	141
31	68	154
34	71	168
37	74	182
37	74	185
	Sy 1.54	
	St 6.0	

+0   +1   +2   +3

SPECIAL PRACTICE AND REFERENCE MATERIALS

44C PERSONAL-BUSINESS LETTERS   Time—nearest ¼′ on Tasks 1 and 2 together

a Use 5-space ¶ indention. **b** Always omit all punctuation at the end of inside-address lines (such punctuation, below and elsewhere in this book, appears only because the letters are "unarranged"—rather than set up in proper form). **c** Aim for a regular right-hand margin; listen for bell, use MR key, divide words as may be necessary.

TASK 1 Use a ½-sheet, long edge vertical, according to the procedures of Lesson 43. Start return address on line 13.

[Your return address and current date] Admissions Office, Wheaton College, Wheaton, IL 60187. Gentlemen: I am completing my freshman year at Canfield College and should like to transfer to Wheaton in the fall. Please send me information about application procedures for transfer students. (¶) Informa-tion about part-time campus employment would also be appreciated. Sincerely yours, [Type your full name, then sign above it in ink.]

TASK 2 You may use a full-size paper (8½″ x 11″) for letters of any length. Retype the letter of Task 1 on a full sheet. Set side margins at 20–65 (pica) or 30–75 (elite). Begin return address on line 21. Address a large envelope [your return address].

Continue with SP–44, p. 112.

45   Personal-business letters □ Error correction

45A STROKE REFINEMENT   Type lines 7–9, p. 121.

45B PERSONAL-BUSINESS LETTERS

At this point in your course, speed gains in typing letters depend less on stroking speed than on knowing what goes where in a letter and on moving from part to part without hesitation. There-fore: Be quick at setting margins and tab stops, inserting paper, and reaching the starting line for typing. Space quickly between parts of the letter; strike keys at a comfortable rate.

TASK 1 To help you remember the order of parts of the letter and the spacing between them, type the letter of 44C (to Wheaton College) over and over (each time on a clean side of a full sheet). If your first trial is perfectly arranged, make your later copies from it rather than from the textbook. With an average of 12 five-stroke words for return address, date, and typed signature, the letter has 85 five-stroke words. How many times can you type it in 15 minutes? 2 times? 2½? 3?

TASK 2 Omit the second ¶ of the message, thus reducing it to 70 five-stroke words. Now see how rapidly you can complete it. **Hint.** For date line, flip down to what you judge to be about 3½ inches; do not take the time to court down to line 22.

Time on TASK 2—nearest ¼′

TASK 3 Address a large and a small envelope to Wheaton College; include your full return address. Then, as shown on p. 157, fold each letter and insert it into the proper envelope.

45C ERROR CORRECTION

1 Correcting an error after you have removed your paper from the typewriter requires reinserting your paper in perfect alignment with previous typing. To avoid that difficult and time-consuming task, correct each error as soon as you notice it. Also, because you will not sense every error when you make it, **always** proofread your work carefully **before** removing your paper from the machine and correct any other errors you find.

2 Some employers prefer that corrections be made by a typing eraser. More often nowadays, special correction strips or tape (for small corrections) or fluid (for more extensive corrections) are used because they are much faster and neater than a typing eraser. Simple directions for use come with the package. For correcting errors on carbon copies, see Lesson 62B, p. 81.

IF YOU USE AN ERASER

a To keep eraser crumbs from falling into and gumming up the machine, use margin release and move carriage to extreme left (for error on left half of page) or to extreme right (for error on right half).

b Lift paper bail. Turn paper to bring error level with erasing table or upper part of roller. If error is toward bottom of page, roll paper toward top of page and bring bottom part over the rear of the roller toward you.

c To avoid creasing or tearing the paper as you erase: Grasp one of the top corners of the paper and pull it tightly away from you, toward the rear of the typewriter—or use an eraser shield.

d Erase l-i-g-h-t-l-y; do **not** scrub—or you might tear the paper. Blow eraser crumbs away from the machine—or use an eraser brush if you have one.

e Return to writing position and type the correction.

Date: Current date

To: Howard R. Nuelle, Floor Manager

From: T. R. Pearl, Vice-President

Subject: Customers' complaints

During the past few weeks many customers have complained of poor service. Examples: no sales-person was available at the counter or two sales-people were engaged in conversation and did not respond promptly to a waiting customer. (¶) Please take these and comparable matters up with the sales personnel and instruct section managers to be alert so as to avoid further cause for complaint.

Date: Current date

To: Sales Manager

From: Advertising Manager

Subject: Customers' addresses

We have not been able to keep a complete and accurate record of our customers for the purpose of mailing circular letters because salesmen frequently omit the customer's address when it is not needed for credit or delivery purposes. (¶) Please instruct salesmen to supply full information on all sales slips. They are surely aware that as our advertising suffers, so do their sales. T. S. Armstrong

B MEMORANDUM (Full Page, Outline Form)

Note the location of the date and the numbering and indention of ¶s. Page placement is the same as for ordinary letters, with no adjustment for memo form because the memo labels use about the same amount of vertical space as an inside address and salutation.

```
                                    Current date

     To:      Leonard Panella
     From:    Robert North
     Subject: Preliminary results of "Princessa" sales campaign

        1. I have examined the first batch of computer printouts
     on the analysis of our sales campaign for "Princessa" and
     thought you would be interested in some of the highlights:

           a. TV is more effective than radio advertising in the
     larger cities; but the two media are about equally effective
```

To: Leonard Panella, From: Robert North, Subject: Preliminary results of "Princessa" sales campaign. 1. I have examined the first batch of computer printouts on the analysis of our sales campaign for "Princessa" and thought you would be interested in some of the highlights: a. TV is more effective than radio advertising in the larger cities; but the two media are about equally effective in the smaller cities. b. "Princessa" is selling best in areas of high concentration of families with young children. c. The medium-size bottle is outselling the other two sizes. 2. I expect to have other details to report to you within the next few days, as soon as the analysis is completed. 3. If there are any analyses of the data you wish me to add to those we discussed two weeks ago, please let me know so that I may issue the necessary instructions to the computer people. They have been most cooperative. George Perkins

Type each sentence exactly as shown; then make the necessary corrections. Can you correct so neatly that no one could tell a correction had been made?

Note. From now on, unless you are told otherwise, correct any errors you make in realistic typing activities (letters, tables, et al.) —but **not** in straight copy or in NS timings or practice.

1	I habe seven.	**4**	Conpare notes.	**7**	Join tge party.
2	He thimks so.	**5**	Tirn left now.	**8**	Corredt errors.
3	Take it awau.	**6**	Cash my checd.	**9**	Depatr on time.

46 Business letter preview □ Short business letters

46A LETTER SEQUENCES   Type the **e** and **f** sequences, p. 121.

46B BUSINESS LETTER PREVIEW

1 A business letter is one **from** a business or other organization. Its form is identical to that of a personal-business letter except that: (a) It needs no typed return address because firm name and address are printed at the top, forming the "letterhead." (b) Additional information follows the complimentary close. (See model, page 64.)

2 Sometimes, but not often these days, a business letter may contain FIRM NAME (in solid caps, a DS below the close)—see #1 at the right. Firm name is usually typed on business postal cards because they have no room for a letterhead.

3 Except for some form letters, a business letter **always** contains the typist's identifying or reference initials (at left margin, 4SS below closing or firm name, in small letters, without periods or spacing). Because the dictator's name is usually typed below the signature, his or her initials may be omitted (#s 3, 4, 5). Some employers, however, prefer to include dictator's initials even when the name is typed. If included, type them in solid caps, separated from the typist's initials by a diagonal (#1) or, more often, by a colon (#s 2, 6, 7, 8).

4 Dictator's title and/or department may be substituted for or added to the typed signature. Variations are: name alone (#s 3, 8), title alone (#1), department alone (#2), or any combination of these items (#s 4, 5, 6). Occasionally, nothing but initials are shown below the longhand signature (#7). If two items follow the longhand signature, always type them on separate lines (#s 4, 6). Type three items on 2 lines (#5).

5 Comma after the closing is optional. Mixed punctuation keeps the comma, as well as the colon following the salutation. Open punctuation omits both the comma and the colon.

6 In full-sheet letters, set tab stop at exact midpoint (pica 42, elite 51) for the closing and the elements below it.

TASK 1 Use full sheet, set tab stop at midpoint and LM 30 spaces left of center. Start on line 3 from the top and type each of the 8 illustrations, in turn, one below the other; TS between them. **Always** use your initials as typist. Space down 4SS from closing (or firm name) to initials; then tabulate to signature. Repeat if time permits.

Continue with Tasks 2–5 on p. 63.

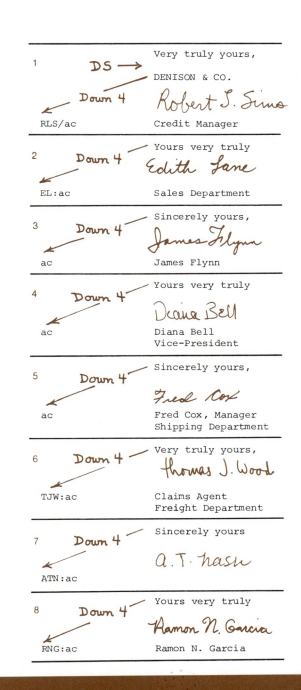

1. DS → Very truly yours,
   DENISON & CO.
   Down 4 — *Robert S. Sims*
   RLS/ac   Credit Manager

2. Down 4 — Yours very truly
   Edith Lane
   EL:ac   Sales Department

3. Down 4 — Sincerely yours,
   James Flynn
   ac   James Flynn

4. Down 4 — Yours very truly
   Diana Bell
   ac   Diana Bell
         Vice-President

5. Down 4 — Sincerely yours,
   Fred Cox
   ac   Fred Cox, Manager
         Shipping Department

6. Down 4 — Very truly yours,
   Thomas J. Wood
   TJW:ac   Claims Agent
             Freight Department

7. Down 4 — Sincerely yours
   A. T. Nash
   ATN:ac

8. Down 4 — Yours very truly
   Ramon N. Garcia
   RNG:ac   Ramon N. Garcia

side head ~~Standards.~~ The use of a 35-wpm [¶] [minimum] standard in some Civil Service ~~exams~~ [tests] for typists ~~results from the fact~~ [means] that such levels ~~of~~ skill are characteristic of available junior typists after a ~~certain~~ [typical] amount of training. Employers tend to set as standards ones that the schools on the average can meet. If the schools regularly [you may be sure that] turned out many 60-wpm typists, 60 wpm would ~~surely~~ be set as a minimum standard.

_____

[1]Wpm means "words per minute." Compute wpm by dividing total words typed by number of minutes. Five typewriter strokes are equivalent to one "word."

Controlled Experimentation in the Classroom, an article by Julian C. Stanley, on pages 195–201 of Volume 25 of the Journal of Experimental Education, published in 1957.

The second edition of Educational Research, by Walter R. Borg and Meredith D. Gall, published in New York, in 1971, by McKay.

Optional Lesson   Interoffice memos

A MEMORANDUM (½-sheet)

A memorandum (plural: memoranda) is generally used for messages within a company or organization. *To, From, Subject,* and *Date* are usually printed on a full- or half-sheet. Inside address, salutation, and complimentary closing are omitted. The message, usually SS (DS permissible if short), begins a TS (DS permissible) below the subject.

Of the several arrangements of the four elements of every memo, two commonly used ones are shown below. If printed forms are not available, use 1-inch top and side margins and **type** the four items, followed by a colon. The corresponding information starts at least two spaces after the colon following *Subject*. The *Date* may be at the left margin, start at the center, or be pivoted from the right margin.

Note (right-hand illustration) that when copies are to be sent to several persons, the name of the person to whom it is to be sent is checked on each copy.

```
TO:        Sales Manager        DATE:  May 5, 19--
FROM:      Advertising Manager
SUBJECT:   "Sirocco" posters

     Our order for 500 additional copies of the "Sirocco"
raincoat poster was due back from the printer on May 10.
However, I was notified by telephone this morning that,
due to last minute changes in the design of the poster,
we shall not be receiving the new copies until May 21.


ld                        Jack Howe
```

```
Date:      July 15, 19--

To:        Mr. J. Kittinger, Account Executive
           Mr. F. Baeur, Art Editor
           Ms. B. DiGrazia, Copy Editor

From:      Mr. D. Keegan, Vice President

Subject:   Whitman account

     This is to remind you that a meeting will be held July 18
at 10 a.m. in the 4th floor conference room to discuss the re-
vised schedule for the Whitman campaign.  Please bring your file
of correspondence concerning this account,
```

For Tasks 2–5 use a full sheet, WL–40, date 3½"–4" from the top (line 22–24). Do **not** copy the commas between the lines of the inside address. If the dictator's name is typed, omit the dictator's initials—but **always** use your own initials as typist. From task to task, next, alternate between blocked and indented paragraphs and between open and mixed punctuation (see ¶ 5, of 46B.)

Proofread and correct all errors **before** you remove paper from the machine.

Your objective. Master the location of letter parts and the spacing between them so that you move rapidly from one part to the next without having to stop to think.

TASK 2 Mrs. Robert Wilson, 275 West 18 Street, Gary, IN 46401. Dear Mrs. Wilson: Our summer sale of kitchenware begins next Monday, June 21. (¶) Please plan to come early and make your selection. Very truly yours, (DS) KREY & CO. (4SS) LK: Sales Department.

TASK 3 Lake Construction Company, Airport Circle, Kansas City, MO 64114. Gentlemen: Enclosed is a complete catalog of our various products. (¶) Please let me know if we can help you further. Very truly yours, (4SS) [Your initials] John L. Exeter, Advertising Manager

TASK 4 Mr. Warren Laine, 831 Elm Avenue, Clinton, IA 52732. Dear Mr. Laine: Your tape recordings were shipped today and should arrive within the week. (¶) Thank you for your order. Yours very truly, Rita M. Diaz, Manager

TASK 5 Mr. Charles Morris, 898 Third Avenue, Norfolk, VA 23523. Dear Mr. Morris: Thank you for notifying us immediately of your damaged shipment. We are investigating and will contact you again shortly. Sincerely yours, H. R. Neuman, Claims Division

47 Business letters □ Folding full-sheet letters for small envelopes □ Letter styles

47A CAPITALIZATION PRACTICE   Type lines 7–9, p. 120.

47B COMPARISON PRACTICE   3′ or 4′ timing; DS, SM–1".

		GWPM		
		3′	4′	CW

This is to acknowledge receipt of your adding machine. As soon as we have had a chance to make a careful examination, we shall notify you of the approximate cost of the repair and the time it will require. We shall begin work as soon as we receive your approval. If we find later that the actual cost of materials and labor is less than our estimate, we shall give you the benefit of the reduced figure. In any event, the charge will not exceed the amount quoted.

We are happy to serve you now and at all times.

3′	4′	CW
4	3	13
9	7	28
14	11	42
19	14	57
24	18	71
28	21	85
31	23	94
34	26	103

| 3′ | +0 | +1 | +2 | +3 | +4 | +5 |
| 4′ | +0 | +1 | +2 | +3 | | |

If you began the copy a second time, compute speed from CW column.

Use a ½-sheet, long edge vertical; indent the ¶s. Sign your first name in ink. Omit a return address.

Dear Uncle Ted, You certainly helped to make my birthday a happy one. The pen set for my desk looks elegant. How did you guess it is something I always wanted? (¶) We are all looking forward to your visit next Sunday. Then I can thank you in person for your thoughtfulness. Love,

73– VERTICAL
75F CENTERING

Center vertically on a full sheet items A–G listed at the beginning of Lesson 73, but omit the letters before each item. Using FINAL TEST ITEMS as a heading, center **each** of the 7 items in the list horizontally on a separate line. Single space the 7 lines, but double space between items B and C.

73– PERSONAL-BUSINESS LETTER
75G

Use your own return address and sign and type your own name.

Mr. David Kent, Personnel Manager, Anderson Tape Co., 43 Park Lane, Duluth, MN 55809. Dear Mr. Kent: I enjoyed my interview with you yesterday for the position of senior typist in the Research Division and am looking forward to the new job. (¶) As you requested, I consulted my present employer about the termination date of my present job. He suggested I complete the week there. Accordingly, I will report for work at my new job on Monday, January 29. Sincerely yours,

73– POSTAL CARD
75H

To: Kinsey Publications, Inc., 1775 Shipwright St., Clifton, NJ 07013 **From:** (Your name and your return address)

Gentlemen: In the May issue of your magazine, *American Business,* you advertised a free booklet entitled "Data Processing Survey." If this booklet is still available, please send me a copy. Sincerely yours, [Type and sign your name.]

73– TABLE
75I

Center on a ½-sheet vertically and horizontally.

TOP SCORERS

January Typing Contest

Student	Speed	Errors
Rose Diaz	43	2
James Kennedy	39	1
Sally Cantor	39	3

Wolff Automotive Supplies

2764 Northwest Highway
Pittsburgh, PA 45202
Telephone: (412) 744-2532

Tab stop at 42 (pica), 51 (elite)

CW

```
....1....2....3....4.|...5....6....7....8....9...
                     Current date                        3

                4SS

Evans Motor Repair Co.                                   8
204-17 Forbes Avenue                                    12
Pittsburgh, PA   45203                                  17
           DS
Gentlemen:                                              19
           DS
Thank you for sending us $50 on account against         29
your overdue bill.  We are crediting it to your         39
account with us.                                        42
           DS
At the repayment rate of $50 a month, your over-        52
due bill will be paid up in three more months.          62

                Sincerely yours,                        65

  Typists'    4SS{  John R. Broom
  initials here
  xx                John R. Broom, Manager               71
                    Claims Department                    75

....1....2....3....4....5....6....7....8....9...
```

	GWPM	
a	b	CW
3	21	17
6	24	31
9	26	45
12	29	59
15	32	73
17	35	86

On May 9 you ordered 5,000 feet of our #4 *Excelsior* white pine @ $69.17. Our invoice for $345.85 is enclosed. Our 2% discount (for payment by June 10) applies. At the same time, you inquired about copper wire, 1/16" in diameter. Stanley & Tate manufactures "Bay-Tech" wire #395, which should fill your needs. The price is $78.20 a reel, with the usual discount of 2% for payment within 30 days. Don't delay!

+0	+1	+2	+3

Time on Items C–J: nearest ½'

73– BUSINESS
75C LETTERS

Type Letter 1 in block style, open punctuation, with moving date starting at center. Type Letter 2 in semiblock style, mixed punctuation, date fixed and pivoted, with carbon copy. Correct all errors on the originals and the carbon.

1 Goring & Howe, 752 Orange Street, Rochester, NY 14617. Gentlemen: We are sorry, but at the present time we are unable to fill your request for two posters advertising our "Sirocco" raincoats. The demand for these posters was so great that our supply was exhausted within five days. (¶) When additional posters become available next month, we shall be happy to send you two. In the meantime, I am enclosing a catalog of our new spring line of leisure wear and a price list. Very truly yours, BEAUMONT, INC., Edward Arliss, Sales Manager

2 Dr. Charles L. Yukawa, Chief, Surgical Services, 6142 University Dr., Pittsburgh, PA 15241. Dear Dr. Yukawa: A well-appointed office and an attractive waiting room play an important role in creating the right "image" for the professional man or woman. You can enhance your image by outfitting your rooms with new furniture, draperies, and floor coverings. Our expert interior decorators are at your service to suit your professional needs and personal tastes. (¶) We have a large stock of office furnishings in all styles ready for immediate delivery. If you prefer, our skilled craftsmen are prepared to carry out any special order you may have in mind. (¶) Why not call and ask us to send one of our consultants to your office today? Very truly yours, Victor Gomez, Manager, Special Sales Dept.

73– ENVELOPES
75D

Address a small envelope for Letter 1, above, and a large one for Letter 2. Type your name in the return address position.

TASK 1

1 Take a 15′ timing on the model letter on the preceding page, repeating it as often as you can and using a clean side of a sheet of paper each time.

2 Use WL–45 (elite SMs of 30 and 75, pica SMs of 20 and 65). On full-sheet letters set tab stop at exact midpoint: 42 pica, 51 elite.

3 You may wish to space down to line 21 for the date (7TS or 10DS + 1SS) or to flip down 3+ inches without counting. Use your initials as typist and the current date.

4 Get total words from CW column + dotted word-count line. WPM = total words ÷ 15.

TASK 2

Use the ¶s of 47B as the message of a business letter to: **Barnes & Weller, Inc., 2400 Clermont Drive, Wilmington, DE 19804. Gentlemen:** Close with: **Very truly yours, Norman Sampson, Manager.** SMs same as for Task 1, date 3″ from the top. NEXT, address a small envelope and insert the letter, folded as shown on p. 157.

Time—nearest ¼′

Continue with SP–47, p. 113.

THE TWO MOST COMMON LETTER STYLES

DATE (in both styles) may be centered or pivoted or it may start at the center. Starting the date at center is most common, pivoted is next most frequent, and centered is rare.

CLOSING ELEMENTS always start at center, even if the date is pivoted or centered.

BLOCK. Date and closing elements on right side of page.

MODIFIED (or SEMI-) BLOCK. Adds paragraph indention to block style.

Date pivoted (ending at right margin —see 50B).

Date starting at center

48–49 Two-day test or review: Part 1 (NS timing □ Table □ Two letters □ Two envelopes)

48–49A PREPARATION
Type 40B, p. 55, for 2–3 minutes.

48–49B NUMBER AND SYMBOL TIMING
5′, DS, SM–1″. TR–NS

	GWPM	
	a	b	CW

	a	b	CW
Olivera & Martin, attorneys, advertised in this morning's *Examiner,*	3	18	17
as follows: "Wanted: stenographer-typist, at least 21 years old; mini-	6	21	31
mum of 2 years' experience, preferably in legal and/or insurance office.	9	24	46
Salary, $175; 37½-hour week; good working conditions. Apply at Hornwell	12	27	60
Building, 126 Flagston Street (Room #849), between 9:30 a.m. and 4 p.m."	15	30	75

+0	+1	+2	+3

	GWPM	
a	b	CW
3	44	13
5	47	27
8	50	41
11	52	56
14	55	69
17	58	83
20	61	98
22	64	111
25	66	125
26	67	128
28	70	141
31	72	155
34	75	169
36	78	183
39	81	197
41	83	206
	Sy 1.52	
	St 6.0	

You take straight copy timings regularly to determine whether you have gained in skill. For several months now, the ones whose scores you have been entering on your record form have been of five minutes' duration. Also, the materials have always been of average difficulty. Why have test length and test difficulty been unchanged? The answer is: because otherwise it would not be possible to determine how much of a change in your performance results from a change in skill and how much from a change in test length or test difficulty. Why five minutes? Because nearly all employment tests for typists use timings of that duration.

Why has a pair of timings been provided on important occasions and why have you been instructed to average your scores? First of all, a person's errors tend to vary from one time to the next. You cannot secure a dependable measure of stroking accuracy in merely one short test. Second, any score should ideally represent a person's typical performance, and typical means "on the average."

+0   +1   +2   +3

3	41	13
5	44	27
8	47	42
11	49	53
13	52	66
16	55	81
19	58	95
20	59	101
23	62	114
26	64	129
27	66	135
30	68	148
32	71	162
35	74	176
38	77	190
39	77	193
	Sy 1.54	
	St 5.7	

Paper containers for letters that were to be mailed appeared in Europe for the first time about the middle of the 17th century. It has never been established with any degree of certainty who was responsible for the invention of this ancestor of the modern envelope.

For more than 150 years people did not realize how useful the envelope could be. Not too much more than a century ago it was still the practice either to wrap letters in paper or to fold them and seal them with wax before mailing them.

A New Yorker whose name was Pearson was the pioneer in the United States in the art of making envelopes. His envelopes were cut, folded, and gummed entirely by hand.

About the middle of the 19th century both the United States and England established cheap postage rates, which encouraged the public to use mail services. In all probability, those cheap rates account for envelopes coming into general use for all correspondence in the decade that followed.

+0   +1   +2   +3

Time on 48C–F—nearest ½'

48–
49C BUSINESS LETTER
86 words

Use a full sheet; same SMs as in 47C, block style, date on line 21.

Mrs. Elizabeth Hunter, 622 Waterbury Ave., Norwalk, CT 06854. Dear Mrs. Hunter: You are correct; your July statement is incorrect. The price of Telco's EL-117 electronic calculator is $27.50, not $37.50. (¶) We are sorry for this billing error. Please disregard your original statement; a corrected invoice will be sent to you shortly. Sincerely yours, Linda Lanza, Customer Service Department

48–
49D TABLE
37 words

Center on a ½-sheet vertically and horizontally. BC–5.

SATURDAY HOBBY COURSES

Course	Time	Fee
Gardening	10:00 a.m.	$ 8.50
Arts and Crafts	1:00 p.m.	17.50
Puppet Making	9:30 a.m.	25.00
Weaving	10:45 a.m.	36.00

48–
49E PERSONAL-BUSINESS LETTER
53 words

Use a ½-sheet, long edge vertical, semiblock style. Use your return address and typed signature.

Discount Appliance Co., 1662 Southwest Highway, Providence, RI 02902. Gentlemen: My Templex Model 602 tape recorder was delivered today. However, the manufacturer's warranty was not enclosed. Would you please send me one? Yours truly,

48–
49F ENVELOPES
15 and 23 words

Address a large envelope for the letter of 48C and a small one for the letter of 48E. Type your own name in the return address position and, on the small envelope, your return address, too. Insert the letters in their envelopes, properly folded.

48–49 Two-day test or review: Part 2 (Straight copy timings □ Rough draft □ Outline □ Personal note)

48–
49G PREPARATION
2–3 minutes on 47B, p. 63

48–
49H STRAIGHT COPY TIMINGS
Use the timings of 44B, p. 60. TR

VII. OUTLINES

A. Within any item, use [SS/DS]. Between items or levels, preferably use [SS/DS].

B. This outline (Lessons 71–72) uses (how many?) _____ levels and requires the setting of (how many?) _____ tab stops.

VIII. MISCELLANEOUS INFORMATION

A. *Manuscript* should preferably be divided [before/after] the *u,* and *movable* [before/after] the *a.* Divide *stirring* [after/between] the *r's* and *calling* [after/between] the *l's.* Dividing *enough* after the *e* and *mighty* after the *t* is [acceptable/wrong]. *Light-ly* is [undesirable/wrong].

B. The abbreviation *etc.* means "_____"; *e.g.* means "_____"; *i.e.* means "_____."

C. A quotation within a quotation is set off by _____.

D. A book belonging to Morris is [Morris'/Morris's] book.

E. 20# means 20 _____; #15 means _____ 15. When used as proofreaders' marks: # means _____; a triple underscore means _____; a circle around a punctuation mark means _____; a diagonal line through a capital letter means _____. A marginal caret should be inverted to show the insertion of a [comma/quotation mark].

71–72C OPTIONAL PRACTICE

1 An original plus two carbons of any earlier letter, table, or ms.

2 Stroke Refinement, Capitalization, Letter Sequences, Keyboard Practice

OR if students begin optional practice together:

3 Paced Practice (4½′–5½′ timings)

4 Progressive or Progressive Number and Symbol Practice

73–75 End-of-semester test (review of all work)

1 The materials on the next four pages include all the important topics and skills covered in previous lessons, as follows:

A Two 5′ straight copy timings
B One 5′ number and symbol timing
C Two business letters (1 with carbon)
D Two envelopes
E One personal note
F Vertical centering
G One personal-business letter
H One postal card
I One table
J One manuscript
K References page

2 The various test items (**A–K**) may be done in whatever order your instructor may assign during the next few days. Proofread carefully and correct all errors in items **C–K**.

48–
49I ROUGH DRAFT   Center on a full sheet, using WL–50 and appropriate vertical spacing.

93 words

THE BUSINESS LETTER

The "business letter" is from a business, *or other organization* and

deals, by definition, with business rather than per-

sonal matters. ¶ As distinguished from the personal-

business letter, ~~it~~ *the business letter* always includes identifying

REFERENCE INITIALS (of the typist and sometimes of

the dictator) and may include the FIRM # NAME of the

sp and l.c. sender a DS below the closing. The dictator's TITLE *u.c.*

sp and/or (DEPT) often accompany a TYPED SIGNATURE.

48–
49J OUTLINE   Start on line 21, LM 18 spaces left of center. Center the heading.

75 words

USE OF THE TELEPHONE

TS ————

   I. The sound of your voice
#————   A. Distance from the mouthpiece
#————   B. Clearness
            1. Pronunciation
            2. Volume of sound
#————   3. Rate of speech
            C. Manner and tone
  II. Placing a call
#————   A. Finding the number
            1. Telephone lists
            2. Telephone directories
#————   3. Information
#————   B. Getting the connection
            1. Use of the dial
            2. Getting the person wanted

 # is used for both horizontal and vertical spacing.

48–
49K PERSONAL NOTE   Use a ½-sheet, long edge vertical, semiblock style; sign your first name in ink.

37 words

Dear Maria, I'm sorry I won't be able to join you Friday evening, but I
must stay over in Chicago an extra day. I'll phone you when I get
home Saturday. Yours,

Turn in your test papers and continue on a practice sheet with OPTIONAL PRACTICE.

IV. MANUSCRIPTS

A. Margins

1. Side and bottom margins should never be less than _____ inch(es).

2. Page 1 uses a top margin of _____ inch(es) or _____ line(s). Later pages use a top margin of _____ inch(es), and the first line of text is on line _____.

3. A sidebound ms. uses a left margin set at _____ on the carriage or margin scale.

4. If an unbound ms. uses a 6-inch writing line, side margins are set at _____ and _____.

B. Footnotes

1. Footnotes end on line _____ and are typed in [SS/DS]. Between the divider line and the first footnote, [SS/DS]; and between one footnote and the next, [SS/DS].

2. To end two 2-line footnotes and two 1-line footnotes on the correct line, the divider line should be on line _____.

3. In footnotes, authors' names are typed [first name/last name] first. Page numbers of direct quotations [are/are not] shown.

C. References

1. References are listed [in the order mentioned in the body of the ms./alphabetically by author].

2. Lines after the first line of each entry in *References* listings are indented _____ space(s).

3. Author's names are typed [first name/last name] first.

4. Of these elements: (a) titles of articles, (b) titles of books, (c) names of journals, (d) publication dates, (e) journal volume numbers, (f) page numbers—the ones that are underscored are lettered _____.

5. The title of an article [is/is not] set within quotation marks.

V. VERTICAL CENTERING

A. In double spacing, each pair of typed lines is separated by _____ blank line(s). In triple spacing, typed lines are separated by _____ blank line(s).

B. If 6 DS lines of typing are centered vertically on a full sheet, the first line of typing is on line _____; if SS on a ½-sheet, start on line _____.

VI. TABLES

A. Horizontal placement

1. To center the column heading *State* over *Minnesota,* starting at the *M* of *Minnesota* you should forward space _____ time(s) and then backspace _____ time(s). Or, by counting instead of spacing methods, to center *Item* over *Dictionary, Item* will begin lined up over the (what letter?) _____ of *Dictionary.*

2. To find the left margin in a 3-column table whose longest items are *James L. Moran, Treasurer, 1974,* start by backspacing for the typed matter a total of _____ time(s); with BC–6, backspace _____ more time(s).

B. Vertical placement

1. Assume a table with a 1-line major heading or title, a 1-line minor head, and 1-line column heads. Between the major and minor heads use [SS/DS/TS]. Between the minor head and the column heads use [SS/DS/TS]; and between the column heads and the first row of the table use [SS/DS/TS]. Between the rows of a 6-row table use [SS/DS/TS].

2. If centered vertically on a full sheet, the major heading or title of the table described above would be on line number _____.

50A KEYBOARD PRACTICE   Type lines 9–10, p. 116.

50B BUSINESS LETTERS

PIVOTING THE DATE OR FIRM NAME

The date in a letter may be "pivoted" (to end it flush with the right margin), rather than begun at midpoint. A pivoted date balances off the inside address lines blocked at the left. Also, since a pivoted date ends at the right margin, its last digit serves as a marker or guide for the desired ending point of each message line.

To pivot, move carriage 1 space past right margin; then backspace 1 for 1 as you spell each stroke in the date. Start to type where the backspacing ends; e.g., assuming right margin at 65, you might set margin stop at 68 to minimize use of margin release key. But pivot by backspacing 1 for 1 from 66. See *Note,* next, for pivoting the firm name.

Note. If a firm name appears to be too long to fit within the right margin if begun at midpoint, pivot it and start the other closing elements (closing, signature, title) where the firm name begins.

ABOUT RIGHT MARGINS

Avoid a right margin wider than the left-hand one; e.g., with margin at 65, it is better to type message lines out to 67 than to stop at 63.

The best typists intentionally hyphenate a dividable word at end-of-line if doing so will improve the evenness of a right-hand margin.

TASKS 1 AND 2 In the letters below, pivot the date (3″ from top); SMs of 20–65 (pica), 30–75 (elite). Do Letter 1 in block style, Letter 2 in semiblock (see models, p. 65). The word count at the right is of 5-stroke words, including an allowance of 4 words for the date and the spacing that follows.

	CW
1 Messrs. Rumford & Hansell, 206 Broad Street,	12
Detroit, MI 48223. Gentlemen: Thank you for	22
asking us to bid on a new heating system for	31
your factory. We are now carefully studying	40
your specifications. (¶) Before submitting our	49
final estimate by Thursday, August 27, I should	58
like our chief engineer, William Leitner, to	67
inspect your facilities and to go over with you	77
personally any special requirements you may	86
have. (¶) He will phone you in a few days for	94
an appointment. Yours very truly, HARRISON	104
& BLACKWELL HEATING CO., John E. Harrison,	113
President	115

	CW
2 Mr. Charles S. Gross, 43 Larch Avenue, Co-	12
lumbus, OH 43202. Dear Mr. Gross: Ms. Noa	21
Lessing has applied for a position as cashier	30
with our firm and has given your name as a ref-	39
erence. (¶) The position calls for a knowledge	48
of bookkeeping, skill in operating business ma-	57
chines, and careful attention to detail. In	66
addition, the employee must be absolutely re-	75
sponsible and trustworthy. (¶) Any information	84
regarding Ms. Lessing's qualifications would be	94
greatly appreciated and will be kept in strict	103
confidence. Very truly yours, Nicole E. West,	114
Personnel Manager	117

TASK 3 Check evenness of right-hand margin. Did you divide words when desirable; that is, in Letter 1: heat-ing, care-fully, Thurs-day, engi-neer, facili-ties, appoint-ment; in Letter 2: posi-tion, book-keeping?

See p. 157 for a listing of major and minor errors in letters.

50C FOLDING LETTERS	Address a small envelope for Letter 1, above, and a large one for Letter 2. Then, according to the instructions and illustrations on p. 157, fold the letters for insertion into the envelopes.

50D TIMED PRACTICE   As many Paced or Progressive or Progressive NS timings as time permits. PF

1 Instead of typing the entire ms. (on this and the next two pages), type only the numbers and letters of its various levels and, as you go along, type the answers that go with each level.

2 The answers require either filling in a blank or selecting the one of the several choices in brackets that is correct. If any item requires more than one answer, separate the answers by commas, as shown below paragraph 4.

3 To save time and space, type down the left half of the page (LM 1 inch)—but stop short of the midpoint on any line. Then continue down the right half of the page, setting a new left margin at the center point.

4 Center the title of the unbound ms. on the proper line. Space between one item and the next as if you were typing the full ms.

```
I.

   A. 8½, 11

   B. larger, 10, 12
```

TYPING PLACEMENT RULES, WITH APPLICATIONS

I. TYPEWRITER ARITHMETIC

  A. Standard-size stationery is _____ inches wide and _____ inches long.

  B. Pica type is [larger/smaller] than elite type. In 1 horizontal inch you can type _____ pica spaces or _____ elite spaces.

  C. From edge to edge across the page there are _____ pica spaces or _____ elite spaces.

  D. In 1 vertical inch in single spacing you can type _____ line(s).

  E. From top to bottom in single spacing a full sheet contains _____ lines; a ½-sheet contains _____ lines.

II. BUSINESS LETTERS

  A. Horizontal placement

    1. A short letter is one whose message contains up to _____ words.

    2. Side margins for a letter of 132 words should be set at _____ and _____.

    3. The closing of a letter starts at _____ on the carriage or margin scale.

  B. Vertical placement

    1. For a letter of up to 60 words, a moving date is on line _____.

      a. For every additional _____ words or fraction of _____ words, a moving date is [raised/lowered] by _____ line(s).

      b. For a letter of 114 words, a moving date should be on line _____.

      c. Between date and inside address, space down _____ time(s).

      d. In a 93-word letter with 3 paragraphs and a 4-line inside address, a moving date should be on line _____.

    2. A fixed date is always on line _____.

      a. For a letter of up to 60 words, between fixed date and inside address space down _____ time(s).

      b. For a letter of 108 words, between fixed date and inside address space down _____ time(s).

    3. Between closing and firm name, space down _____ time(s). If there is no firm name, between closing and typed signature space down _____ time(s).

    4. The typist's initials are preferably typed in [small/capital] letters [on the same line as/below] the typed signature.

      a. If the dictator's name (John L. Ray) is typed below his signature by Sue Kent (his secretary), the reference initials should preferably be [sk/JLR:sk].

      b. Enc. or Encs. is typed _____ line(s) below the reference initials.

III. ENVELOPES

  A. Addresses are typed in [single/double] spacing. Return addresses use [SS/DS].

  B. On a small envelope the address starts on line _____; on a large envelope, on line _____.

51A STROKE REFINEMENT   Type lines 10–12, p. 121.

51B ALIGNING
If any change or correction has to be made after paper is removed from the typewriter, the paper should be reinserted so that the new typing will be aligned (lined up) perfectly with previous typing.

1 Type (on one line): I believe the delivery may be delayed until a month from now.

2 Without spacing down, push back or backspace to middle of sentence. Fix in mind the relation (distance) between bottom edge of typing and top edge of aligning scale. Vertical marks on scale point to center of each letter (see illustration). Check (in your sentence) the letters: i, l, v.

3 Remove paper from machine and reinsert it. Use paper release to adjust paper horizontally across full length of your sentence; use variable line spacer or ratchet release to make finer vertical adjustments; use aligning scale for exact line-up.

4 Type over the *l* of *believe*. Check exactness of strikeover and adjust paper, if necessary. Then type over the entire word.

5 Repeat the process of removing, reinserting, aligning, and typing over for each of these words: delivery, delayed, until.

51C BUSINESS LETTER TIMING   20 minutes on the letters of 50B

1 Set margins to extreme left and right; clear all tab stops. Since speed of work includes preparation for typing, wait for start signal before inserting paper and making machine settings.

2 Use any letter style(s) and method(s) of date placement you or your instructor prefer.

3 **Speed scoring.** For total words, add words on partial line (strokes ÷ 5) to figure for last completed line. WPM = total words ÷ 20. *Example:* If you reach *bus* (line 6 of second letter), you have typed:

115 + 48 + 38/5 = 171 words, and
171 ÷ 20 = 8.55 = 9 wpm.

51D PERSONAL NOTE (With Enclosure)

Often, an item such as a check is sent with a letter. To remind the writer to enclose it and the reader to look for it, *Enc.* or *Encl.* or *Enclosure* is typed as shown at the right. It is also helpful to name the item on the next line, indented 3 spaces.

Your friend,

Sue

Sue Rankin

Enc.
        Manuscript

Type the personal note below on a full sheet, including your return address, starting 3½″ from the top.

Dear Jim, I was sorry to hear that it will be another few days before you are well enough to return to school. (¶) I know you have to write a report for your American History class, so I am sending you some information about manuscript typing that I prepared in today's typing class. I hope you will find the information useful. (¶) I hope to see you again soon. Yours, Enc. [Type your name.] Manuscript

51E PACED or PROGRESSIVE PRACTICE   As many timings as time permits. PF

The writer is not always free to choose the citation style he or she prefers. It is therefore desirable to learn to use both citation styles: (1) footnotes and (2) author's name and publication date in parentheses within the text.

Whatever the style, the purpose of citation of sources has been well stated by a leading authority on English usage, as follows:

> Any paper based on the writings of others should acknowledge the sources used. Common courtesy and honesty require that credit be given where credit is due, and a scrupulously documented source allows the reader to judge for himself the evidence an assertion is based on . . . . College students are expected to draw their materials from various sources, but they are also expected to make a frank acknowledgement of these sources. Fundamentally, the forms of documentation are symbols of courtesy and consideration shown by scholars to each other.[1]

---

[1]Porter G. Perrin. *Writer's Guide and Index to English* (5th ed.). Chicago: Scott, Foresman, 1972, p. 418. In an earlier edition of Perrin's book (1939,

A footnote must be begun on the page on which it is mentioned in the text. If it cannot be completed on that page, continue it at the bottom of the next page. If each of the two columns in this report were on a different page (e.g., left-hand column is page 3, right-hand column is page 4), the footnote reference to Perrin's book, below, is illustrative.

Footnote and parenthetical citations are rather formal. In an informal report a source might be included in the text, as in:

> It has been remarked that if a given construction makes good sense, it usually makes good English (Barrett Wendell, *English Composition,* page 78).

or

> In his *English Composition,* page 78, Barrett Wendell has remarked that a construction that makes good sense usually makes good English.

Whatever the citation style within it, a report ends with a list of references.

---

p. 365), the author referred to the "decency" of citing one's sources.

70C TIMED PRACTICE   As many Paced, Progressive, or Progressive NS timings as time permits. PF

71–72 Review of typing rules and procedures (Ms. in outline form)

71–72A LETTER SEQUENCES   Type the sequences for **m** and **n**, p. 119.

| SHORT (up to 100 words) | MEDIUM (101–200 or 250 words) | LONG (more than 200 or 250 words) |

52A LETTER SEQUENCES

Type the sequences for **g** and **h,** p. 118.

52B LETTER PLACEMENT

1 Attractive appearance or placement is a requirement for all realistic work at the typewriter. As shown above, short letters have wider margins (vertical and horizontal) than longer letters.

2 Letter placement is based mainly on the number of actual (dictionary) words in the body or message and, in addition, on the features described below the upper table on p. 156. Examine that table **now,** including its footnotes. It describes two methods of date placement, as follows:

  a Moving. Distance from top of page to date varies with letter length, and date is always followed by 4 line spaces down to the inside address. See MEDIUM and LONG models above.

  b Fixed. Date on line 14 regardless of letter length. Distance from date to inside address varies with letter length. See SHORT model above.

Both placement methods are widely used, so it is important to learn both of them.

3 The fastest way to determine how many lines to subtract from 21 (moving date) or from 12 (fixed date) is to COUNT ON YOUR FINGERS BY 20's, from 60 (the first finger is 80), until you reach the number of words in the body of the letter. Then subtract number of fingers counted off from 21 (moving date) or from 12 (fixed date). *Example:* For 108-word message, count "80-100-120" (3 fingers). Therefore, moving date = 21 − 3 = 18 lines from top; fixed date = 12 − 3 = 9 carriage returns between date (on line 14) and inside address. See the table below for other illustrations.

4 Before selecting letter margins, estimate the number of words in the body of each letter, according to the instructions of 54B, p. 72.

Message words	Count	Number of fingers	Moving date	Date fixed on Line 14 (Distance to address)
52	None	0	21 − 0 = 21	12 − 0 = 12
73	80	1	21 − 1 = 20	12 − 1 = 11
96	80-100	2	21 − 2 = 19	12 − 2 = 10
135	80-100-120-140	4	21 − 4 = 17	12 − 4 = 8

TASK 1 Assume that you are to type a basic letter (2 ¶s, 3-line inside address, no additional elements). For each of the message lengths shown, count on your fingers to determine (a) moving date line and (b) fixed-date distance to the inside address. **1** 64 words, **2** 128 words, **3** 86 words, **4** 145 words, **5** 109 words, **6** 172 words

TASKS 2 AND 3 Study the footnotes to the upper table and ¶s 2 and 3 under the letter placement table on p. 156 and apply the information to the typing of each of the 2 letters below. Correct all errors.

Hereafter, **you** are responsible for noticing whether the body of any letter mentions enclosures. If it does, add the appropriate enclosure notation at the end of the letter.

1 Block, moving date starting at midpoint

Ms. Alice Gallagher, 62 Coster Street, Cincinnati, OH 45202. Dear Ms. Gallagher: We are very sorry that the Regency table you ordered was delivered in poor condition. We can only surmise that the damage was caused in transit, and we are checking with the trucking company about this. (¶) We would be happy to send one of our expert carpenters to your home to make the necessary repairs, or, if you prefer, you may come into our store to select another table. (¶) Please call this department (751-7020) and let us know your preference. Yours very truly, John Sill, Manager, Customer Service Dept.

2 Semiblock, date fixed and pivoted

Mrs. Jane H. Kahn, 45 Dover Street, Ames, IA 50010. Dear Mrs. Kahn: Thank you for inquiring about Gould Brothers' new, exclusive "Take-It" charge card. (¶) I am enclosing an application form for you to complete that folds as a self-sealing envelope addressed to us and needs no postage. (¶) Upon receipt of your completed application form, we will process it as quickly as possible. Very truly yours, Robert Dunois, Credit Manager

Are you remembering to continue with Optional Practice when time permits?

69B PERSONAL NOTE AND ENVELOPE — The ms. of 68A is part of the report referred to in this personal note. Type the note on a full sheet, omitting all addresses. Complete the salutation and address a large envelope to one or both of your parents or to some other relative or friend at an appropriate address.

Dear _____, I'm immensely enjoying my course in Industrial Psychology. In fact, I'm so proud of the report I wrote on "The Working Environment" that I'm attaching a copy. You can see from the dates of some of the references that many things people still argue about were settled long ago! (¶) Also, last week in typing class I learned a great time-saver in typing term papers. Instead of footnoting source information, which takes a great deal of planning, I'm now using the journal style of parenthetical citation, which is more professional, as well as much faster and easier to type. (¶) I'm looking forward to seeing you at intersession. Love, [Sign your first name.]

69C REPORT TABLE — Always number tables in reports serially (preferably with Arabic—not Roman—numerals). SS before and DS after the divider line before table footnotes. Center the table on a full sheet, BC–5.

Table 2

Sales Trends of Manual and Electric Standard Typewriters

(In percentages)[a]

Type of Machine	1955	1962	1972
Manual	74.1	48.9	16.6
Electric	25.9	51.1	83.4

[a] Data from Census Bureau reports.

70 Long quotations

70A STROKE REFINEMENT   Type lines 19–21, p. 121.

70B LONG QUOTATIONS

In both correspondence and reports, short quotations (up to 2–3 lines) appear within the text, set in quotation marks. Longer quotations are

1 Typed as a separate paragraph

2 Typed in single spacing

3 Indented on both the left **and** right sides

Quotation marks are omitted because the indention on each side shows that the materials are quoted. In a letter with a long quotation the unquoted paragraphs should preferably be blocked.

Type the ms. on the next page as p. 2, SM–1", 5-space ¶ indention.

Perrin has remarked that "Properly used, punctuation reflects and supplements the spoken signs of meaning." He then goes on to observe (1972, p. 294):

> Though accurate punctuation can't redeem a mixed-up sentence--one that requires rewriting--it may save a weak sentence from ambiguity, and it can make the meaning of a complicated sentence precise and clear.

All authorities on punctuation make two major observations. The first is that overpunctuating is as much to be avoided as un-

53A CAPITALIZATION PRACTICE   Type lines 10–12, p. 120.

53B TITLES (In addresses and closings)

The placement of an addressee's (or signer's) title—if any—depends on its length. Type it on line 1 or 2 of the inside address (or with the typed signature or department or by itself in a letter closing)—whichever will make the lines more nearly of equal length.

Use Ms. (instead of Miss or Mrs.) if a woman prefers that title or when you write to a woman whose marital status you do not know.

TASK 1 Examine and type the addresses on the 3 upper lines and the closings on the 2 lower lines. LM pica ½″, elite 1″; space 3 times between illustrations.

On same line as name	On same line as department	On a separate line
Mr. John Ames, President Mutual Insurance Company 122 Parsons Boulevard	Mr. Robert H. Anderson Manager, Claims Division Crop Adjustment Bureau	Ms. Ruth L. Kent Editorial Director Rand Book Company
John King, Chairman Sociology Department	Carole P. Vandersteen Head, French Department	Warren F. Goldsmith Assistant Comptroller

TASK 2 Take balanced line length into account **before** you type, in proper form, the inside addresses (items 1–3) and the letter closings (items 4–5) below.

1 Mrs. Roberta Sands, Chairman, Secretarial Studies Department, Grover Cleveland High School

2 Mr. Alfred N. Harrison, Chief, Insurance Section, Veterans Administration

3 Mr. Benjamin Mott, Vice President, Kahn & Co., Inc.

4 Dean Ward, Chief Clerk, Insurance Division

5 William R. Howerington, Head, Bond Department

53C ABBREVIATIONS (In inside and envelope addresses)

To balance the line lengths in addresses, compass directions (North, South, East, West) may be abbreviated (N., S., E., W.); so may Street (St.), Avenue (Ave.), Boulevard (Blvd.), Drive (Dr.), Company (Co.), and Department (Dept.). Inc. (Incorporated) and Corp. (Corporation) are generally abbreviated, rarely spelled out.

TASK 3 Before you type the addresses below in proper form, examine them to decide which spelled-out words should be abbreviated to make the address lines more nearly of equal length.

1 Mr. Everett Sloan, 56 North Baldwin Street

2 Coughlin, Barrett & Company, 2144 Hansen Boulevard

3 Mr. Richard L. Andrews, Head, Industrial Department

4 John Masers & Company, 48 State Street

Noise, Music, and Other Distractions

Chapanis has remarked that "In some cases industrial noises have been replaced with other noises—commonly known as music—which are supposed to make work more pleasant."[1] However, noise appears to have only temporary effects on work.[2,3] Soon after the onset of noise the worker expends greater energy, more force in keystroking.[4]

Recovery, however, is rapid; and speed, accuracy, and other measures of production do not appear to suffer.[5] There were, for example, no performance differences between standard and noiseless typewriter operators.[6]

[1]A. Chapanis, W. R. Garner, and C. T. Morgan. *Applied Experimental Psychology.* New York: Wiley, 1949, p. 393.

[2]F. K. Berrien. The Effects of Noise. *Psychological Bulletin,* 1946, *43,* 141–161.

[3]D. A. Laird. The Measurement of the Effects of Noise upon Working Efficiency. *Journal of Industrial Hygiene,* 1927, *9,* 431–434.

[4]J. J. B. Morgan. The Overcoming of Distraction and Other Resistances. *Archives of Psychology,* 1916, *5,* No. 35.

[5]L. W. Crafts, T. C. Schneirla, E. A. Robinson, and W. R. Gilbert. *Recent Experiments in Psychology.* New York: McGraw-Hill, 1938, p. 218.

[6]L. M. E. Nordgren. An Experimental Comparison of Beginning Students Writing on Standard and Noiseless Typewriters. Master's thesis, Stanford University, 1931.

TASK 2 All reports that draw information from other sources—whether typed in book or in journal style—require a reference list at the end. As p. 3, prepare one for the ms. of Task 1. Keep in mind the two differences between the form of a footnote entry and a reference list entry and remember to list entries in alphabetical order of authors' names.

69 Repeated footnotes □ Personal note □ Report table

69A REPEATED FOOTNOTES

A source of information may often be referred to more than once in a report. At the first occurrence, publication information is given in full. If the same source is used again, the footnote information is shortened, as follows:

1 If a footnote refers to a work cited in the immediately preceding footnote, use *Ibid.* (Latin for "same") plus the page number(s).

2 If other works are cited between one mention and the next of the same work, use *op. cit.* (the work cited) if a new page number is referred to; but *loc. cit.* (the place cited) if the same page number is involved. Modern usage, however, favors a shortened form of the title in place of either *loc. cit.* or *op. cit.*

Examples

[1]John Bruce. Elements of Modern English Style. New York: Adams Press, 1974, p. 3.

[2]Ibid., p. 69.

[3]Ben Day. Today's English Usage. Boston: Kay & Dun, 1954, p. 128.

[4]Bruce, op. cit., p. 86.

or

[4]Bruce, Elements, p. 86.

[5]Day, loc. cit.

or

[5]Day, Today's, p. 128.

Assume that you are to type a ms., using WL–6". Start with a divider line on line 48 (pica) or 49 (elite); then type the five examples above. For Footnotes 4 and 5, use the shortened form of the title.

53D BUSINESS LETTER   Time—nearest ¼'. Use any acceptable style; correct errors.

Mr. T. K. Curry, Credit Manager, March & Lane, Inc., 304 Grove Street, Ames, IA 50010. Dear Mr. Curry: Mrs. Jane H. Kahn, of 45 Dover Street, wishes to open a charge account with Gould Brothers. On her application form, Mrs. Kahn states that she has been a charge customer of yours for the past five years. Would you please verify this and also indicate the terms under which you have extended credit to her. (¶) I should appreciate any other information concerning this account that you can provide and assure you that it will be kept in the strictest confidence. (¶) Thank you very much for your help. Sincerely yours, Robert Dunois, Credit Manager

53E TIMED PRACTICE   As many Paced or Progressive or Progressive NS timings as time permits. PF

54   Correspondence practice

54A PREPARATION   Type 48B, p. 65, for 2–3 minutes.

54B STRAIGHT COPY TIMING   5', DS, SM–1". TR. Read before you type.

	GWPM		
	a	b	CW
It is impossible to imagine any employer instructing a typist to	3	42	13
"type this seventy-word letter." It is the typist's responsibility to	5	45	27
estimate letter length (words in the body) so that proper margins can	8	48	41
be set.	9	48	43
For that, it is certainly not necessary to count every word. In-	11	51	56
stead, for any materials—typed, printed, or longhand—just count the	14	54	70
number of words on each of a few complete lines chosen at random from	17	56	84
the body of the letter; consider a divided word as half a word. Next,	20	59	98
determine average number of words per line and multiply that average by	23	62	113
the number of lines in the message, adding up any fractional lines.	25	65	126
In the letter of 53D, for instance, almost any three or four lines	28	68	140
average 9 words per line. Because the body uses 10 lines, you should	31	70	154
estimate the message to contain about 90 words—not far from the exact	34	73	168
count of 88 words.	34	74	172
From now on, before selecting letter margins, estimate the number	37	77	185
of words in its message, excluding materials outside the body.	40	79	198

Sy 1.54
St 5.5

+0   +1   +2   +3

Type in outline form in DS. In pica, use SM–1"; in elite, WL–6". End the footnote on line 60 (see 54B, p. 72, and 64B, p. 83, about estimating footnote space and locating the divider line).

REFERENCE LISTINGS

I. Order of Listings

  A. All references (to articles, books, etc.) are in *one* list, alphabetized by last name of senior author (the one named first if there are several authors). If no author is given (personal or institutional), alphabetize by title.

  B. The order given in sentences 4, 5, and 9 of 67A also applies to the reference list.

    1. Alphabetize the last names in cases of multiple authorship (e g., Sears and Davis precedes Sears and Wilson; Sears, Adams, and Cox precedes Sears and Baker).

II. Typing of Items Within the List[1]

  A. Underscore (italicize) the titles of books and the names and volume numbers of journals.

Type issue numbers in parentheses.

  B. Each of the three sections (author, title, publication information) ends with a period. Use commas within sections, but a colon after the city of publication in a book reference.

    1. Include page numbers only for articles.

_____

[1]There are many different referencing styles. The one illustrated in Lesson 66 is a highly professional one, slightly adapted from the one recommended in the style manual of a major publisher of professional reports. In other styles, publication information is given in a different order; the month of issue is included in journal references, major sections of an entry are separated by commas—not periods, and so on. In short, the style recommended in this book is an efficient one, but it is not the only one.

68   Manuscripts in journal and book style □ References page

68A MANUSCRIPT IN JOURNAL STYLE

The portion below is adapted from a technical book. Type it as p. 2, WL–6"; use 5-space ¶ indention and make a carbon copy.

<u>Noise, Music, and Other Distractions</u>

Chapanis has remarked that "In some cases industrial noises have been replaced with other noises —commonly known as music—which are supposed to make work more pleasant" (1949, p. 393). However, noise appears to have only temporary effects on work (Berrien, 1946; Laird, 1927). Soon after the onset of noise, the worker expends greater energy, more force in keystroking (Morgan, 1916). Recovery, however, is rapid; and speed, accuracy, and other measures of production do not appear to suffer (Crafts, Schneirla, Robinson, and Gilbert, 1938, p. 218). There were, for example, no performance differences between standard and noiseless typewriter operators (Nordgren, 1931).

68B MANUSCRIPT IN BOOK STYLE / REFERENCES PAGE

The journal style of the ms. of 68A puts source information in parentheses. In book style, as shown in the version of the same ms. on the next page, full citation information is instead given in footnotes. Footnote form differs from reference-list form in two respects. **In footnotes:**

1 Authors' names appear in signature style (first name first).

2 Page numbers for direct quotations and other source information are at the end of the footnote (including p. or pp.).

Alternate from letter to letter (full sheet) between block and semiblock styles and between open and mixed punctuation. Use whatever method(s) of date placement you or your instructor may prefer. Correct all errors. In Letter 2 (personal-business letter) include your return address and type and sign your own name. Letters 1 and 3 are business letters. Score for speed according to ¶ 3 of 51C, p. 69.

	CW
1 Mr. Howard Stein, Pierce, Burnet & Co., Gros-	12
venor Building, 175 Bragg Avenue, Knoxville, TN	21
37901. Dear Mr. Stein When you have a good	31
thing going, you hate to see it end. For more	40
than 15 years, our customers have enjoyed read-	49
ing our monthly newsletter. However, due to	58
rising costs, we must discontinue publication	68
with our April issue. (¶) Nevertheless, much	76
of the information once found in our newslet-	85
ter will now be included in our spring and fall	94
catalogs. As a newsletter subscriber, you may	104
order both catalogs for only $1.50—a saving	113
of 50 cents an issue. (¶) Why not fill out the	122
enclosed postal card and drop it in the mail	131
today? Very truly yours GIROUX PAPER SUP-	139
PLIES, William McMahon, Customer Service Dept.	150

	CW
2 Service Department, Kagan Electronics, 499	170
Eighth Avenue, Wilmington, DE 19899. Gentle-	179
men: The Kagan Model 352 cassette player/re-	188

	CW
corder that I sent you for repair on October	197
2 arrived in this morning's mail in damaged	205
condition. The box in which it was packed was	215
crushed at one end, and the insurance number	224
pasted on the package was partly torn off. (¶)	232
Would you please send me a duplicate copy of	242
your insurance receipt so that I may file a	251
claim with the post office? Very truly yours,	260
[type your name]	

	CW
3 Mrs. Isabel Montez, 94 Arcadia Street, Tampa,	278
FL 33608. Dear Mrs. Montez After bringing	286
together the finest selection of women's foot-	295
wear in the world, we are at last ready for our	305
grand opening. Only one thing is missing—	314
you! (¶) When you come in, please ask for our	322
manager, Mr. Jamison. He will be happy to pour	332
you a free cup of coffee while you make your	341
selection. Yours very truly Harold R. Sulli-	351
van, Customer Service	355

55 Envelope addressing □ Minor headings in tables □ Spacing between columns

55A KEYBOARD PRACTICE   Type lines 11–12, p. 116.

55B ENVELOPE ADDRESSING   Time—nearest ¼'

In a business office it is quite common to address envelopes for a group of letters after all the letters have been typed. How long will it take you to address envelopes for the six letters of 52B, 53D, and 54C (the ones to: Gallagher, Kahn, Curry, Stein, Kagan Electronics, Montez)?

Use large envelopes for the first three letters, small ones for the last three. When the writer's name is given, type it in the return address position.

Try flipping out each completed envelope with the same spin of the cylinder knob used to insert the next envelope (old one out, new one in—with one or two spins of the knob, as illustrated on p. 156).

67A CITIONS IN JOURNAL STYLE   In journal style, a portion of source information appears in the text rather than in footnotes.

FEATURE ILLUSTRATED		SAMPLE CITATIONS WITHIN A REPORT
Year of publication in parentheses	1	The report by Smith (1963) was . . . .
Author and year in parentheses	2	A later study (Fox, 1964) confirmed . . . .
Authors alphabetical, semicolon between	3	Others (Cox, 1965; Poe, 1964) found . . . .
Same author, two publications in same year	4	Cook (1966a, 1966b) presented . . . .
Same author, publications in different years	5	Jones (1967, 1968) tested . . . .
Particular chapter in book	6	Dunn's theories (1968, Chap. 4) are . . . .
Particular pages in book	7	Beck (1969, pp. 240-258) discussed . . . .
Page number of direct quotation	8	Wynn (1970, p. 38) said: "It seems . . . ."
One author before that author plus others	9	Others (Poe, 1972; Poe and Eng, 1971) . . . .
Source at end of sentence —*inside* the final period.	10	Wynn said: "It is clear . . ." (1970, p. 38).
	11	The theory was tested later (Grayson, 1973).

Type the first 9 items above, in 1 DS paragraph, WL–60, but omit the sentence numbers. In place of the ellipsis (the 3 or 4 spaced dots showing missing words), complete the sentences, in turn, as follows:

1 interesting. **4** a new theory. **7** them at length.
2 Smith. **5** Cook's theory. **8** difficult to explain."
3 mistakes in Fox's work. **6** different. **9** agreed with Wynn.

Like this:

    The report by Smith (1963) was interesting. A later study (Fox,
1964) confirmed Smith. Others (Cox, 1965; Poe, 1964) found mis. . . .

Note. Your paragraph is make-believe and not to be taken seriously. It is only intended to illustrate the various ways to show the sources of information within a report, avoiding footnotes.

As illustrated at the right, tables contain two major sections: heading and body. Always leave more space between sections than within them (TS between the minor head and the body, but DS between the major and minor heads and between the rows in the body of the table). Notice, also, that major or minor heads of more than one line are typed in SS.

Spacing Between Columns. Unless a table is unusually wide or unusually narrow (and in a few other special instances), leave 6 spaces between columns. That will result in an attractive, easy-to-read appearance.

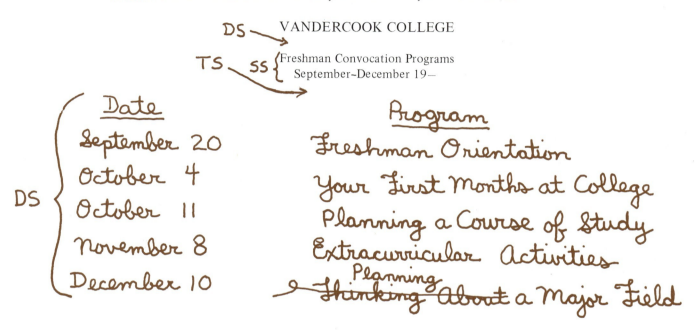

TASK 1 Center the table below vertically and horizontally on a ½-sheet, BC–7.

TASK 2 Retype the table with the following changes: (1) Change major head to Whitman University, (2) Omit second minor head line, (3) Omit the program of October 4, (4) Use BC–10.

55D TIMED PRACTICE   As many Paced or Progressive or Progressive NS timings as time permits. PF

56 Error correction by crowding and spreading □ Enclosure listings

56A STROKE REFINEMENT   Type lines 13–15, p. 121.

1 Journal paged by issue	Cook, Fred S. and Maliche, Eleanor. Office Machines Used in Business. <u>Delta Pi Epsilon Journal</u>, 1966, <u>8</u>(3), 1–16.
2 Journal paged by volume	Little, Ruth C. Effect of Class Size on Learning. <u>NEA Journal</u>, 1951, <u>40</u>, 215–216.
3 Encyclopedia article	Pribram, Karl H. Training of the Brain. In <u>Encyclopedia of Education</u> (Vol. 1), 478–486. New York: MacMillan, 1971.
4 Monthly popular magazine	Schrag, Peter. America Needs an Establishment. <u>Harper's</u>, December 1975, 51–58.
5 Weekly popular magazine (no author named)	Test of the Best on Snow and Ice. <u>Time</u>, February 2, 1976, 56–63.
6 Institutional author	U.S. Bureau of Labor Statistics. Employment Projections by Industry and Occupation, 1960–1975. <u>Monthly Labor Review</u>, 1963, <u>86</u>, 240–248.
7 Newspaper article (discontinuous pages)	Vartan, Vartanig G. Stock Prices Ease Amid Profit Taking. <u>The New York Times</u>, January 28, 1976, 45, 54.

TASK 2

Type the items above as p. 12 of an unbound ms., using the heading *References* and a 6-inch writing line.

REFERENCE LIST

TASK 3

With rare exceptions, reference entries of all kinds and from all sources are typed and printed in one continuous list, in alphabetical order of sole (or senior) author's last name. When you type a term paper or report of your own, you will have to type the entries and the parts of each entry in the right order. To give you practice in doing so, the entries and their parts listed below are in scrambled order, and the usual ways to show titles (underscoring, quotation marks) are intentionally omitted. Unscramble the entries: Type them in proper form **and** order, using the heading *References*, as p. 14 of a sidebound report.

Know Your Typewriter, by David Kent, published in 1975 on pages 111–115 of Volume 9 of a trade journal called Office Machines.

The third (3d) edition of Measurement and Evaluation in Psychology and Education, by Robert L. Thorndike and Elizabeth Hagen, published in 1968, in New York, by Wiley.

Opera—From Stage and Studio, by Roland Gelatt, on pages 51–52 of the January 24, 1976 issue of the Saturday Review.

Educational Psychology, by David Ausubel, published by Holt, Rinehart and Winston, in New York, in 1968.

The article on Shorthand, by Helen Reynolds, on pages 746f–750 of Volume 24 of the Encyclopedia Americana, published in New York by the Americana Corporation in 1969.

The chapter on The Nature of Measurement, by Lyle V. Jones, on pp. 335–355 of the second edition of Educational Measurement, edited by Robert L. Thorndike, published in 1971, in Washington, D.C., by the American Council on Education.

James S. Coleman's article on Recent Trends in School Integration, published in 1975 in Volume 4, Issue No. 7, of the Educational Researcher, on pages 3–12.

This typewriting textbook (see the title page and its reverse side).

56B ERROR CORRECTION (Crowding and spreading on **Manual*** typewriters)

1 Some corrections require replacing a word by one that has one letter more than the original word (crowding) or that has one letter less (spreading). By crowding or spreading in such instances, you avoid having to correct an entire line or having to retype an entire page.

2 Crowding leaves a ½-space, rather than a full one, before and after the new word:

See him now.
See them now.

3 Spreading leaves 1½ spaces before and after the new word:

Go for it.
Go to it.

4 To halfspace, depress and *hold down the space bar while you strike the letter key*. Then release the space bar, depress again, strike the next key. Alternately, depress-strike-release.

AFTER REMOVING THE ORIGINAL WORD

5 **To crowd** (using the illustration of ¶2): Position the carriage at the space after the preceding word (the space after the final *e* of *See*). Then depress-strike-release for the letters of the new word, in turn.

6 **To spread** (using the illustration of ¶3): Position the carriage at the first letter of the old word (at the *f* of *for*). Then depress-strike-release for the letters of the new word, in turn.

7 If your space bar does not halfspace forward, depress and hold the backspace key just halfway down (with printing point indicator just midway between the marks on the alignment scale). Use the sequence: depress-strike-release-space.

To crowd: Position carriage at first letter of old word before your first ½-backspace.

To spread: Position carriage at second letter of old word before your first ½-backspace.

*On *typebar electrics* that do not have a ½-space bar or key, hold the carriage firmly by hand at each ½-space position (with printing point indicator just midway between the marks on the alignment scale). On *Selectrics* and other ball-type machines without a ½-space bar or key, push the carrier (the platform on which the ball sits) slightly to the left, holding it there as you strike each key. The sequence is: push back-strike-release-space.

In turn, type each sentence as printed; then make the correction shown in longhand.

1 Close ~~the~~ *that* door. **2** Take ~~your~~ *his* book. **3** Read ~~John's~~ *Tom's* letter. **4** Take ~~eight~~ *Twelve* pens.

56C ENCLOSURE LISTINGS

Read the instructions; then type the letters in any of the acceptable styles. List the enclosures, as in the model. Time—nearest ¼'

In a business letter the enclosure notation is typed a DS below the reference initials. By showing the number of enclosures and listing them in condensed form, as illustrated at the right, the typist is reminded to enclose them and the addressee alerted to look for them. Take the added lines into account when determining letter placement. The illustration of an enclosure listing uses three added lines.

```
                                    Sincerely yours,

                                    Erica West

ac                                  Erica West
                                    Systems Division
Encs. 2
    1-Table
    2-Ms.
```

1 Miss Susan North, Office Manager, McMasters & Lee, Inc., 4138 River Front Dr., Memphis, TN 38104. Dear Miss North: I have examined the procedures for typing formal reports, as described in a number of reputable style manuals, and I am enclosing a table and a brief report that describe the methods most widely used today. (¶) Feel free to use the enclosed materials in revising your company manual for technical typists. Sincerely yours, Erica West, Systems Division

2 Clive Daniels & Company, 2 Fairweather Ave., Baltimore, MD 21206. Gentlemen: Thank you for inquiring about our Triton water coolers. You will be glad to learn that they are available in a wide variety of sizes. I am enclosing a brochure describing our various models, together with a price list. (¶) To find out more about Triton coolers, please phone us. A sales representative will be happy to visit your office to discuss your needs. Very truly yours, John G. Huey, Sales Manager

56D PROGRESSIVE or PACED PRACTICE   As many timings as time permits. PF

66A KEYBOARD PRACTICE   Type lines 15–16, p. 116.

66B REFERENCE LIST

List the sources of information in a report, starting on a separate page after the last report page. Center *References* as the heading when all items listed are mentioned in the report. Use *Bibliography* as the heading only when items for background or further reading are also included.

List entries alphabetically by author, last name first. SS within and DS between entries.

Each entry consists of three major sections: author(s), title, publication information. Use commas within and a period after each section.

BOOK ENTRIES

1 Underscore book titles. Use (ed.) for edition and (Ed.) for editor. No quotation marks are needed around the title of a chapter in an edited book (see *Weaver,* below); its position immediately following the author's name shows that it is a title. The editor's name is given first name first.

2 The publication information consists, in order, of: city of publication, name of publisher, year of publication. Use the colon after city of publication; if the city is not large and well-known, include the state (abbreviated, as in *Ebel,* below). The name of the publisher need not be accompanied by such words as *Publishing, Book, Co., Inc., & Sons;* but include Press (e.g., Ronald Press).

---

1 Book

Ebel, Robert L. <u>Measuring Educational Achievement</u>. Englewood Cliffs, N.J.: Prentice-Hall, 1965.

2 New edition of book

Hodges, John C. and Whitten, Mary E. <u>Harbrace College Handbook</u> (7th ed.). New York: Harcourt Brace Jovanovich, 1972.

3 Edited book with various chapter authors

Weaver, Warren. Probability. In Abe Schuchman (Ed.), <u>Scientific Decision Making in Business</u>. New York: Holt, Rinehart and Winston, 1963.

TASK 1

Type the 3 items above as p. 17 of an unbound report with 1-inch side margins. Use *References* as the heading.

ARTICLE ENTRIES (See next page.)

1 Magazines, newspapers, professional journals, encyclopedias, et al., contain *articles*.

2 The issues of a *professional* journal for a year make up a "volume." If each issue starts with page 1, show both volume and issue numbers. If issues are paged consecutively throughout a volume, show only the volume number.

3 Publication information for a journal article (**1** and **2,** next page) consists, in order, of: name of publication (underscored), year of publication, volume number (underscored), issue number (if needed and in parentheses without spacing), and page numbers.

4 Because their position in a reference shows what they are, article titles need no quotation marks, and (except as stated in ¶5, next) the abbreviations *p.* or *pp.* and *Vol.* are not needed.

5 If an encyclopedia has several volumes, always show the volume number (in parentheses, including the abbreviation *Vol.*), then the page numbers, and finally, the book publication information, as in **3,** next page.

6 If no author is given (as in **5,** next page), alphabetize by title of the article.

57–58A PREPARATION 2–3 minutes on 55B, p. 73.

57–58B STRAIGHT COPY TIMINGS 5′, DS, SM–1″. Enter average scores on TR. Read before you type.

	GWPM	
a	b	CW
3	40	13
4	42	22
7	44	36
10	47	51
13	50	65
14	51	71
17	54	84
20	57	98
23	60	113
25	63	127
28	65	141
31	68	155
34	71	170
37	74	184
37	74	186

This essay explains a leading feature of the manuscript or report typing that starts in Lesson 59 in this book.

First, in this book the two terms—manuscript and report—are used interchangeably. A manuscript is a handwritten or typewritten document, as distinguished from a printed copy. Many manuscripts, whether or not later printed, are reports.

Next, many reports include information from other sources. If so, it is both ethical and professional to mention the source of each such item of information, as in the footnotes used for years in books. Footnotes, though, are time-consuming to type and costly to print. A more modern style, used in professional journals, does away with footnotes. Instead, the last name of the author and year of publication (of the article or book, for example) are shown in parentheses in the text of the report. A reference list at the end of the report gives full publication data.

Sy 1.55
St 5.9

+0   +1   +2   +3

a	b	CW
3	40	13
5	43	26
8	46	40
11	49	54
13	51	67
16	54	80
18	56	92
21	59	106
24	62	120
24	62	122
27	65	135
30	68	149
32	70	162
35	73	176
38	76	189

In a survey of typing activities (Featheringham, 1965), it was found that manuscript work was the most common one among high school and college students who had taken a personal typing course in high school. Among adults not in school, it ranked second for frequency. In another study, Perkins, Byrd, and Roley (1968) found report typing to be the sixth most common job of secretarial employees.

When you were in high school, you may have written reports for some of your classes. In most colleges, writing term papers and reports is very common. You would be wise, therefore, to learn how to type reports.

The first line of this essay shows source information (author's name plus date of publication) in parentheses. Later in the first paragraph the writer's style puts only the date in parentheses. The writer could also have said that research shows report typing to be very common (Featheringham, 1965; Perkins, Byrd, and Roley, 1968).

Sy 1.53
St 5.7

+0   +1   +2   +3

65A CAPITALIZATION PRACTICE   Type lines 16–18, p. 120.

65B TABLE FOOTNOTES / 2-LINE COLUMN HEADS

The table at the right shows that:

1 Because most tables include numbers, footnotes are lettered rather than numbered.

2 Footnotes are typed directly below the table, **not** at the bottom of the page; and they must **not** extend beyond the table margins.

3 The 1-line heading of col. (column) 1 is lined up with the lower line of the 2-line heads of cols. 2 and 3.

There are two ways to center the 2-line heads of cols. 2 and 3:

By Machine. From the *M* of *Margin*[a] in col. 2, space forward 1 for 2; then backspace 1 for 2 to center *Top*.

By Spelling and Counting (as described in 41A). Spell *T-o-p* as you point with your pencil to the *M-a-r* of *Margin*[a]; then count 1-2-3-4 as you point at *g-i-n-a*. Start *Top* over the third letter of *Margin*[a] (the *r*).

Typing Hint. Type the longer heads of line 5 immediately after typing the table title; then turn back 1 line to type the shorter heads of line 4.

		MANUSCRIPT MARGINS	
Binding	Top Margin[a]		Left Margin
Unbound	1"		1"[b]
Sidebound	1"		1½"

SS
DS

[a]Applies to pages after page 1.

[b]A 6-inch writing line requires side margins of 1¼ inches.

TASK 1 Center the table above on a ½-sheet; use BC–8.

TASK 2 Center the table below on a full sheet. Use BC space shown by circled numbers.

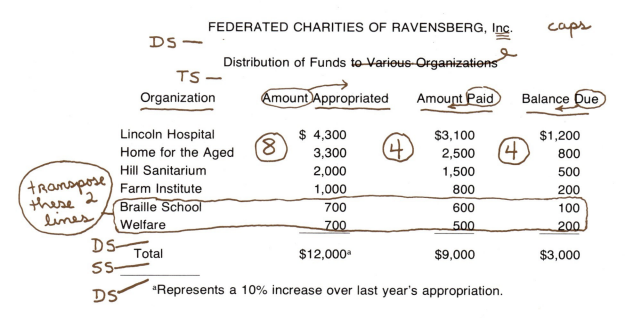

FEDERATED CHARITIES OF RAVENSBERG, Inc. *caps*
DS
Distribution of Funds to Various Organizations
TS

Organization	Amount Appropriated	Amount Paid	Balance Due
Lincoln Hospital	$ 4,300	$3,100	$1,200
Home for the Aged	3,300	2,500	800
Hill Sanitarium	2,000	1,500	500
Farm Institute	1,000	800	200
Braille School	700	600	100
Welfare	700	500	200
Total	$12,000[a]	$9,000	$3,000

transpose these 2 lines

DS SS DS

[a]Represents a 10% increase over last year's appropriation.

65C PROGRESSIVE PRACTICE or OPTIONAL PRACTICE   As many 2′ timings as time permits. PF

57–58C   LETTERS AND ENVELOPES

Type Letter 1 in block style, open punctuation; include your return address in it and on a small envelope. Type Letter 2 in semiblock style, mixed punctuation; address a large envelope. Use any of the methods of date placement you or your instructor prefer.

1 The Ondine Bookstore, 438 Marlborough Street, Boston, MA 02115. Gentlemen: While vacationing in Boston last August, I visited your bookstore. At that time, I noticed that you had the Merton Press edition of George Bernard Shaw's *Pygmalion* on sale for $5. If you still have that edition in stock, I should like to order a copy. I enclose my check for $5.75 to cover the price of the book and shipping charges. Yours very truly, [Type and sign your own name.]

2 Mr. Howard Bentley, 2165 Oak Post Rd., Columbus, OH 43229. Dear Mr. Bentley: Did you ever wish you could get away for an exciting weekend in a city like New Orleans? Now you can—thanks to Tackett Weekend Tours. (¶) You'll spend two days riding the streetcar named Desire past beautiful nineteenth-century homes in the Garden District, shopping in exotic boutiques on Canal Street, and watching a minstrel show on a Mississippi steamboat. (¶) You'll spend two nights dining in gourmet restaurants in the French Quarter, strolling through Pirate's Alley, and listening to jazz in a club on Bourbon Street. (¶) And the cost? Cheaper than you might think. Return the enclosed, postage-paid card to learn more about this and other fabulous Tackett Weekends. Sincerely yours, Daniel S. Pollock, Sales Manager

57–58D   TABLE

Center on a full sheet; make the indicated changes and use appropriate vertical spacing between parts of the table. Because the table is rather wide, use BC–3.

SUFFOLK ELECTRIC COMPANY, Inc.

Members of the Board of Directors, May, 19– *Substitute the current month and year.*

Name	Principal Occupation	First Elected
Edward Dellman	President, Dellman Brothers	1968
Augusta F. Elson	Secretary, Budd, Inc.	1975
Victor Fehr	Treasurer of the Company	1960
Julian V. Hobart	Attorney at Law	1974
Evelyn A. Mason	Attorney at Law	1973
Daniel T. Lemson	President of the Company	1969
Howard H. Stanton	Vice-President of the Company	1972

57–58E   OPTIONAL PRACTICE

Continue on a practice sheet with one or more of the following: Stroke Refinement (pp. 121–125), Letter Sequences (pp. 118–119), Capitalization (p. 120), Keyboard Practice (pp. 116–117). Make PF entries when you finish.

64A LETTER SEQUENCES   Type the sequences for **k** and **l**, p. 118.

64B STRAIGHT COPY TIMING   5', DS, SM–1", TR. Read before you type.

Footnote space must be estimated in advance. Indeed, because one often cannot know beforehand how many footnotes will appear on a page, it is vital to estimate the lines necessary for each one as soon as you reach its raised number in the body of the text. For short footnotes, count words; for longer ones, use the estimation processes of 54B. Recognize, next, that manuscript margins in elite permit 12–13 words per line; in pica, 10–11 words per line. A 35-word footnote requires three elite lines, four pica lines—plus a blank line. If in doubt, type the footnotes on scrap paper beforehand. To locate the divider line, subtract footnote lines—typed plus blank ones between footnotes—from 60.

To reach that divider line, first identify your present line number. How? Just count by two's from the top line (7, 9, 11, etc., taking into account triple spacing *before* centered and side heads, if any). Better yet, use the line counting side of a typing ruler or a numbered backing sheet. As illustrated in Lesson 63, you sometimes SS, at other times DS, between the last line of text and the divider line.

GWPM a	GWPM b	CW
3	48	13
5	51	27
8	54	42
11	57	56
14	59	70
17	62	84
20	65	99
23	68	113
25	71	127
28	74	141
31	76	154
34	79	168
37	82	185
40	85	200
43	88	214
45	91	226
	Sy 1.51	
	St 5.7	

```
+0            +1            +2        +3
```

64C MANUSCRIPT WITH FOOTNOTE

Omitting ¶3d, type ¶'s 1–3c within the colored box of 63B as p. 2 of a ms., using WL–6" and 3-space ¶ indention. Begin with the sidehead Footnote Typing. Type the divider line on line 56 and number, do not star, the footnote. As shown at the right, use outline form, DS, and bring lines after the first line in each ¶ out ot the left margin.

```
   3 . xxxxxxxxxxxxxxxxxxx
xxxxxxxxxxxxxxx .
      a . xxxxxxxxxxxxxxxx
xxxxxxxxxxx .
```

64D ESTIMATING FOOTNOTE SPACE

TASK 1 Use the procedures of the first ¶ of 64B to estimate number of footnote lines and to find the location of the divider line in each of the following instances. Assume each footnote to be the only one on its page. Just do the arithmetic; do not type.

1 In 15C, the items within the colored box (p. 26), assuming an unbound ms. with 1-inch side margins.

2 In 20B, bottom of left column (p. 33), assuming a 6-inch writing line.

3 In 32C, the items within the colored box (p. 47), assuming a sidebound ms.

4 At bottom left of 37B (p. 52), assuming 1-inch side margins.

TASK 2 Type the footnotes of Items 2 and 3, above. Number them serially and place the divider line on the proper line.

59–60A LETTER SEQUENCES Type the sequences for **i** and **j**, p. 118.

59–60B UNBOUND MANUSCRIPT

Page 1 of Unbound Manuscript

Partial Page 2

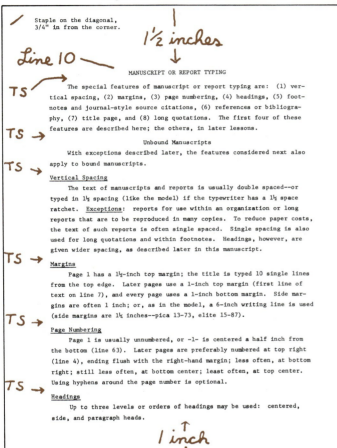

Staple on the diagonal, 3/4" in from the corner.

Line 10

1½ inches

TS

MANUSCRIPT OR REPORT TYPING

The special features of manuscript or report typing are: (1) vertical spacing, (2) margins, (3) page numbering, (4) headings, (5) footnotes and journal-style source citations, (6) references or bibliography, (7) title page, and (8) long quotations. The first four of these features are described here; the others, in later lessons.

TS

Unbound Manuscripts

With exceptions described later, the features considered next also apply to bound manuscripts.

TS

Vertical Spacing

The text of manuscripts and reports is usually double spaced--or typed in 1½ spacing (like the model) if the typewriter has a 1½ space ratchet. Exceptions: reports for use within an organization or long reports that are to be reproduced in many copies. To reduce paper costs, the text of such reports is often single spaced. Single spacing is also used for long quotations and within footnotes. Headings, however, are given wider spacing, as described later in this manuscript.

TS

Margins

Page 1 has a 1½-inch top margin; the title is typed 10 single lines from the top edge. Later pages use a 1-inch top margin (first line of text on line 7), and every page uses a 1-inch bottom margin. Side margins are often over 1 inch; or, as in the model, a 6-inch writing line is used (side margins are 1¼ inches--pica 13-73, elite 15-87).

TS

Page Numbering

Page 1 is usually unnumbered, or -1- is centered a half inch from the bottom (line 63). Later pages are preferably numbered at top right (line 4), ending flush with the right-hand margin; less often, at bottom right; still less often, at bottom center; least often, at top center. Using hyphens around the page number is optional.

TS

Headings

Up to three levels or orders of headings may be used: centered, side, and paragraph heads.

1 inch

Line 7

-2-

Centered. The title of a report is centered in solid caps and must not be underscored. Centered heads are also used for the major divisions of a report, with initial caps for important words (i.e., except for articles, connectives, and prepositions of fewer than five letters). It is permissible, but not desirable, to underscore centered division heads. "Unbound Manuscripts" (page 1 of this report) is an example of a centered head.

DS

Side Heads. Side heads are typed flush with the left margin and are underscored. Important words use initial caps. Vertical Spacing (on page

1 Study the illustrations and read—for the information it contains—the 3-page ms. (manuscript), "Manuscript or Report Typing," that begins at the bottom of this page and continues on the next page.

2 Apply the information to the typing of the copy as an unbound ms. Use SM–1″ and 5-space paragraph indention. In DS you will not get as many lines on the page as the model, which uses 1½ spacing. Before inserting paper, make a light pencil mark about 1½ inches from the bottom of each page at the right edge —to warn you when you have room for only 1–2 more lines before you must start a new page.

3 Ms. instructions assume the use of DS. If 1½ spacing is available, use it instead of DS and substitute DS where TS is specified below.

4 Correct any errors you may make. Be sure to proofread each page **before** removing it from the machine. Use the underscore for italics.

5 Before you stop work today, complete the line you are typing —out to **your** margin. Save your work for completion in the next lesson. **Note.** The plural of ms. is mss.

MANUSCRIPT OR REPORT TYPING

The special features of manuscript or report typing are: (1) vertical spacing, (2) margins, (3) page numbering, (4) headings, (5) footnotes and journal-style source citations, (6) references or bibliography, (7) title page, and (8) long quotations. The first four of these features are described here; the others, in later lessons.

Unbound Manuscripts

With exceptions described later, the features considered next also apply to bound manuscripts.

Vertical Spacing

The text of manuscripts and reports is usually double spaced—or typed in 1½ spacing (like the model) if the typewriter has a 1½-space ratchet. *Exceptions:* reports for use within an organization or long reports that are to be reproduced in many copies. To reduce paper costs, the text of such reports is often single spaced. Single spacing is also used for long quotations and within footnotes. Headings, however, are given wider spacing, as described later in this manuscript.

63A STROKE REFINEMENT   Type lines 16–18, p. 121.

63B FOOTNOTES

---

1 A footnote is a *note* placed at the *foot* of a page, below the last line of the text. One type of footnote is a comment or remark that would otherwise interrupt the main discussion. Examples of these are in 15C (p. 26), 20B (p. 33), 32C (p. 47), 37B (p. 52), and here—at the foot of this column.

2 If a footnote occurs only occasionally (as in these lessons so far), use an asterisk in two places: immediately after the item in the text to which the footnote refers and immediately before the footnote. More formally, footnotes are numbered in series, as in the 2-footnote example below this colored box,* or lettered serially, as in the Letter Placement table on p. 156.

3 The 2-footnote example below this colored box shows that:

   *Serial numbering of footnotes applies throughout a ms.; do *not* start with 1 on each new page. But serial lettering is preferred in tables (because they often contain numbers).

a The main text on the page ends with just enough room to bring the last footnote line to 1 inch from the bottom (line 60, or within 1 line of line 60). Therefore, estimate in advance the number of footnote lines needed (see 64B).

b Footnotes are typed as separate paragraphs, with paragraph indention. SS within and DS between footnotes.

c A *divider line* of 1¼–1½ inches (in this book, 15 underscores in both pica and elite type) is always typed a DS above the first footnote—1–2 lines below the last ms. line on a full page.

d A "superior" figure (raised a ½-line) is used in the text and before the footnote. Use the ratchet release and turn the roller a ½-line before typing the footnote number or letter. *Example:* [1]Begin the footnote.

	Line	
	50	In its latest shipment our zoo received an aardvark[1] and
	52	a koala.[2] The animals arrived in fine condition and are sure
SS	54	to delight the public. They will be on display starting on
	55	————————
DS	56	
	57	[1]From Africa; also called ant bear, anteater, or earth
DS	58	pig.
	59	
	60	[2]From Australia; looks like our Teddy bear.

TASK 1 Use WL–60 in copying the example above. Align top edge of paper with alignment scale and space down to line 50 (16TS + 2SS or, if you have no TS, 25DS).

TASK 2 Turn the page used for Task 1 upside down and type the example again, omitting the second footnote (and, of course, the superior 2 after *koala*). Start on line 52.

TASK 3 Start on line 52 on a clean side of paper, this time omitting the first footnote. Make the necessary changes to convert what was Footnote 2 into Footnote 1. **Question:** To end on line 60, should you SS or DS before the divider line?

63C PROGRESSIVE PRACTICE   As many 2′ timings as time permits, PF. See 59–60E (p. 79) for 2′ timing instructions.

Margins

Page 1 has a 1½-inch top margin; the title is typed 10 single lines from the top edge. Later pages use a 1-inch top margin (first line of text on line 7), and every page uses a 1-inch bottom margin. Side margins are often 1 inch; or, as in the model, a 6-inch writing line is used (side margins are 1¼ inches—pica 13–73, elite 15–87).

Page Numbering

Page 1 is usually unnumbered, or –1– is centered a half inch from the bottom (line 63). Later pages are preferably numbered at top right (line 4), ending flush with the right-hand margin; less often, at bottom right; still less often, at bottom center; least often, at top center. Using hyphens around the page number is optional.

Headings

Up to three levels or orders of headings may be used: centered, side, and paragraph heads.

Centered. The title of a report is centered in solid caps and must _not_ be underscored. Centered heads are also used for the major divisions of a report, with initial caps for important words (i.e., except for articles, connectives, and prepositions of fewer than five letters). It is permissible, but not desirable, to underscore centered division heads. "Unbound Manuscripts" (page 1 of this report) is an example of a centered head.

Side Heads. Side heads are typed flush with the left margin and are underscored. Important words use initial caps. _Vertical Spacing_ (on page 1) and the three headings that follow it are examples of side heads.

Paragraph Heads. This paragraph and the two above it begin with paragraph heads. They are indented and underscored, and they use initial caps for important words. They are followed by a period, then two spaces, and by text on the same line. (Incidentally, both in long reports and in reports to be printed, paragraph indention is typically three, not five, spaces.)

Spacing with Headings. After you type the report title, triple space. Because centered and side heads are also important, triple space _before_ them. Elsewhere, use double spacing: _before_ paragraph heads and _after_ centered and side heads.

Bound Manuscripts

A short manuscript (up to about 30 pages) could be stapled at the upper left corner (see model). A longer report would need two or three staples at intervals down the left side. Formal reports are usually enclosed in a binder. For school reports an ordinary file folder makes an excellent, inexpensive binder. It requires heavy staples at the side that will go through the folder and its contents. Because of its binding, it must use the wider left margin that goes with sidebound manuscripts.

Sidebound. The instructions for unbound manuscripts apply, except for the left margin and centering of headings. Use a 1½-inch left margin (15 pica or 18 elite spaces) on all pages. Other margins remain 1 inch. Center headings from the midpoint of the page: from 45 pica, 54 elite.

Topbound. In a few special cases (e.g., legal papers) manuscripts are topbound; pages turn like those of this typing text and are numbered at the bottom. Page 1 has a 2-inch top margin; other pages, 1½ inches. Side and bottom margins are 1 inch.

59–60C SIDEBOUND MANUSCRIPT

Reread the section on sidebound mss. above. Then retype the ms. for side binding—until the end of the _Vertical Spacing_ section. Center headings from the center of the WL, not the center of the page.

59–60D UNBOUND MS. (WL–6″)

Using a 6-inch writing line, retype p. 3 of the ms., arbitrarily starting with the _Topbound_ paragraph.

Continue with Optional Practice until it is time for 59–60E.

59–60E PROGRESSIVE PRACTICE

Change from 1′ to 2′ timings—as many as time permits. PF

Using the 2′ column at the right of the materials (pp. 127–130), start with speed practice at a speed 1 wpm more than your average gross wpm on the straight copy timings of Lessons 57–58. Follow the usual "up 5, down 2" rule. Enter and maintain your 2′ schedule on your PF. When you succeed at any timing, line it out on your PF and progress from 1 whole wpm to the next, skipping in-between paragraphs. _Example:_ From 24 wpm (¶53) move to 25 wpm (¶55). For speeds of 33–39 wpm, use the 1′ column of Series A (p. 128), and type the paragraph twice in 2 minutes. For speeds of 40+ wpm, use Series B (pp. 131–134).

62A KEYBOARD PRACTICE   Type lines 13–14, p. 116.

62B SIDEBOUND MANUSCRIPT   First read the ms. and then the personal letter of 62C about spacing before side heads. Follow their instructions in making 1 carbon of the ms.

CARBON COPIES

Except when an office copying machine is preferred and available, the typist uses carbon paper and makes copies on light-weight paper called "tissue sheets" or "onion skin." Using supplies of the proper weight, you can make about 4–6 copies on a manual typewriter and about 8–10 on an electric.

Assembling a Carbon Pack

If only one or two copies are needed, it is convenient to assemble the "carbon pack" alongside the typewriter: tissue sheet at the bottom, carbon paper above it (waxy or shiny side *down*), then another tissue and another carbon, with the original or "bond" copy on top. Align the pack evenly and pull the paper release forward to start feeding the pack behind the roller; then lock the release and continue turning the pack into the machine. The bond copy should then be on top, facing you.

There is a superior method that avoids having to straighten the pack after it has been inserted into the typewriter. Just insert the top edges of the assembled pack under the flap of an envelope or into the crease of a folded sheet of paper. After full insertion of the pack into the typewriter (including the envelope or folded sheet), remove the envelope or sheet.

Correcting Carbon Copies

To make corrections on carbon copies, be sure to use a soft pencil eraser or the special correction tape made for carbon copies. Equally important, to prevent smudges on carbon copies when making corrections, *always* place a stiff card or slip of paper *behind each* carbon sheet beforehand. Remove the cards or slips before typing the corrections.

62C PERSONAL LETTER AND ENVELOPE   Use a full sheet; make one carbon copy. Address a large envelope and complete the salutation of the letter to a (if necessary, make-believe) sister of yours in high school. Use your home address on the envelope, but omit all addresses in the letter. Make the necessary adjustment in vertical placement, as described at the top of p. 156.

Dear _____, In her latest letter Mom told me you are working very hard on a term paper for your high school history class. I'm taking a Report Writing course here at college, and I thought you might find useful some of the information I've learned. (¶) First, it is a good idea to prepare a title page. A copy of one of mine is enclosed to show you how to arrange it. Second, it is wise to enclose school reports in a binder. If so, remember that centered items in a sidebound report are backspaced from 54 (elite) or 45 (pica), including all title page lines. Third, to show that centered and side heads apply to what follows, not to what precedes, always triple space before such heads. (¶) Do make a carbon copy of your report so I can read it when I get home on vacation. I'm looking forward to seeing you then. Love,

62D TITLE PAGE   Prepare a title page for the ms. of 62B, written by **you** for your typing class.

About 3" down
Title —— MANUSCRIPT OR REPORT TYPING
William A. Henderson ← Triple space
Author
Name and number of class or course
Instructor —— Report Writing 201 / Mr. Harkin / December 19, 1977
Date
About 2" from bottom

61A CAPITALIZATION PRACTICE   Type lines 13–15, p. 120.

61B UNBOUND MS.   Read before typing. SM–1″.

REPORT WRITING
MANUSCRIPT HIGHPOINTS   *more # after title*

If you have access to a typewriter outside of class--perhaps a portable typewriter at home *or on campus*--you ~~may already have used it for school work.~~ You should certainly ~~be able to~~ begin now to type *college* ~~school~~ reports and term papers ~~on the typewriter.~~ Here are a few pointers that sumarize some of the main ideas about report typing.

Headings. Generous use of headings is an aid to the reader. They *correspond to* ~~parallel~~ the entries in a formal outline and help the reader to perceive the organization of the report. Usually, only long reports require all three orders of headings (centered, side, paragraph). More often, side and paragraph heads are *sufficient* ~~enough.~~ In a short report, side headings alone or paragraph headings alone *are usually adequate* ~~might suffice.~~ Use good judgement about *assigning* ~~selecting~~ ~~the number and kinds of~~ headings ~~to include.~~

Source Citations. Showing source information in parentheses within the body of the report (see pp. 76 and 87) simplifies the typing *#* enormously; the older method of *footnoting* ~~showing full~~ publication information ~~in footnotes~~ is very time-consuming. However, not all college faculty members or professional disciplines, have adopted, as yet, the newer style; They continue to require footnoting of publication information. ~~For that reason~~ it is *therefore* important to *learn to* use both the "journal style" of parenthetical citations and the "book style" of footnote citations. Besides, even in journal style, footnotes are used for "asides," comments or examples that would otherwise interrupt the main discussion in the body of the report. Even so, ~~the chief~~ *a leading* point in favor of parenthetical citations is that a college report or term paper parallels a journal article--not a book.

TASK 2 Remove your completed ms. from the typewriter; than make the corrections shown below. Align the reinserted page carefully (see 51B, p. 69, and 56B, p. 75).

¶1, last line (crowd)	¶2, first line (replace)	¶2, second line (spread)
chief the ~~main~~ ideas	*a help* is ~~an aid~~ to	*aid* and ~~help~~ the

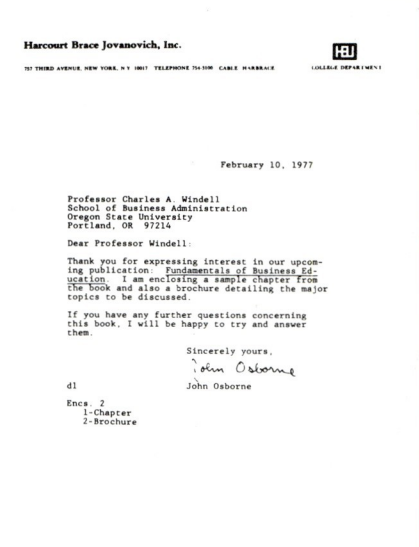

Business letter, block, date pivoted

Business letter, modified block, date starting at center, firm name

Business letter with enclosure listings

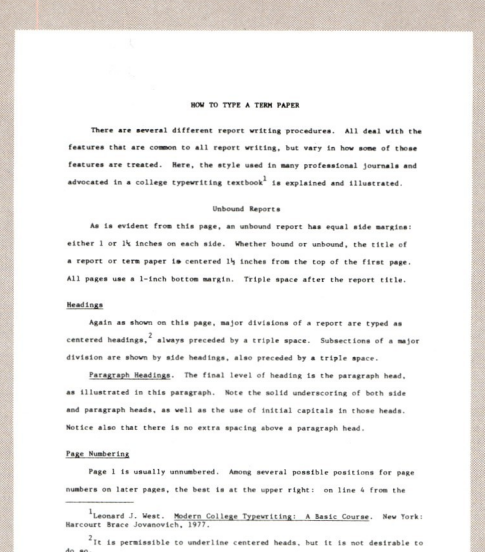

Page 1 of an unbound report with 1-inch side margins, including footnotes

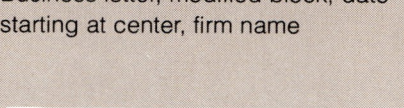

Partial page 2 of a sidebound report

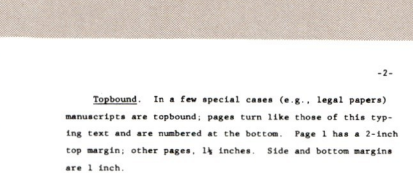

Partial References page

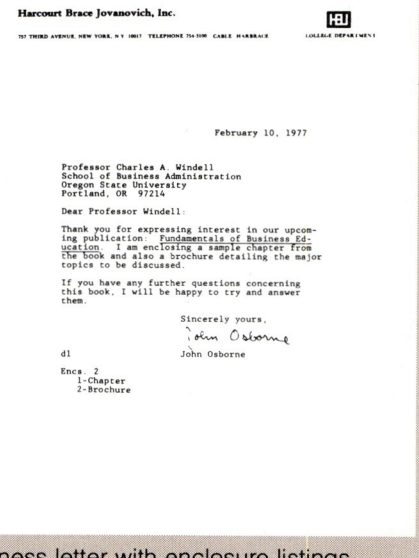

Personal-business letter on a 1/2-sheet with return address

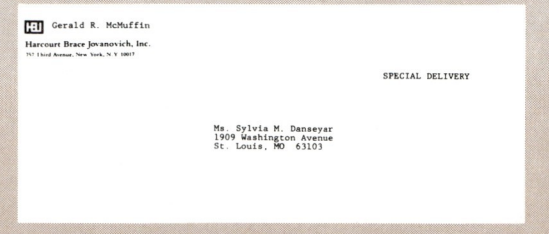

Envelope with dictator's name above printed return address and postal notation

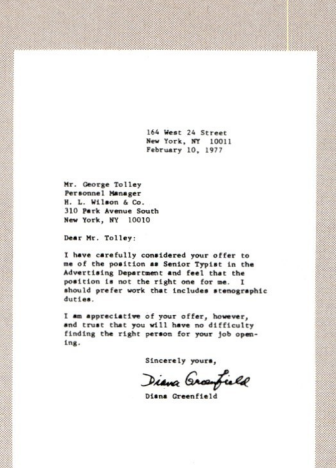

Envelope with addressee notation

Index

Abbreviations
  c/o 31
  Enc. 75
  in addresses 71
  initials 37
  in letter closings 71
  latin 37
  n. and m. 54
  periods with 37
  spacing with 37
  special, inside front cover
  two-letter state, inside front cover

Accuracy
  during timings 11
  how to type with 44, 142
  lesser importance in relation to
    speed at the start 8
  program for developing 44, 142
  relationship with speed 44, 142

Address(es)
  abbreviations in 71
  envelopes 39
  postal cards 41
  personal-business letters 59
  return, envelopes and postal
    cards 39, 41
  titles in 71

Aligning
  $ sign 55
  numbers in columns 35, 54
  reinserted paper 69
  roman numbers by
    backspacing 50
  scale 69

Ampersand ("and" sign, &) 34
Anchor finger 9
"And" sign
  See: Ampersand

Apostrophe
  as "feet" 28
  as "minutes" 28
  as single quote 33
  in exclamation point 28
  major uses 28

Articles
  references to 85–86
Asterisk or star (*) 33
  as footnote sign 82
"At" sign (@) 37

Backspacing
  aligning roman numbers 50
  centering column heads 49
  continuous, electric typewriters 35
  for planning tables 47
  horizontal centering 26
  underscoring 35

BC (between-column) spacing
  backspacing for 47
  in tables 24
  unequal 53
Bell
  ringing of 21
Bibliography
  See: References
Block style 65
Blocked paragraphs 59
Blocked tables
  See: Tables
Book style of footnoting source
    citations 80
  in manuscripts 88–89
Books
  references to, in reports 85
  underlining titles of 36, 85
Business letters
  addressee's and signer's titles 71
  closing elements 62
  enclosures 75
  estimation of length 72
  folding 157
  inventory xi
  parts 62, 64
  placement 70, 156
  punctuation styles 62
  review of procedures 92
  styles 65

Call-the-throw
  first practice 22
  practice materials 127
  PF entry 115
Capitalization
  in report headings 79
  practice materials 116
Carbon copies 81
Carriage return
  electrics and manuals 6
  practice 22
Carriage scale
  for alignment 69
  location 2
Centering
  horizontal 26
  in sidebound mss. 79
  vertical 31
  See also: Column headings,
    centering
Cent sign (¢) 71
Chaining of motions 60, 140
Chapters (of books)
  in reference lists 85
  in journal style 87
Citation of sources
  See: Source citations

Closing elements
  adjusting for long firm name 68
  business letters 62
  personal-business letters 59
  personal notes 58
  postal cards 41
  See also: Reference initials
c/o (care of) 31
Colon 36
Column headings
  centering
    by forward and backspacing 49
    by spelling and counting 57
  two-line 84
  See also: BC spacing
Columns
  setting tab stops 24
  See also: BC spacing
Comma
  between place names 14
  spacing with 13
Comparison practice 51, 54, 56, 64
Compound words and expressions
  hyphen in 20
Correspondence
  review of procedures 92
  See also: Business letters, Memos,
    Personal-business letters,
    Personal notes, Postal cards
Crowding 75

Dash 20
Date line in letters
  horizontal location 65
  pivoted 41, 68
  vertical placement 70, 156
Decimal point 29
Diagonal (slant) 30, 31
Dictator's (initials, name, title or
    department)
  location in a letter 62
  omission of initials 62
Difficulty measures (indices) 27
Divider line
  in manuscripts 82, 83
  in tables 84
  variable spacing before 82
Division sign
  diagonal for 31
Dollar sign ($)
  aligning in money columns 55
  key 29
Double spacing
  between double-spaced
    paragraphs 23
  between lines 7
  between single-spaced
    paragraphs 21